THE STRATOCASTER CHRONICLES

CELEBRATING 50 YEARS
OF THE FENDER STRAT

BY TOM WHEELER

"The whole guitar was pretty good."
— Leo Fender

ISBN 0-634-05678-6

Published by Hal Leonard Corporation
7777 W. Bluemound Rd.
P.O. Box 13819
Milwaukee, WI 53213

Library of Congress Cataloging-in-Publication Data has been applied for.

Printed in China

First Edition

Visit Hal Leonard Online at **www.halleonard.com**

10 9 8 7 6 5 4 3 2 1

THE STRATOCASTER CHRONICLES

Table of Contents

A CD is included with this book. A Listening Guide appears in Chapter 10.

For Leo Fender,
who brought it into the world
and Jimi Hendrix,
who took it beyond

The Stratocaster Chronicles is intended neither to replace other books devoted to Fender's flagship guitar nor to fulfill functions better left to catalogs, price lists, or web sites. The landmarks in the Stratocaster's evolution are noted here (along with scads of minor details), but *The Stratocaster Chronicles'* larger function is to broaden what we know about the origin of this extraordinary instrument, and to lend perspective to all the facts, dates, and specs reported here and elsewhere. It gives voice to the people behind the guitar, providing a forum for them to recount the tale of the Strat as a reflection of musical tastes, manufacturing necessities, industry competition, and economic trends.

This book also recognizes that the Strat's deeper significance lies in the music guitarists have created with it. We will hear what Strat players have to say about their instrument — and their music, and each other — providing a glimpse into what might be called the family of Strat. The intent is to deepen our appreciation by hearing from a diverse chorus of voices — Strat players, Fender executives and craftspeople, even rival manufacturers.

The Fender Stratocaster both reflects and influences popular culture worldwide. *The Stratocaster Chronicles* is a Golden Anniversary celebration of the people who conceived it, the designers and builders who refined it, and the players who took it from there.

ACKNOWLEDGEMENTS

Fender's Senior Vice President of Market Development Ritchie Fliegler and editor Brad Smith at Hal Leonard approached me in the fall of 2002 with the idea of writing a book commemorating the Stratocaster's 50th anniversary. I owe my old friend Ritchie and new friend Brad a great deal for their encouragement and good counsel at every step. Although I've been writing magazine columns and contributing to other writers' guitar books in recent years, *The Stratocaster Chronicles* is the first full-fledged guitar book of my own in more than a decade, and writing it has been exhilarating.

I am deeply appreciative of Eric Clapton's writing the foreword and, as any guitar player will understand, profoundly honored to have his name associated with this project. Thanks also to his associates Lee Dickson and Vivien Gibson.

I could not have asked for a more highly qualified team of advisers and collaborators. Art director Richard Slater has done a beautiful job, designing the book I dreamed about for more than a year. When it comes to photographing instruments, John Peden is simply the best in the world (and an astute connoisseur of vintage guitars), and I am pleased to have an opportunity to share his work in these pages. Don Randall once said of Richard Smith, "He knows more about Fender's history than I do." Richard read portions of the manuscript and offered valuable insights. Artist/photographer Bob Perine was instrumental in fashioning Fender's image in the heyday of the '50s and '60s; it was a thrill to meet someone who many years ago had stimulated my teenage imagination, to review his archives, and to present a few of his images.

Thanks to author/editor Jim Roberts, who reviewed the manuscript, and to Alan Rogan, whose roster of current and former clients reveals his esteem among artists and fellow guitar techs — Keith Richards, Mick Jagger, Eric Clapton, George Harrison, Pete Townshend, John Entwistle, Joe Walsh, and Graham Nash, to name a few. Perry A. Margouleff contributed detailed comments about many of the instruments pictured here. The Experience Music Project generously opened its archives; special thanks to Collections Manager Michele Wallace. I am also indebted to the dazzlingly talented and funny Greg Koch, who recorded the enclosed CD and makes the book come alive in the best possible way — rippin' on a Strat.

When I asked for help, Fender rolled out the Fiesta Red carpet. Executives, designers, and Custom Shop Master Builders all read portions of the manuscript and provided corrections and clarifications. Ritchie Fliegler, Richard McDonald, George Blanda, and Mike Lewis all were interviewed several times and read the entire manuscript in one version or another. Special thanks to my old friend Dan Smith; despite his enormous responsibilities at the factory, he found time for several lengthy interviews and for patiently reviewing the text, some sections repeatedly.

Included here are excerpts from my previous interviews with the late Leo Fender, Freddie Tavares, and Forrest White, all of whom I remember with respect and affection. Also included are recent interviews with Don Randall and George Fullerton, to whom I am deeply grateful. It was especially gratifying to speak again with Bill Carson, who provided many insights and reflections. Additional current and former Fender employees interviewed for this book include J.W. Black, Joe Carducci, Mike Eldred, Bob Hipp, Mark Kendrick, Todd Krause, Larry Moudy, John Page, and Bill Turner. Other interviewees who gave generously of their time: Vince Cunetto, Lee Dickson, Clay Harrell, Iain Hersey, Norm Isaac, Mary Kaye, and Bob Sperzel. Thank you all.

Fender's Rich Siegle and Jason Farrell scoured the company vaults and assembled most of the images seen here from Fender's recent history. They enlisted the aid of other employees and associates already mentioned here, as well as Patrick Cheung, Doug Crouch, Connie Herron, Jake Hill, Paul Jernigan, Joel Meine, Bill Mendello, Morgan Ringwald, Andy Rossi, Bill Schultz, and Mark Van Vleet. Thanks also to Fender Europe's Michael Charalambous and Jamie Crompton.

My colleagues at *Guitar Player* magazine, where I spent 14 rewarding years, generously allowed me to quote from their unparalleled archive of interviews (having been removed from their original contexts, some excerpts have been lightly edited, with care, for clarity). Special thanks to old pals and former editorial partners Dan Forte and Jas Obrecht, several of whose interviews are quoted. Videographer Dennis Baxter freely allowed me to reprint brief excerpts from his interviews with William Schultz, Forrest White, Don Randall, Dick Dale, Steve Miller, Richie Sambora, and Elliot Easton.

In the last half-century, countless musicians have recorded or performed memorable music on the Stratocaster; a small sample of those players is pictured in these pages. Thanks to Ken Settle, Neil Zlozower, Jon Sievert, and the other photographers who contributed a fine gallery of evocative images; to authors A.R. Duchossoir and the previously mentioned Richard Smith, whose books are cited here in several places; and to Andy Babiuk, Sterling Ball, Rose Bishop, Peter Blecha, Susan Carson, Karen Cavill, Jol Dantzig, Teisco Del Rey, Tricia Earl at the Buddy Holly Center in Lubbock, Dan Erlewine, Steve Fishell, Dónal Gallagher, Diane Gershuny (who interviewed Ernie Isley), *Rockin' 50s* editor and Buddy Holly historian Bill Griggs, Eddy Grigsby at the Lubbock Memorial Civic Center, George Gruhn, Bill Harkleroad, Stanley Jay, Henry Kaiser, John Kaye, Sonny Landreth, Don Latarski, Robb Lawrence, Brian Majeski at *The Music Trades*, Amy Rogers, Paul Reed Smith, Steve Soest, John Sprung, Richard Thompson, Rick Turner, and especially my wife Anne for her good cheer and support.

I never did meet Leo Fender, but I wish I had. If I could go back and somehow talk to him about the Stratocaster, I'd say, "You've created something that can't be bettered, really. How did you do that?" I know there were prototypes with the Telecaster and the Esquire, and some early experimental stages, but nevertheless, the fact that he got to this conclusion so quickly is remarkable, isn't it? Leo Fender was so far in advance of anybody else, developing the Strat to the point where it just can't be bettered, even now. My hat's off to him.

One reason why I hadn't played Strats earlier was that the necks always looked so narrow I thought, I won't be able to bend any strings, no room, but in fact I was wrong. And any Strat that I'd seen up until that time had a rosewood fingerboard, and I had an aversion to rosewood fingerboards — don't ask me why — even though some of my earlier guitars had them. I'd always preferred ebony. I liked that silky finish. Of course, when I got my hands on a maple-neck Strat with the white fingerboard, I was surprised at how easy it was to play.

I had a lot of influences when I took up the Strat. First there was Buddy Holly, and Buddy Guy. Hank Marvin was the first well known person over here in England who was using one, but that wasn't really my kind of music. Steve Winwood had so much credibility, and when he started playing one, I thought, oh, if he can do it, I can do it.

Picking up a Stratocaster makes me play a bit differently. I find that over the last few years I play more with my fingers because of the way my hand sits on the guitar. I don't feel the need to use a pick quite so much as I would with any other guitar, where the bridge sits higher off the body. With the Strat the bridge is almost flush with the guitar, so my hand

rests on the body, part of my heel rests on the bridge, and then my fingers rest on the scratchplate. It's really easy to play either way, but I've found more and more that I'm using just my fingers.

It's got those famous lead tones, but it's so versatile you can use it in any kind of rhythmic sense as well — great big power chords, or that really light kind of Tamla/Motown chord sound with very little volume. Unlike most other electric guitars, it sounds almost better when the guitar's volume knob is on 2 or 3, really under-amplified and quiet.

My first Strat was Brownie, and I played it for years and years, a wonderful guitar. Then I was in Nashville at a store called Sho-Bud, as I recall, and they had a whole rack of old '50s Strats in the back, going second-hand. They were so out of fashion you could pick up a perfectly genuine Strat for two hundred or three hundred dollars — even less! So I bought all of them. I gave one to Steve Winwood, one to George Harrison, and one to Pete Townshend, and kept a few for myself. I liked the idea of a black body, but the black one I had was in bad condition, so I took apart the ones I kept and assembled different pieces to make Blackie, which is a hybrid, a mongrel.

I played those old ones so much they wore out. Blackie's neck was actually narrower because of all the playing I'd done on it, and the frets were quite low. I hadn't done much restoration on my old ones, so I gave Blackie's neck to Fender as a template, and they built the Eric Clapton Signature guitars I'm playing now, which are more robust, with more power in the pickups.

I keep coming back to the Stratocaster because it's so practical. It doesn't move very much, it's stable, it stays in tune, and has a great sound. It's fairly invincible, quite difficult to damage. I really like the old coil pickups, especially that middle and bridge combination. I used that for the solo in "Bell Bottom Blues," which would be a classic example of that sound. But I've got those new Noiseless pickups now, and active circuitry, and I get so many different sounds coming out of the Stratocaster that it's hard to compare it to any other guitar. My other guitars, I only visit them from time to time. I very rarely use anything else but the Strat.

My feelings about a perfect design is that it has to be functional, and with the Strat, its functionality really steers it. That's what makes the design so beautiful. It's superbly thought out. At first I thought it was odd to have only one volume control, but that's only because I was used to a different set-up. All the things I love about it aesthetically are there for a real purpose, like the contoured back. If those things were based just on the way they looked, that would be fine, but everything on that guitar is there for a reason. Like the pegboard, with all the tuning pegs on the top. That's such a logical thing to do when you think about how accessible it is.

I come back to the fact that I don't think there's anything on that guitar that doesn't come from pure logic. I would challenge anybody to come up with a better design for a guitar. The Stratocaster is as good as it gets, isn't it?

Eric Clapton

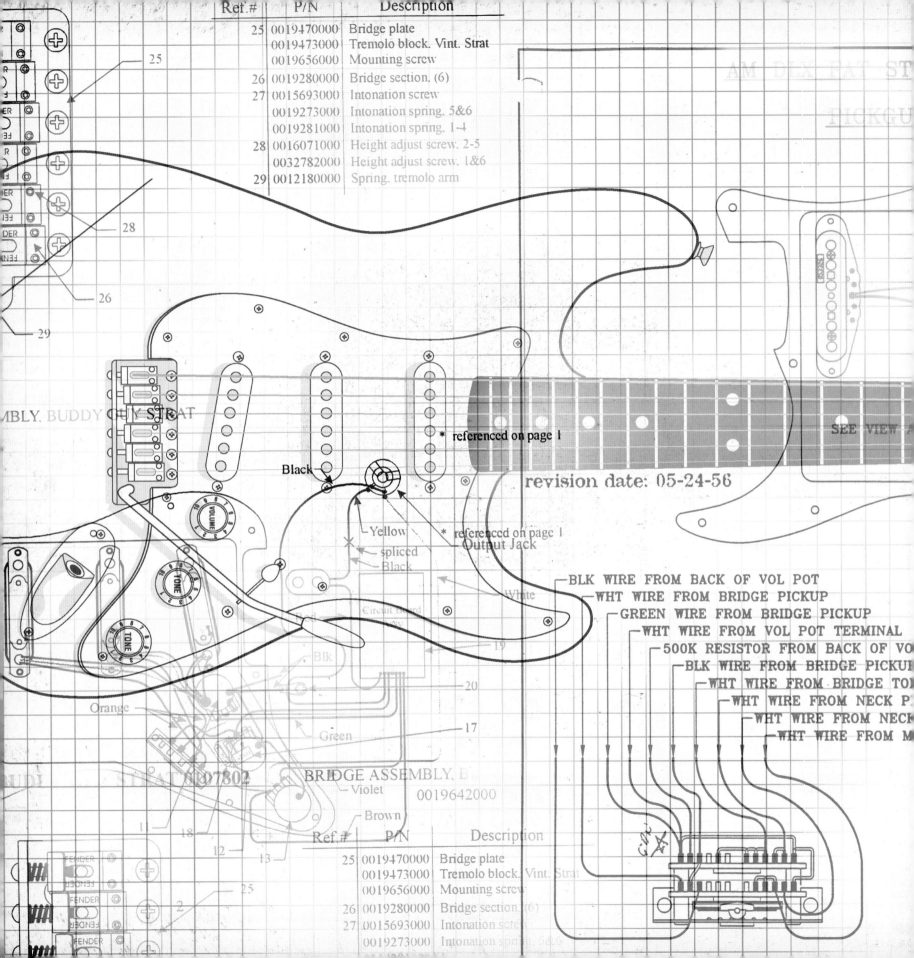

SEE VIEW A—A

BACK OF VOL POT
FROM BRIDGE PICKUP
WIRE FROM BRIDGE PICKUP
WIRE FROM VOL POT TERMINAL
OK RESISTOR FROM BACK OF VOL POT
BLK WIRE FROM BRIDGE PICKUP
WHT WIRE FROM BRIDGE TONE POT
WHT WIRE FROM NECK PICKUP
WHT WIRE FROM NECK/MID TONE POT
WHT WIRE FROM MID PICKUP

INTRODUCTION

BRIDGE ASSEMBLY

VIEW A—A
SCALE : NONE
date: 10-11-72

VOLUME

TONE

TONE

f#	P/	Description
25	0019170000	Bridge plate
	0019473000	Tremolo block. Vint. Strat
	0019656000	Mounting screw
26	0019280000	Bridge section. (6)
27	0015693000	Intonation screw
	0019273000	Intonation spring. 5&6
	0019281000	Intonation spring.
28	0016071000	Height adjust screw. 2-5
	0032782000	Height adjust screw. 1&6
29	0012180000	Spring. tremolo arm

"In some cases,
a musician likes an
acoustic guitar better.
Well, fine and dandy.
In other cases,
an acoustic won't
do the job. That's
where we come in."
– Leo Fender

Reflections on the Stratocaster

When 21-year-old Buddy Holly appeared on the Ed Sullivan Show in late 1957 strumming the living daylights out of a maple-neck Stratocaster, typical viewers might well have asked, "Is that a guitar?" After all, Leo Fender's latest innovation, only three years old and not particularly well known, seemed as far removed from conventional guitars as, say, a baritone ukulele or even a banjo. Its twin-horned body wasn't shaped like any guitar anyone had ever seen. It had no acoustic chamber, no soundholes. It had all its tuning gears on one side of the peghead. It was slim, solid and, for its day, positively bristling with electrical and mechanical doodads.

Plenty of professional musicians saw the new Fender as unworthy of serious consideration — merely a tool, a gimmicky contraption, even a joke. It had neither the figured woods nor the understated Old World charm of an expensive arch-top like the kind played by Johnny Smith or Freddie Green or even Scotty Moore. It hardly looked as though it had been crafted on the workbench of a reputable artisan. The new slab-bodied "plank" out of California looked more like it had come from … a *factory*, which of course it had.

And yet, when I look up "electric guitar" in my American Heritage College Dictionary, the generic illustration pictures one of the countless copies of the Stratocaster. Webster's New World Student Dictionary shows another. Could the very same instrument that once appeared so radical it made people wonder if it were actually a guitar have had so profound an influence over the past half-century that, somehow, it has come to epitomize the public's idea of what an electric guitar looks like, what an electric guitar *is*?

Well, yes. But how did that happen? By what extraordinary chain of events did a revolutionary and once maligned deviation become not only popular but the standard — literally a dictionary definition of "electric guitar"? Looking at the instrument and its inventor, some answers are apparent. Simply put, Mr. Fender considered existing products, saw flaws, thought he could do better, and went ahead and did it. The outcome was an instrument so far ahead of its time that other manufacturers' models — even some that came along years later — looked stodgy by comparison.

How was such an ultimately dominant product created by a newcomer to the business who seemed to have several strikes against him? Leo Fender wasn't a serious musician, had little background (or interest) in the traditional crafts or lore of instrument building, and was even less interested in associating with the old-boy network of acquaintances who ran the major guitar companies and might have helped him get on his feet.

But I've come to think that Mr. Fender's status as a non-player and industry outsider was an advantage, because it freed him from orthodoxy, gave him a blank slate. Could anyone, no matter how brilliant, have dreamed up the Stratocaster if he had been rooted in established notions of how electric guitars looked, sounded, and were supposed to work? No focus group, no marketing committee could have come up with the Strat. It had to be the brainchild of a stubborn visionary, one who not only felt unbound by the customs of his industry but also clearly didn't give a damn.

"Once you start playing one,
    it's hard to play anything else."

– Eric Johnson

From Mr. Fender's point of view, the Strat wasn't about radical visions or revolutionizing the industry or anything so momentous. He was interested in seemingly mundane pursuits: methodical analysis, trial and error, improving existing guitars (specifically his own Telecaster) feature by feature, and assessing feedback from musicians, including some who shared county fair stages with sequin-encrusted western music stars, and others who played in dinky dives and bowling alley bars. The result may have been the sleekest, sexiest guitar anyone's ever seen, enshrined as an artwork as well as an instrument, but it was rooted in long days and nights at a sheet-steel workbench, in midnight oil and elbow grease. Longtime associate Bill Carson: "Leo used to say, if we've only got a hundred dollars to develop this item, it's got to be reliable, and it's a life or death matter for the musician for that thing to perform every time. We will spend as much of that hundred dollars as necessary to get that. If we've got four or five dollars left over, we'll work on the cosmetics."

Leo Fender had plenty of help, from Bill Carson, George Fullerton, and Freddie Tavares, all of whom contributed to the design; Don Randall, a marketing genius without equal in the annals of the music industry; Forrest White, who straightened out the factory operation; and a crew of skilled workers, some of whom spent decades winding pickups and sanding bodies for their plain-spoken boss.

Still, even a grasp of the raw genius of Leo Fender, the impressive list of his guitar's attributes, and the contributions of talented associates aren't enough to explain the Stratocaster's journey from the outback of the guitar market to its summit.

Something else is at work here.

Since the dawn of the last century, music technologies have produced not only intended results such as improved methods of recording musical signals but also any number of unintended consequences, including changes in the forms and styles of the music itself. The mechanical-acoustic recording methods of the early 1920s favored the instruments whose volumes and timbres allowed them to be heard, as well as

 The "Derek" Clap-Tone, Track 31

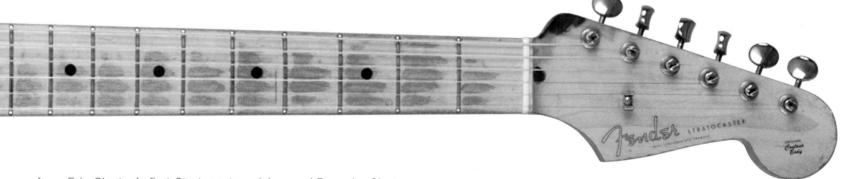

 Eric Clapton's first Stratocaster, nicknamed Brownie. Clapton used it on his 1970 masterpiece *Layla*. Nearly two decades later, the June 1956 2-color sunburst guitar (serial no. 12073) brought nearly half a million dollars at an auction to raise money for The Crossroads Centre, a rehabilitation clinic founded by Clapton in 1998. According to Fender Europe's Michael Charalambous, Clapton purchased Brownie in London while touring with Cream in May 1967.

vocalists who sang in a certain range. But when the old tin horns and glass diaphragms were displaced by microphones and electrical systems, no longer were tubas favored over string basses, banjoes over guitars, tenor vocalists over baritones. Aside from providing higher fidelity, the new technology permitted a softer, up-close vocal delivery, with nuance and detail. As documented in a 2002 NPR program, Bing Crosby was quick to capitalize on the opportunity, singing with a compelling intimacy that redefined what it meant to be a pop singer.

Similarly, the introductions of magnetic tape, multi-track, long play records, stereo, and FM radio not only realigned the processes and economics of music but also rekindled at every step an exhilarating experimentalism that broadened musicians' techniques, aesthetics, and repertoire.

Buddy Holly & The Crickets, 1958, with Joe B. Mauldin on bass and Jerry Allison on drums. Mauldin recalled in the video *The Real Buddy Holly Story*, "When Buddy bought something, he bought the best there was to get. Like when he bought his first Fender Stratocaster — and I think that was the first one in Lubbock, Texas — I couldn't believe that was a guitar. That was the first solidbody guitar I'd ever seen, you know, with a gearshift on it … I was very impressed with it, and I think a lot of other people were, too. After we did our first tour in Europe, seems like everybody wanted to talk to Buddy about that guitar." Jeff Beck: "I saw Buddy Holly live, and it was the best thing I've ever seen."[1]

 Harmonious Hollyism, Track 13

"Buddy came to me and asked me for a loan so he could buy a new guitar and amplifiers....

I asked him how much he needed, and he said a thousand dollars.... I wondered if it was wise to spend money that way... and he said, 'No, I know what I'm doing. I'm going to be a star now, and everything I do has got to be the best, and my guitar has got to be the best.'"

– Buddy's brother, Larry Holley, from the book *Remembering Buddy*

Sculpted by Grant Speed and unveiled in 1980, this larger-than-lifesize bronze statue of favorite son Buddy Holly was commissioned by the city of Lubbock, Texas, where Holly was born on September 7, 1936.

The electric guitar, of course, is another example. Its rich vocabulary of techniques, tones, and effects is so much a part of today's musical landscape that it's easy to forget its original intent was not to expand freedom of expression or to push guitarists into the spotlight but merely to amplify the familiar sounds of strummed acoustic guitars.

USA Today once asked me to write an article about how the first-generation solidbody guitars were designed to accommodate rock and roll. I explained that those guitars weren't designed for rock and roll at all. They appeared in 1950 (Fender's Telecaster), 1952 (Gibson's Les Paul, a direct response to the Tele) and 1954 (the Strat, among other things a response to the Les Paul), up to six or seven years before Elvis and Little Richard began giving Mitch Miller and Patti Page a run for their money in record sales and airplay. The Strat was already there when rock and roll arrived, a sleeping dragon waiting for someone to come along and poke it, tap into some deeper potential, and awaken in it a new kind of life.

Someone did. In fact, many did, in ways no one could have foreseen, certainly not Leo Fender. While the Stratocaster is still Mr. Fender's guitar in terms of its design and construction, in other respects the incandescent, unruly offspring slipped away from its father a long time ago. Indeed, the ingenuity of the Strat's inventor is only the beginning of its story; the rest is found in the boundless creativity of the players who picked it up and plugged it in. No one suggests that Jimi Hendrix or Eric Clapton or Jeff Beck couldn't have made interesting music on guitars other than Stratocasters (they all made plenty of interesting music on other guitars), but their Strats were essential not only to their sounds but to their influence and legacies as well.

Ike Turner (here with Tina in an early publicity photo) performed blistering, whammy-wranglin' solos on the Stratocaster he bought soon after the model's introduction (and other Strats). His inventive style is a classic example of an artist discovering the Stratocaster, adapting to its features, and fashioning something remarkable. Explaining his radical approach to the tremolo bar, he said, "That's what I thought it was for!"

As George Fullerton wrote in his book *Guitar Legends*, "With these new [Fenders] came a new breed of players. They had some of their own suggestions about new sounds and different ways of establishing their music." As Jeff Beck put it, "I think I can sound more like myself with a Strat."

During the June 1957 recording session for "Peggy Sue," Niki Sullivan's assignment was to throw the pickup selector on Buddy Holly's Stratocaster guitar so the singer wouldn't have to miss a single stroke when he launched into his now-classic strumfest solo. Players have been adapting to the Strat's advan-

tages and quirks ever since: balancing its pickup switch to select the "in between" tones Mr. Fender never liked; plugging it into high-volume amplifiers to produce the kind of distortion Mr. Fender tried to avoid in his own world-dominating amps; generating the howling feedback that was the bane of archtops and one of the reasons Fender went with a solid body in the first place; exploring drastic vibrato-bar techniques that Mr. Fender and anyone else of his generation would likely have considered bizarre and unmusical; and purchasing or jerry-rigging a pile of accessories and fix-its to customize the guitar or to compensate for its perceived shortcomings.

Still, the connection between the inventor and the musicians who play his guitar to this day is real and meaningful, rooted deep in Mr. Fender's radical vision, his getting so many things right the first time, and his all-important commitment to function. As if taking their cue from Leo himself, some of the players who adopted his Stratocaster redefined it again and again to suit their visions, as Mr. Fender had redefined the electric guitar to suit his own.

The story of the Strat is typically told in terms of the bulging gallery of its players and their milestone albums and legendary performances. Its physical evolution is also well documented, to say the least, with entire volumes listing structural variations in exhaustive detail — not only in the fingerboard thickness and peghead dimensions but also in pickup impedance, the digits in the decals, even the metallic composition of bridge saddles. We know the names of workers who penciled their initials inside Strat bodies a half-century ago.

Pee Wee Crayton. Several of his hits made *Billboard's* "race" charts in the '40s, and Leo Fender gave him one of the very first Custom Color Strats (note anodized pickguard). "The music, the guitar playing, was already in me, but I don't play the guitar. God plays the guitar through me. Just play what you know, what's inside of you."

Don Wilson, left, and Bob Bogle were founding members of the Ventures, the instrumental combo that inspired countless bands and helped to sell countless Fenders.

THE VENTURES

That same history churns with inconsistent accounts and sometimes bitter feuds among Leo Fender's old associates about what happened when, or who suggested which feature, whose voice had the most influence on the man himself. The drama is further agitated by incessant debates among players about the merits of vintage instruments vs. reissues or updates, and speculation about, say, the sonic effects of different fabrics used to sheath interior wires. One illustration of the Strat's allure: No aspect of its history or construction is too obscure to escape scrutiny.

But far removed from the screw-by-screw minutiae, beyond the now fading echoes of squabbles about long-ago events, apart from the buzz of this season's musical trends and industry chatter, the Stratocaster floats transcendent in the ether of its own uniqueness, high above the drama and the din. Its

essence seeps into recording studios and across arena stages and magazine covers, into neighborhood rehearsal garages, glitzy supper clubs and rank, sticky-floored roadhouses. It drifts into the private vaults of secretive collectors, under teenagers' beds in suburban homes, and into the dreams of youngsters just now learning the howdy-partner chords to "On Top Of Old Smokey" or the black-leather riff to "Enter Sandman." Apart from the weight of its own history, the Strat abides. Its structural evolution is important, but the real marvel, a deeper phenomenon beyond documentation, is the unique 50-year relationship between the guitar, its players famous and obscure, and the music they made and continue to make together.

More than any other electric model, the Strat is all guitars to all people, a period-perfect vintage object, yet timeless as well. It strikes us at various moments as an example of the beauty of pure function, a futuristic space vehicle, a sexy prop, an elegant piece of sculpture, a badass weapon, a holy grail among collectibles, an investment commodity to be hoarded or traded, a vehicle for personal expression, a tool for making a living, or all of the above. What more do we need to say about the versatility of an instrument that was adopted by the guitar players with both Lawrence Welk and Pink Floyd?

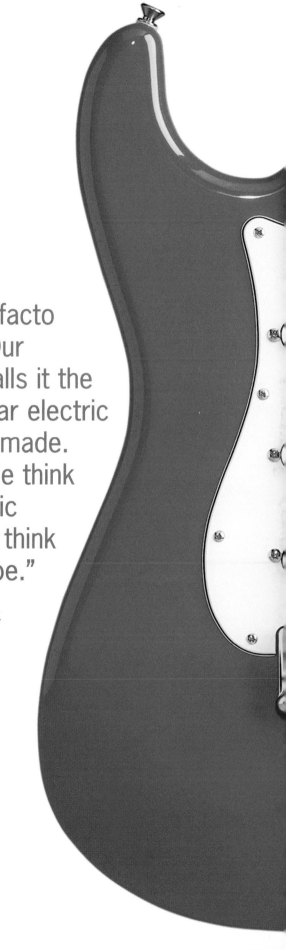

"It's the de facto standard. Our literature calls it the most popular electric guitar ever made. When people think of an electric guitar, they think of that shape."

– David Riddle, of NBT, maker of lithographed guitar illustrations

'50s cool: Ronnie Dawson and admirers onstage during Dawson's stint with the Light Crust Doughboys.

The Strat is now exalted routinely, even predictably, as a cultural icon. *Rolling Stone* went so far as to include it in its May 2003 "American Icons" cover story, along with Elvis Presley, the American flag, the Corvette, and "blonde bombshells"; note that the magazine picked only one musical instrument for this 35th Anniversary Special Issue, and it was the Fender Stratocaster rather than the generic electric guitar. As David Fricke wrote, the Stratocaster "looks and sounds like America."

But if we can chisel away the accumulated crust of its rumors and legend, let's remember that underneath it all this icon is "just" a guitar, succeeding decade after decade for the same old reasons, the same advantages Mr. Fender and his small crew built into the originals in the early months of 1954. It still looks cool, and it still makes you look a little cooler than the other players in the band. It's still comfy, still durable, and it still sounds … well, like a Stratocaster. *That* sound.

As we celebrate the golden anniversary of the Stratocaster, Mr. Fender's vision still unfolds, still reveals itself. Fifty years out, we stand in awe at the essential rightness of the Strat as generation after generation responds to its call with passion and creativity, taking the guitar — and music — to places Clarence Leo Fender never could have imagined. As a musical instrument, the Stratocaster will always be Leo Fender's guitar. As a dream machine, it belongs to the world.

— Tom Wheeler, 2004

"The amazing thing about the Stratocaster is that Leo did not have Jimi Hendrix in mind when he designed it, and look where it went. For musicians to pick up an instrument that was designed so completely in one direction, and take it in such a different direction, speaks of the almost unconscious mind of Leo Fender."

– Rick Turner, designer & luthier, Renaissance Guitars

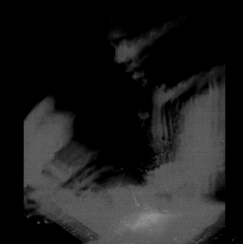

"The Strat is the most expressive of all the electric guitars, the nearest to the human voice you can get."

– *Robin Trower*

Is this the most widely heard Strat of all time? Hard to say, but among guitars heard on long-running hit singles, this one at least deserves some sort of marathon award. It was used for the solo on a tune in constant radio rotation for years by the time "Purple Haze" or "Layla" hit the airwaves. The original continues to inspire renditions heard at brass-band parades, sporting events, frat parties, or beer-intensive wedding receptions. You're just as likely to hear this Strat on the radio today as you were 20 years ago. Or 30 years ago. Final hint: The song title is two words — or one word, depending on how you look at it. Answer on p. 276.

IN THE BEGINNING

The father of the solidbody electric guitar

The Stratocaster's originality was so startling that it's easy to overlook its connection to the Telecaster, but as George Fullerton said, "The Stratocaster evolved from the Telecaster." In fact, while Tele and Strat lovers

cherish their instruments' distinct personalities, Mr. Fender believed back in 1954 that the newer guitar's advantages would render its older sibling obsolete. The Tele's venerability has proved him wrong on that point, but the story of the Strat does indeed go back to the Tele, and further.

If historians can't pinpoint the first solidbody electric Spanish guitar, it's partly because of a lack of agreement on criteria that would define it. Was it a Hawaiian lap steel modified by some obscure soul who hammered frets into

his guitar, tuned it to standard pitch and flipped it on its side? Was it Lloyd Loar's short-lived, seldom seen Vivi-Tone of 1933, with its impractical pickup and oddball construction (sort of a full-length neck assembly with a guitar top attached to it)? Was it Rickenbacker's Model B Spanish guitar of 1935, with an inconveniently small, chambered body of Bakelite, a short scale, and its frets and neck molded into a single unit? Or Slingerland's late-'30s Songster Style 401, called by some the first "modern" solidbody with its full 25" scale, real frets, and wooden body?

Some point to Les Paul's "Log," a makeshift contraption consisting of a neck, hardware and strings attached to a 4x4" pine board with body "wings" stuck on the sides. There were more than a few drops of bad blood among various parties concerning a guitar designed by Merle Travis and built in 1948 by Paul Bigsby; my own contender for the "first modern solidbody" title, it had neck-through construction, a headstock profile that foreshadowed the Stratocaster, and a somewhat Les Paul-like body silhouette. Leo Fender borrowed it prior to the introduction of the Telecaster, although its influence on him was disputed. (In the September '76 *Guitar Player*, Travis declared, "I designed the Fender guitar." Mr. Fender dismissed the exaggeration.)

Leo was once asked by a co-worker why he ate canned spaghetti instead of buying a hot sandwich from the lunch truck like the rest of the factory crew. He replied, "Because for the difference in price between the spaghetti and the sandwich I can buy a handful of resistors."

"Leo was a deep, relentless thinker, and when you got an idea across to him he could put it into being. He could figure the size of the screws, the amount of threads per inch — *in his mind* — and write it down on an envelope and then go out there and make it. In my estimation, the working musician never had as good a friend as Leo Fender."

— *Bill Carson*

The Vivi-Tone, Rickenbacker, and Slingerland were innovative, to be sure, but aside from suggesting to anyone who was aware of them that the solidbody concept might be worth pursuing, it would be hard to document their influence on the pioneers who designed practical solidbody guitars. Although the ingenious Paul Bigsby almost certainly influenced Leo Fender to some degree, he never wanted to be a major manufacturer, and according to former Gibson president Ted McCarty, the time-honored Les Paul of 1952 was not so much a fulfillment of Les Paul's request for a solidbody but rather a response to the Telecaster.

As much as we might revel in the romance of a tidy, straight-line evolution traceable to some hallowed First Guitar, the story of the solidbody's development is rather a tale of sometimes simultaneous efforts by independent builders, each with his own influences and insights. A few of their ideas are still with us every time we play or hear an electric guitar, but most are long forgotten. As with many species, the solidbody's story is marked with more than a few evolutionary dead ends.

Debates about who influenced whom, however fascinating, sometimes obscure an essential fact: It was Leo Fender who put the solidbody on the map. He possessed something beyond a knack for mechanics, or foresight, or a belief in a dream: He could make it happen, and therein lay the singular genius of Fender. He designed an electric Spanish guitar with no discernible connection to the Vivi-Tone or the Slingerland, one that looked nothing like the little Rickenbackers or Les Paul's ungainly "Log," one that even Merle Travis admitted was superior to his own Bigsby, one that would later prove its practicality with continuous production over half a century (and counting). Mr. Fender's next move was just as important but often overlooked: He developed a process by which the new instrument and its more glamorous sibling, the Stratocaster, could be profitably manufactured on a large scale. By any and all meaningful cri-

teria, it was Clarence Leo Fender who was the father of the solidbody guitar.

Fender's radical guitars and their profound, even subversive effects seem all the more impressive given Mr. Fender's low-key personality and the distinctly conservative tenor of the Orange County, California, surroundings where he grew up. But his calm demeanor diminished neither his passion for things mechanical nor his relentless inquisitiveness. He routinely annoyed representatives who sold him parts and supplies by grilling them about their own products and then

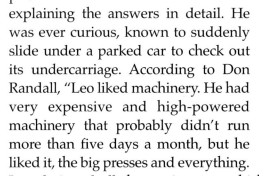

A Custom Shop craftsman installs a pre-wired pickguard assembly. The modular production process devised by Mr. Fender cut costs and helped make the Stratocaster more affordable.

explaining the answers in detail. He was ever curious, known to suddenly slide under a parked car to check out its undercarriage. According to Don Randall, "Leo liked machinery. He had very expensive and high-powered machinery that probably didn't run more than five days a month, but he liked it, the big presses and everything. Leo designed all the equipment, which was unique, and he was a genius for figuring out the manufacturing process. A very clever man." By his own estimate, Leo Fender owned up to 75 patents. Clever, indeed.

It's difficult to overstate Mr. Fender's impact on his industry. Almost like a glitzy trend-setter, he helped to alter the look, the sound, and the personality of American music, and yet it would be hard to imagine a man of plainer appearance or fewer affectations. The late Freddie Tavares said, "He never wore any kind of clothes that you'd expect a person in his position to wear. People didn't have the slightest idea he was any kind of a wheel. I would have to

Leo Fender began work on the Strat in this shop on the corner of Santa Fe and Pomona Avenues in Fullerton.

point him out to someone who didn't know him. 'See that man over there? He owns everything.' Leo never flew off the handle, never raised his voice. One time someone made a costly mistake, and Leo just said, 'I wish they knew how often I made a mistake.' With all of his stresses and strains, he still tried to keep everyone's spirits up."

A similar account, told by the late Forrest White, concerned a new employee who, not recognizing Mr. Fender, responded to some casual advice from Leo by saying, "Look buddy, you take care of your job, and I'll take care of mine." "Leo just sort of grinned and didn't say anything," Forrest recalled with obvious affection. "But that gives you an idea of what kind of man he was. He was easy to get along with because he didn't have to impress anyone. He was a living example of what a successful man should be."

Although Mr. Fender was not an outgoing individual, his offbeat sense of humor often entertained employees. One of his favorite techniques was the play on words; an example: "You know, everybody thinks we make custom instruments, but that's because we make them so good that our competitors have always cussed 'em." He liked a good car, meaning one that was mechanically sound, but he shunned most trappings of the successful executive. He rarely wore a suit, and was almost never without his leather holster full of screwdrivers. In his shirt, he kept a plastic pocket protector stuffed with pens, pencils, and a little metal ruler.

When someone did a job for Leo Fender, no matter how good it was, it rarely met his standards. He split hairs, he looked over shoulders, and he could be meddlesome (he offered employees much advice, solicited or otherwise, on subjects such as which new car they should buy). Yet his employees liked him; some practically worshipped him. Forrest White's opinion — "I wouldn't trade the years I spent with Leo for anything" — was not uncommon.

Leo Fender neither drank nor smoked and had few close friends. He was described by more than one associate as something of a recluse. While he dabbled in photography, liked to play pinochle on a Saturday night, and owned an expensive boat, his only true hobby, perhaps his obsession, was his work. He was a man of few words. He did not play guitar.

"Leo Fender is a personal hero. I was fortunate to be able to spend time with him and I cherish his words and insights. To me, his genius is the simplicity of his thinking and the purity of his execution—all (at the time) unencumbered by tradition. The Strat is the most copied guitar not because of its musicality (which it has in spades) but its ease of manufacture. As a musician, I love the brutal clarity a Strat brings to music. As a builder and designer, I stand in awe of the completeness of the Stratocaster's statement as a production-friendly appliance. The fact that it is possibly the most musical electric guitar seems like icing on the cake."

– Jol Dantzig, cofounder,
Hamer Guitars

"California has always had kind of a renegade reputation, not wanting to do anything like the rest of the country. Those early guitar pioneers in California were definitely out there on the leading edge. We also had the influence of Hollywood being just up the road from Orange County, where both Rickenbacker and Fender were, so there was a lot of communication with the Hollywood musicians."

– John Hall, who heads today's Rickenbacker company
and whose father, F.C. Hall, ran Radio-Tel,
Fender's first distributor

"There is a good chance that his office would disappoint the lowest federal bureaucrat in Washington. It's a small room, sparsely furnished — no carpet, functional lighting, with a drafting table piled high with blueprints; the monotonic paint is vaguely institutional. A metal bookcase is crammed with speaker parts and catalogs from electronics suppliers. On the modest desk is a Styrofoam coffee cup that, while disposable, is nevertheless being saved; it is labeled with a name carefully printed on masking tape in ballpoint pen: *Leo.* A side door opens into a large, concrete-floored room full of industrial drills and punch presses. There are no clues to the fact that the occupant of the office is a millionaire executive and a leader of his industry, though the absence of frills and the palpable air of utility and frugality befit the man who designed it, Clarence Leo Fender."

– Tom Wheeler, Guitar Player

Leo Fender designed electric guitars and amplifiers as matched sets, like this early production Stratocaster and its all-tube, tweed-wrapped partner. Photo by Mr. Fender.

"My family and Leo Fender go back to about 1951. My dad was one of the very early endorsees and was so taken with Leo's designs that he opened the first electric guitar store in 1953. At 18 I had the honor of being asked by my godfather [Leo's partner in Music Man, Tom Walker] to come check out Leo's new bass. The first surprise was that Leo was hard of hearing. He really had a hard time hearing high frequencies. When it sounded like butter to Leo it was over-the-top harsh for the rest of us. Back then it was a hard fought battle to get Leo to agree to softening the high end. I think that in a funny way Leo's hearing difficulties really shaped the way the world hears the guitar. He would love to have people come into his lab and put a screwdriver on a guitar's bridge and the plastic on the hard cartilage of your ear and listen to the string ring, the more vibration the better. My last memory of Leo is in his lab smiling at just how much that string rang."

– Sterling Ball, President, Ernie Ball/Music Man;
Sterling's dad is Ernie Ball

The works: Mike Parker's mint 1955 sunburst with amp, case, catalogs, endorser photos and, as photographer Robb Lawrence put it, "every type of accouterment imaginable, all the case candy — strap, cord, polishing cloth, strings, pick case, and instructions."

A Conversation with Leo Fender

As Editor in Chief of *Guitar Player*, I was fortunate to meet many fascinating players, some of whom were my heroes. Once in a while I even had a chance to jam with them, and those were dreams come true. But nothing ever topped being taken out to lunch by Leo Fender, to go to Carl's Jr. for a sandwich and some lemonade or iced tea, to have George Fullerton or Forrest White along for the discussion, and to have Mr. Fender walk me through his recollections, his opinions, and the processes of his mind.

The following is an edited composite of late-'70s interviews that took place in and around Leo Fender's shop at CLF Research; Leo's comments on the Strat appear in the Imaginary Roundtable, p. 56; excerpts can be heard on the CD that accompanies this book. As in the Roundtable, the comments here were mildly edited to enhance clarity, to remove redundancies, or to locate in one spot Mr. Fender's thoughts on a particular topic.

Leo Fender, January 1967

let aesthetics get in the way of utility. *[On the CD that* *accompanies this book, track 4 is only a few seconds long, but you can hear in Mr. Fender's own voice an assertion of his cardinal principle: utility comes first.]*

What were you trying to accomplish with the Broadcaster? What were your criteria?
At that time, the steel guitar was extremely popular, and we wanted a standard guitar that had a little bit more of the sound of the steel guitar. I always liked western music, and it was popular. There were problems with the guitars that had gone before. On an acoustic electric guitar you have a string fastened to a diaphragm top, and that top does not have one specific frequency. If you play a note, the top will respond to it and also to a lot of adjoining notes. A solid guitar body doesn't have that, and so you're dealing with just a single note at a time; this went along with the concept of the individual polepieces [on Fender pickups].

Your guitars were so radical, so unlike anything that had come before; what was your inspiration for the designs, the shapes?
I had so many years of experience with work on radios and electronic gear, and my main interest was in the utility aspects of an item; that was the main thing. Appearance came next. That gets turned around sometimes. To digress just a little bit, perhaps you heard a while back where they designed a car that looked a certain way, but then you had to hoist it up just to get at the spark plugs when you needed to change them. See, there, someone along the way had

How did the neck design come about?
On most of the necks at that time, all of the ones that we ran into, the frets weren't properly spaced for noting, and that had gone undetected in the acoustic style guitar because the diaphragm top gave you a tone that had these adjoining tones, so it wasn't so specific and clean. You could be a little out of tune and not know it. But on our guitars, it was clean, and you had to play just the right pitch, or it wouldn't sound good. So I devised a system for our fret measurements, and that was a whole new ball game. We found that the European

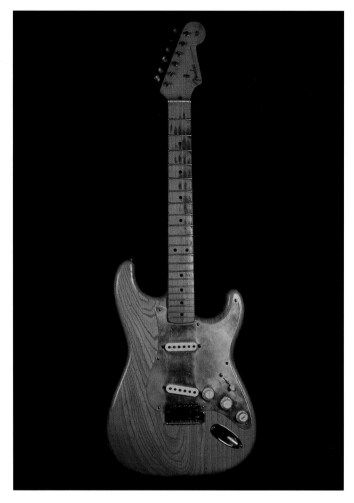

"This guitar doesn't exist — officially," says collector/author John Sprung of Parts Is Parts, Wilmington, VT. "It's a factory Strat with two pickups and a really wide neck, almost 2" at the nut. Larry Briggs at Strings West in Tulsa loaned it to me for the photo. I've been looking at old Fenders for decades, and this thing is authentic." Sprung explained in *20th Century Guitar* magazine that some of the pickup routing was done by hand. The wiring is odd yet practical in some respects. In the neck position, the two tone controls work simultaneously, providing a broad range of tones, including a "super mellow Jazzmastery sound" (Sprung speculated that this guitar could have been one experiment in Leo Fender's development of the two-pickup Jazzmaster). Aside from the fabulous one-piece body, other details include a metal pickguard (lightly anodized on the back), an aluminum (rather than plastic) spring cover in back, a neck date of Dec. '55, potentiometer dates of early '56, and serial no. 7070.

schools had trained their people to lay out frets by using a big chart. They'd draw this big graph, and it required some estimation, and it wasn't very satisfactory for our purposes, since it wasn't accurate enough. So we developed a method that allowed us to measure fret placement to one thousandth of an inch. A normal sheet of paper is about three thousandths, so we were as close as one third the thickness of an average sheet of paper. On the fretboards that you could just go and buy from suppliers, the frets were visibly misplaced.

Did anyone use the process of bolting on necks before you?
Yes, I think they bolted necks onto banjos. I did it because when you build a guitar and neck that are joined in one piece or bonded, then when you have a flaw in the neck, you have to decide between putting up with it or junking the whole damn thing — body, neck, and all. So I decided that it'd be best for the customer if I built the body and neck separate. See, a lot of times, even if the neck doesn't have to be replaced, it may just need an adjustment. It's better for the owner just to remove it for shipping. It's much easier than shipping the whole instrument. Sometimes a guitar would get injured; maybe a neck might be ruined, let's say. Well, we could check out a neck, put it into air transit the same day, and the customer would have his new part the day after the accident. It's functional. That's why we did it.

Your maple fingerboards looked different and felt unlike previous fingerboards. What was your aim in using maple?
I don't know if I actually remember, but at the time, there was a big trend toward instruments with blonde finishes on the body. Epiphone was very popular, and some of them were just about as blonde as you could make an instrument. People seemed to like that look, and I think that might have had a little to do with it.

Did you realize the potential for what you were doing? Were you setting out to revolutionize guitar manufacturing?
I didn't look at it in that way, no. I wanted to build a guitar that would have the sound that I thought that a stringed instrument should have. The guitar has

such a range, from the first string to the sixth, and two octaves up the neck, to expect a diaphragm top to respond to all of those frequencies with equal volume treatment, it's kind of an unreasonable demand. I never had too much feeling for the acoustic guitars. I always felt the guitar could do a much better job if it wasn't limited by the properties of that vibrating top. I didn't really think about revolutionizing the industry or anything of that sort. We were spending all of our time thinking about doing a better job for the musician. We wanted to get rid of the feedback that you get with the acoustic guitar, and we took care of other problems as they came up as well. We weren't trying to harm the acoustic guitar or anything like that, just come up with something that would do a better job for the player.

"I didn't really think about revolutionizing the industry or anything of that sort."

Did you originate the headstock with the tuners all on one side?
Well, that was my design, but I shouldn't just say that without telling you a little about it. It was originally a Croatian design, or maybe it's even older. *[On the CD that accompanies this book, track 7, Mr. Fender explains how the inspiration for the headstock came from his seeing instruments played by visiting Croatian musicians. Track 8: more details on Mr. Fender's reasoning behind the 6-on-a-side peghead.]*

Do you think that perhaps you work too hard?
Well, it's what I know. Most every evening I'm up until twelve or one o'clock, sketching at home — guitar bodies, pickups, or whatever's necessary.

Do you get a chance to spend much time on your boat?
Yes, but not like I used to. Going fishing tomorrow with a couple of friends, though.

Your catalogs often pictured musicians. Did many come by the factory?
It seemed like a part of every day we'd have some visiting musician. Hank Thompson, Hank Snow's group, Roy Acuff's group, Speedy West, Jimmy Bryant. They contributed ideas for new products, aside from being our friends. They're the ones who play the gear. We have a lot of musicians today, too. I can pick up the phone and get a dozen fellows over here tomorrow morning to give advice. We've always worked real close with the musicians.

Did you ever meet any of the guitar superstars who helped to popularize Fenders — Jimi Hendrix, Eric Clapton?
No, but I met Bob Wills.

Any favorite guitarists?
There are several, but one I really like is Roy Clark. I really admire him, not only his playing, but his singing, too.

But doesn't he usually play a Gibson?
Well, we can't all have the best [*laughs*]!

What would you like to do in the future?
Oh, I don't know, just have a small company and build more guitars, I guess. All I've ever really done is work in the guitar business. I like the people in it, and that's a good part to have in your work — it's important — and I like working with musicians and the people who help me.

How did you feel about other companies climbing on the bandwagon with their own solidbodies after your success?
I was too busy, I guess, to pay much attention to it. I didn't give it much thought. But I will say this: Their first reaction to our solidbody guitars was to make a lot of fun of them, but you know, I believe that eventually our dollar volume put us into the number one position in the whole world. Those other companies, they laughed at us at first, thought we were real amusing. [*Pauses, then laughs out loud.*] Maybe they've changed their minds by now!

Country/jazz artist Eldon Shamblin worked with one of the greatest bands of all time, Bob Wills & His Texas Playboys, and was dubbed "the world's best rhythm guitar player" by *Rolling Stone*. Bill Carson wrote, "I think Eldon Shamblin was the person most responsible for getting the Stratocaster out onto the market and getting it noticed by other musicians." Mr. Shamblin died in 1998 at age 82. His Strat, serial no. 0569, has a body dated June 4, 1954 and was signed inside the neck cavity by Gloria Fuentes; the neck is dated 5/54 and was initialed by Tadeo Gomez. Note its round string retainer, extensive neck wear, and the worn pickup tips, like those on Buddy Holly's '55 and other early Strats. According to Bill Carson, this is the first Custom Color Strat. The few greenish spots are due to oxidation. Eldon jettisoned the tremolo handle, blocked the trem assembly, and installed "chicken head" amp knobs. John Sprung wrote in *20th Century Guitar*: "Here lay a guitar that had seen more dance halls, state fairs, bars, and the like than a jukebox repairman … I find it to be the best sounding Strat I've heard."

Eldon recalled: "This was given to me by Mr. Fender in 1954. It was a demonstrator. It's been banged and beat, and the frets is wore, but I've had no problems with it whatsoever. It's been a good one. I can't find one that compares to this for rhythm. Leo Fender himself used to come out to wherever we were playing and service our amps … his equipment was probably the best there was." Eldon is shown here in front of historic Cain's Academy Ballroom in Tulsa, where the Texas Playboys rocked the house many a night.

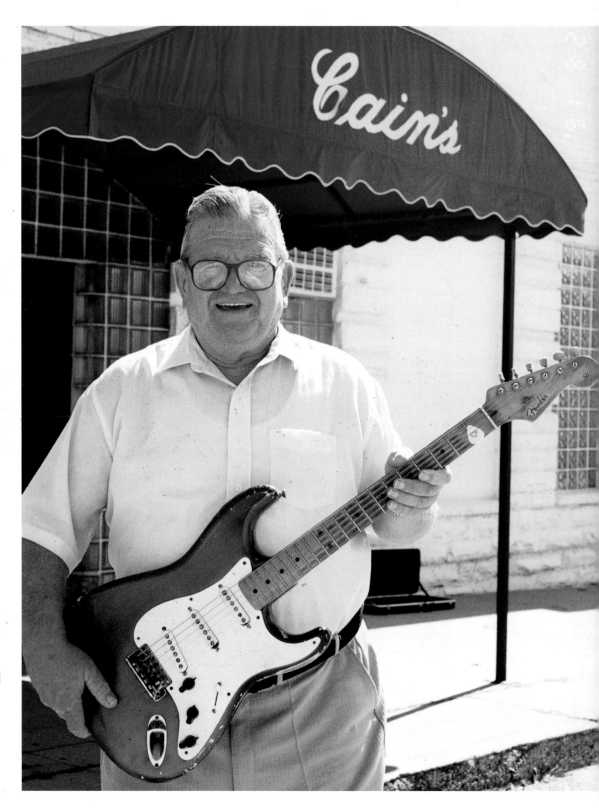

Swing-A-Billy!, Track 11

John Burks, *Guitar Player*: "Remember Bob Wills & His Texas Playboys?"

Jimi Hendrix: "[*Laughs*] I dig them. The Grand Ole Opry used to come on and I used to watch that. They used to have some pretty heavy cats, heavy guitar players."

"The Stratocaster is unbelievably successful on two levels. It's comfortable, and it's played more than any other guitar, so it's earned its popularity. It works when you're standing up, and when you're sitting down. My hat's off to Leo Fender for being an incredible innovator."
– Ned Steinberger

In January 1993 *Guitar Player* inaugurated the Leo Award for innovation in guitar equipment design: "We've named the award after the late Leo Fender for obvious reasons. His towering genius and his efforts over a lifetime perfectly embody the spirit of the award. Even if he had never designed a guitar — even if the words Telecaster and Stratocaster had never been dreamed up — Leo's perfection of the modern electric bass and his amplifier designs, achievements that radically altered popular music, could easily have justified the honor."

Broadcaster, serial no. 0027. In designing his first commercial electric Spanish guitar (the Broadcaster, soon renamed Telecaster), Mr. Fender approached the challenge from two perspectives. Whereas Gibson adapted its first electrics from the fine acoustic arch-tops it had been building for decades, Leo had no such experience; in fact, he didn't particularly like acoustic guitars. He had been building an utterly different instrument, a lap steel, with a small, solid body and a singing treble tone (lap steels are played flat on the lap, as opposed to the conventional "Spanish" or upright position). That type of guitar, and that sound, and the way the instrument interacted with its essential but underrated partner, the amplifier, were his starting points. The other key factor was production efficiency. As Richard Smith has written with insight, "Contrary to conventional readings of Leo's philosophy, the first requirement of his design was an easy-to-make body, not necessarily a solid one."

So Mr. Fender sought not to convert acoustic Spanish electrics to solid-body versions, but rather to convert his own solidbody electric lap steel guitars to Spanish versions, and to do it in a way that would maximize efficiency for the builder and, consequently, affordability for the customer. Such a guitar demanded several things from its designer: considerable technical know-how, mechanical intuition, and a willingness to try, to fail, and to try again. Perhaps more than anything else it took audacity. With the Telecaster, the otherwise softspoken Leo Fender effectively announced to the world: Let's take everything we think we know about electrifying guitars and throw it out the window; let's start over. This attitude reached its fullest expression in the design of the Telecaster's even more audacious successor, the Stratocaster.

"I took the first guitar to the [1950 music trade] show, and it was, 'What's that thing?' We got all kinds of comments. 'Do you paddle your canoe with that thing? Swat flies?' They all laughed."
– Don Randall

"When Leo's guitar came out we weren't too surprised, because we were familiar with the custom solidbodies Paul Bigsby built. I was fortunate in having a group of men who had been trained in the old country, a lot of Hollanders. Their whole life was woodworking and crafting. We experimented with different pickups on guitars, and they were accepted by players. But then we discovered that out in California there were solidbody guitars and they were beginning to get a little section of the business away from us, so we decided that we had to do something to compete with what Leo Fender was doing. We had to buck this competition from the West Coast."
– former Gibson president Ted McCarty, on the origin of the Les Paul

"With the Broadcaster/Telecaster, Leo got more guitar out of less materials than anyone has ever been able to do, and it's never been beat."
– Rick Turner

"That thing'll never sell."

– Fred Gretsch to Harmony's Jay Krause, upon seeing the Broadcaster for the first time.

Freedom, culture, and the electric guitar

If Leo Fender's goal was to mass-produce down-to-earth musical appliances, how did the Tele and especially the Strat ultimately ascend to the cloud-wreathed Mount Olympus of culture totems, alongside Levi's jeans, the Chrysler Building, and Flathead Harley-Davidsons? As with those other icons, purity of function and form was essential.

So was timing. The introduction in 1950 of the high-quality and, crucially, affordable Broadcaster/Telecaster would have been remarkable in any case, but its injection into the broader mix of post-War technological advances, urban migrations, cultural cross-pollination, and surging sociological realignments multiplied the revolutionary potential of the Telecaster, the even more versatile Stratocaster, and their competitors from Gretsch, Danelectro, Harmony, Rickenbacker, Gibson, Guild, Kay, Supro, Epiphone, and others.

The expansion of radio, television, photo-based magazines, and pop-music record labels provided not only new forms of entertainment but also methods by which influences of fashion and musical styles could leap across once formidable barriers of geography, race, and class. Migrating Mississippi sharecroppers brought their rural music to Detroit and Chicago. Stetson-hatted cowboys in Corpus Christie listened to Kansas City jazz on their new Bakelite-bodied radios. City-bred Manhattan songwriters listened to Delta blues. Elvis Presley listened to everyone from Big Boy Crudup to Dean Martin. White kids in their Leave It To Beaver households saw wondrous sights on their black & white televisions they never would have seen in their neighborhoods — Screamin' Jay Hawkins and Bo Diddley on *American Bandstand*, Howlin' Wolf on *Shindig*.

The great Otis Rush at Pepper's Show Lounge on 43rd St., Chicago. In the book *Michael Bloomfield: If You Love These Blues*, Bloomfield's childhood friend Fred Glaser said of Pepper's and other South Side clubs, "Here was this other world that was totally unimaginable to us. And we were just overwhelmed by this music."

The advent of smaller tape recorders, smaller recording studios, and independent record labels all helped to dissolve the monopoly of a few big record companies and allowed a much wider variety of musicians to be heard. During the decade or so between the end of World War II and the dawn of the space age, vibrant musical hybrids such as urban blues, western swing, honky tonk, rhythm and blues, and rock and roll sizzled across the airwaves coast to coast and blasted out of malt-shop jukeboxes and living-room hi-fi's, and the electric guitar twanged and chimed and snarled through every one of them. (While Mr. Fender's Tele was an instant success, his Strat got off to a slower start. According to Richard Smith, during '54 and '55 Fender shipped 720 Strats, compared to 1,027 Teles and Esquires.) Ultimately, the new Fenders would help to make the electric guitar pop music's most significant instrument, rivaled only by another Fender milestone, the electric bass.

Timing and coincidence would continue to be Leo Fender's allies. His Stratocaster was advertised in the spring of 1954 but not produced in significant numbers until October. By then, Elvis Presley had walked into Sam Phillips' Sun Records studio in Memphis, recorded "That's All Right, Mama," and lit the fuse on the rock and roll powder keg.

> "As a kid, when I got that first electric guitar, and it went *braannggg* and I took the wang bar and it went *rurruurrurr*, and I heard what a new electric guitar sounds like through a little Fender amp with some reverb — things changed."
>
> – *Steve Miller*

> "The first black blues that flipped me out was Howlin' Wolf. Between his voice and Hubert Sumlin's guitar, I just could not believe it. This was coming from another planet. That voice was, 'Is this a human?' and I was going, 'What is that guy doing, bending those strings? What is that instrument?' I couldn't even relate it to anything I'd heard before. And here was this little white 15-year-old kid who'd never even seen a black person, basically. . . . It completely took me over. I didn't really think of it as black music; I just wanted to do it. I mean, I started off listening to Fats Domino and Chuck Berry, and I didn't know they were black. Color never mattered."
>
> – *Duke Robillard, to* **Guitar Player***'s Dan Forte*

Chicago blues giant Howlin' Wolf manhandles his white Strat. On developing a signature voice, Mark Knopfler once said: "It's not going to happen by buying a videocassette tape that shows you how to play like some guy in a heavy metal band. You'd be much better off listening to Howlin' Wolf and then taking it nice and slow from there."

"The freedom and individuality suggested and provided by the electric guitar was brought into even sharper relief against the racial segregation and restrictive social pressures of the 1950s and the Cold War. The electric guitar was a way for players to defy stereotypes thrust upon them by society. It provided a tremendous freedom of expression, of attitude."

– Charles McGovern,
the Smithsonian Institution

Buddy Guy, to *Guitar Player's* Jas Obrecht: "There was a television show called *Shindig*, and they asked the Rolling Stones to be on it, and the Stones said, 'We'll do this show if you bring on Muddy Waters,' and they asked, 'Who was that?' Mick Jagger and them got offended by this. 'You mean to tell me you don't know who Muddy Waters is? We named ourselves after one of his famous records.' So [Carlos Santana, the Stones, Eric Clapton, and others] have done as much for us as any record company just by saying, 'This is where I got it from. This is John Lee Hooker, Muddy Waters, and Little Walter music we're playing.'"

Fantasy Blues Jam, Track 59

Perspectives on the Origin of the Strat

One man's vision, and "a world of suggestions from many people"

Leo Fender designed the Stratocaster while receiving feedback from many people, some of whom later disagreed as to which person offered which suggestion, and when. Notwithstanding several irreconcilable recollections and occasional gaps in the historical record, one fact rings as bright and clear as a Strat through a Twin: the Stratocaster was ultimately the responsibility of one person, Clarence Leo Fender. No one ever pretended otherwise. The world's most popular electric guitar was Leo's baby, top to bottom, and he was proud of it. He once described it in terms that for the taciturn Mr. Fender fairly bubbled with enthusiasm. He called it a pretty good guitar.

When did Leo get started?

Regarding who came up with this or that idea, previous accounts are contradictory in several respects. Some of the confusion is due to semantics: Did Leo Fender "begin working on the Strat" a year or so after the Broadcaster/Telecaster's introduction in 1950, back when he began to conceive improvements that in some form or another eventually found their way onto the new guitar? Or was it a couple of years after that, when he called on Freddie Tavares to help him take several works-in-progress and blend them into a refined, cohesive whole with the familiar features of the production version?

First, it's impossible in retrospect to fix a date on which a project was begun by someone who never actually stopped working. Bill Carson echoed every Fender associate when he said, "Leo was totally immersed, seven days a week. You'd go by there on a Sunday afternoon after you got out of the movies, and he was still there. It was his entire life."

Second, a peculiarly Leo-esque complication was the way Mr. Fender regarded his designs. As Richard Smith revealed in his landmark book, *Fender: The Sound Heard 'Round The World*, Leo saw the Tele and Strat and even his later Fender, Music Man, and G&L models not as utterly discrete entities (like the rest of us do) but rather as stages in a continual refinement of "the Fender guitar." On occasion, even a "finished product" wasn't finished; Leo was known to make changes to specs in the middle of a production run — on his own, sometimes without telling the foreman. To Leo, then, a Fender guitar was *always* a work in progress.

Third, suppose we could go back in time to 1953. Imagine we're standing outside Fender's new three-building factory on the corner of South Raymond and Valencia in Fullerton. As we wipe away a clear spot on the window and peer inside, we might see parts of the embryonic Stratocaster stocked on metal shelves, already rendered in final form. But looking through another window around the corner we might see other components still in the prototype stage and scattered in pieces across a work table, while others are mere sketches on a drawing board, a notepad, even a napkin from that day's lunch at the local cafe.

So it's no wonder the notions of Leo's "refining the Telecaster," "working on the Strat," and "fine tuning the Strat" are less than distinct. In fact, Mr. Fender told Richard Smith that work on the Stratocaster began all the way back in '43 or '44 — meaning, back when he built his first electric Spanish model, the rudimentary "radio shop" guitar.

The Arrival of Freddie Tavares

Our recognizing differing interpretations of the phrase "working on the Strat" may shed light on several discrepancies, one regarding Freddie Tavares. Some accounts place Mr. Tavares' arrival at Fender at the very beginning of the Strat's design process. Freddie laid out the drawings for the new guitar, and Bill Carson recalled working with Freddie on essential features — the body shape, individual saddles, the vibrato. In fact, Freddie's involvement goes so far back that Dick Dale, who contributed ideas to several Fender products and described Leo as "like a second father to me," remembered that "Leo brought in Freddie to *perfect the Telecaster* [emphasis added]."

But Mr. Tavares arrived in 1953. The Broad-caster/Telecaster was three years old (older, if we count prototypes), and by several accounts work on the Strat was well under way. When I asked Mr. Fender when he began working on the Stratocaster, he said it was "mostly before Freddie came to work. It'd be around '51. *We had the neck and body designed, and the pickups.* I remember because it was done before we moved from Pomona Street over to Valencia [in June '53]. I had most of the materials tooled and *the parts in stock* [emphasis added]."

George Fullerton, an eyewitness to these events, concurs in some respects but sets the dates just a bit later: "Around the end of 1951 and the early part of 1952 … Leo started working on the pickups … By the latter part of 1952 a lot of work had been done on getting the new guitar project completed…."

These accounts might be less incompatible than they seem if in addition to asking whose memory we should trust, we also ask, once again, what does "working on the Strat" mean, exactly? Dick Dale's comment doesn't prove or disprove any particular account. Rather it sheds light on how these events were perceived at the time by participants and witnesses. It also illustrates the folly of trying to pinpoint when "perfecting the Telecaster" evolved into "working on the Stratocaster." For a period of time, they were one and the same.

The Telecaster as "Drawing Board"

It's not that Mr. Fender originally intended merely to fine tune the Telecaster and only later refocused his energy on a new model. Given his belief that "it's not so good to alter a model…. It's better just to go to a whole new model," it seems likely that he was working on a new guitar early on (George Fullerton agrees). Remember, the Strat was more than a successor to the Tele; it was a direct outgrowth of it, both generally in terms of Mr. Fender's conception of his ever-evolving "Fender guitar," and also specifically regarding essential Telecaster features that he carried over to the new design. It's a stretch, but not much of one, to say that in one sense Mr. Fender came to view the Telecaster as a Stratocaster prototype.

Given the connotations of the term "drawing board," we might assume the very first step in designing a typical guitar would be just what Freddie Tavares helped Leo to do in April or May of 1953 — draw a body shape on paper. But the organization of the Fender shop was anything but typical, and Leo didn't begin the Strat's design process with a blank sheet of paper. He started with his existing instruments. Bill Carson recalled that in early '53, the new body's rough prototypes, although contoured, still resembled the Telecaster, at least to some extent. Given that Leo was, by several accounts, already working on the vibrato, new pickups, a new neck, the body's contouring, and individual saddles prior to Freddie's arrival, perhaps the refinement of the body shape occurred midway or even relatively late in the process (both Bill Carson and George Fullerton support this assessment).

Freddie Tavares is fondly remembered by all who knew him. Bill Carson called him "the greatest man in both musical talent and personal integrity that I worked with at Fender."

A Strat Shape in '51?

Freddie Tavares drew the Strat on paper. The question is: What are the implications of those drawings? Did his work at the drawing board make him the Strat's co-designer? George Fullerton, with all respect, doesn't think so (see the next chapter). When a publication carried an article that credited Freddie as the Strat's co-designer, Leo Fender told this author: "Freddie Tavares, when this article came out, came over and apologized and said he didn't have anything to do with it being written." Richard Smith added: "Freddie never felt he was the Strat's co-designer."

Remember, Leo Fender's first twin-horned solidbody was not the Strat. That honor belongs to the Precision Bass. Freddie's drawings either pre-dated or post-dated near-final prototypes of the new guitar, but either way it's unreasonable to conclude the Precision's silhouette had no influence on the Strat's; they are just too similar. Dale Hyatt went to work for Leo at K&F and was already an eight-year Fender veteran when the Strat was introduced. As he put it: "To make it balance more evenly, Leo extended that body horn on the Precision, and that carried over to the Strat." The P Bass had been around since 1951, which suggests the Strat's silhouette was Leo Fender's design, although it may well have been refined in important ways by Freddie Tavares. Certainly, it is not only smaller but much sleeker than the early, non-contoured version of its 4-string companion. (As we will see, Freddie's work on the body shape was only one of his contributions to the Strat.)

While the Strat may have ended up resembling the P Bass in its general outline, Bill Carson recollected that early prototypes more closely resembled the Telecaster and "grew" horns during the development phase. It is reasonable to conclude that both factors came into play — the alteration of the Telecaster's body, and the influence of the Precision's.

Individual Components vs. a Cohesive Blend

All of the following were in place prior to Mr. Tavares' arrival: the Precision Bass (from whose body

This 1952 advertisement unveiled the Precision Bass, a double-cutaway Fender that predated the Strat by more than two years.

the Strat's silhouette seems to have been distilled), the Telecaster (with several features carried over to the Strat), the Bigsby/Travis guitar (whose peghead shape was seemingly blended with the Tele's to form the Strat's), plus Leo's various works in progress — new pickups, a vibrato, etc.

But none of this proves that Freddie Tavares' involvement was unimportant to the Stratocaster's inception. While most of the Strat's elements were already there in embryonic form, it's still a significant step from a pile of prototype components to a masterpiece guitar. Freddie Tavares helped Leo Fender take that crucial step.

His own perspective on all this differed from Mr. Fender's. Notwithstanding Carson's and Fullerton's recollections of having working prototypes by early '53, Freddie told A.R. Duchossoir: "The design *started* in April or May of 1953 and it took less than a year [emphasis added]." Don Randall generally agreed. He told authors Ray Minhinnett and Bob Young, in *The Story of the Fender Stratocaster, A Celebration of the World's Greatest Guitar*: "... although Leo Fender had been experimenting with different pickup designs ever since the launch of the Precision Bass, it was *not until Tavares joined* that work on the new guitar started in earnest [emphasis added]."

So, assessing Mr. Tavares' role depends in part on how much value we ascribe to designing individual parts vs. melding them all into an integrated whole.

Bill Carson

Bill Carson brought several of the Telecaster's perceived shortcomings to Leo's attention — the sharp-cornered body, two strings per saddle, the lack of a vibrato, the limitations of two pickups — and provided essential feedback as Leo worked to "improve" his earlier guitar. In Carson's view the result of that ongoing exchange was the Stratocaster — "just a guitar that I hammered out of Leo." Indeed, the body contouring, individual saddles, vibrato, and third pickup all ended up on the Strat, not on some improved Tele. But as with his recollections regarding Freddie Tavares, Leo remembered working on the Strat before he even met Carson. Again, the accounts may be somewhat more compatible than they seem if we recognize the elastic interpretation of "working on the Strat."

Mr. Carson recalled that after several refinements, the prototype he used on gigs was generally similar to the production Stratocaster, although it had aluminum

Tele-style knobs and an impregnated-fiber pickguard. Other pre-production aluminum pickguards have been described as both "anodized" and "not anodized but similar — electroplated." In any case, according to Carson, the aluminum guard was promptly abandoned "because the anodizing was so thin it wore out right away, and the player's fingers turned black."

Bill Carson was an in-demand western guitarist who field-tested Strat prototypes for Leo Fender and made suggestions on essential aspects. His insights and no-nonsense feedback have benefited the Fender company for half a century. The pre-production guitar he's holding here acquired the nickname "Carson's guitar" among local musicians.

Faulty Memories, Proud Men

Some discrepancies are due to inevitable glitches in various parties' memories of what happened 50 years ago. Forrest White, who arrived a month after the Strat's official announcement, doubted that Strat bodies and necks had been designed quite as early as Leo recollected but suggested that Leo may have indeed worked on the pickups and vibrato back in '51.

Other disparities are surely matters of pride. While Mr. Fender acknowledged certain mechanical attributes of Paul Bigsby's vibrato, to this author's knowledge he never credited Bigsby for influencing the Stratocaster's headstock design, despite its unmistakable resemblance to several Bigsby guitars, most notably the historic solidbody built for Merle Travis some six years before the Strat's debut. George Fullerton admits to some similarity but is reluctant to give much credit to Bigsby on this matter.

On the other hand, Forrest White (as staunch a Fender loyalist as ever lived) wrote in his own book, *Fender: The Inside Story*: "I think you would have to look at the solidbody guitar Paul Bigsby made for Merle Travis to form your own opinion. I personally don't think there is any doubt that it influenced the shape of the neck head on the Stratocaster." As with other aspects of the Strat, the headstock was the result of multiple influences: Bill Carson specifically mentioned the Bigsby headstock when enumerating his preferences to Leo, and in some accounts, Freddie Tavares shares credit with Leo for the headstock's design.

Paul Bigsby wasn't the only person whose influence was rarely if ever mentioned by Mr. Fender. "You never heard Leo give anybody any credit for anything," said Bill Carson. "The closest he ever came to telling me anything was the last time I saw him [Mr. Fender died in 1991]. It was one of our NAMM show things. There were all these Fender guitars around, many of them Strats. Leo was in his wheelchair and he got ahold of my shirt and I knelt down beside of him. He got right in my ear — he could barely whisper — and he said, 'Let's do it again,

Bill!' Hell, it made me cry. That was the closest he ever came to giving me any recognition."

The ironic counterpoint to Mr. Fender's sometimes waiting years, even decades, before acknowledging the contributions of others was that at the time an individual was speaking to him, Leo could make him feel special. Perhaps it's not so surprising that Jimmy Bryant reportedly believed the Strat was going to be called the Jimmy Bryant model, even though Carson remembers a prototype's acquiring the nickname "Carson's guitar."

Overlapping Suggestions

Given that some suggestions were received repeatedly from multiple, overlapping sources who were likely unaware of each other's input, it's no wonder that accounts of the Strat's history have been told from different perspectives. Some reports may seem inconsistent only because they are incomplete, and may all be true. Carson remembers details from his one-on-one exchanges with Leo Fender; from Don Randall's point of view, Bill was only one of several players who were constantly providing feedback.

In his own book, George Fullerton credited Bill Carson with contributing essential suggestions regarding the Strat's adjustable saddles, among other features: "The field testing that Bill did brought about the awareness for individual bridge sections for each string." Carson said the same thing. These statements are not inconsistent with Richard Smith's report that salesman Bud Driver had written to Don Randall way back in 1950, prior to Leo Fender's meeting Bill Carson, suggesting that the Telecaster's three saddles were inadequate; nor are they inconsistent with Fullerton's conviction that Fender would likely, perhaps inevitably, have arrived at the same conclusion in any case.

Another example: Carson's claim that "95 percent of the ideas that ended up on the Stratocaster were mine" generally echoes Forrest White's recollection that regarding input from musicians, "[Freddie Tavares] thought that Bill Carson gave Leo most of the

A Bigsby headstock (note inlays and metal nut), along with two Strat headstocks: a small pre-CBS type and a CBS bullet-rod.
Forrest White said of the Bigsby, "I personally don't think there is any doubt that it influenced the shape of the neck head on the Stratocaster."

ideas." These claims are not incompatible with undisputed accounts that over a period of months or years other people also contributed ideas, some of which overlapped and reinforced Carson's suggestions.

Still other disputes are matters of who-came-first. Bill Carson claimed credit for the Strat's body contouring, although Mr. Fender recalled that guitarist Rex Gallion had previously made the same request. White and Fullerton credited Gallion *and* Carson, although Forrest speculated it was Carson who first came up with the idea.

Trem Dilemma

The new tremolo was the source of additional confusion. Generally, there were two versions. The first entailed a length of string between its saddles and tailpiece, somewhat like Leo's later Jazzmaster and Jaguar units, and also a set of roller bridges (perhaps not unlike "inventions" that appeared twenty years later). It was field-tested and pronounced adequate. Leo finalized the design — or so he thought — and tooled up for production.

George Fullerton tested one of the finished guitars and discovered to his alarm the vibrato's inadequacy. He alerted Leo: "It sounds like a tin can!" Carson did the same, wasting no time and calling Leo from a gig to tell him it sounded like "a damn cheap banjo." Freddie Tavares told Bill Carson he believed the problem was in the tremolo's light weight and its lack of what would come to be called (in the production version) the inertia bar. Despite considerable investments of time and money, Leo was forced to scrap the unit.

A second vibrato was designed from the ground up in consultation with several players, notably Freddie Tavares. After still further testing and modifications, some suggested by Bill Carson, the second version was pronounced ready, and Fender's new guitar was unveiled to the world. Carson and Fullerton both recall the vibrato fiasco postponed the Strat's introduction by about a year, from mid '53 until mid '54. Mr. Tavares thought the delay was more like six months, which is in keeping with his recollection that the entire design process "took less than a year."

Prototype vs. production

Once again semantics plays a part, this time regarding definitions of "prototype," "pre-production," and "production." Fullerton's account is that finished, production-ready components of the first-vibrato guitar had to be scrapped, but Leo's view, apparently, was that *all* guitars prior to the official announcement in 1954 (including any with the first vibrato, whether rough experiments or finished guitars) were prototypes.

Finished guitars with the first vibrato have never surfaced, and Fullerton recalls actually assembling only one of them. In fact, no legit '53 Strat has ever surfaced, so the first-vibrato guitar was indeed a prototype, even if it was briefly considered the first unit off the production line. (My best guess is that Leo's memory failed him when he told me the new, revised vibrato was developed by the middle of '53; if it were, why wait a year to introduce the Strat? Richard

Smith: "Detailed inventory sheets from December 1953 do not even show Stratocaster decals, much less bodies, necks, or pickguards.") In any case, the Strat was officially announced in April 1954, in the May issue of *International Musician*, and a letter sent from Fender Sales to dealers specified that "shipments are expected to begin May 15."

In Richard Smith's *Fender: The Sound Heard 'Round The World*, Rex Gallion is pictured holding an early Stratocaster. Richard did some detective work on a calendar visible in an uncropped version of the photo, and he dates the picture to January or February 1954. Unless the Jan.-Feb. '54 calendar was left open after February, which is possible, the photo indicates that the Strat appeared prior to the April announcement. In fact, an advertisement appearing on newsstands in April 1954 may well have been produced a month or two earlier, given typical publication turnaround times, so it is reasonable to speculate that production Strats may have existed in January or February. (In fact, guitarist/historian Robb Lawrence reported he has seen close-up photos of a January 1954 model and has personally examined a few Strats from February and March.) The guitar in the Gallion photo certainly looks like a production model, with details such as the circular string retainer, the *Original Contour Body* peghead decal, the top-mounted output jack (which George Fullerton says was the last element to be designed), and plastic knobs (the earliest prototype with the refined tremolo had metal knobs, somewhat like the Telecaster's).

Forrest White called all such guitars "prototypes" or samples. His view was that guitars built until *autumn* of '54 "were considered to be prototypes and guinea pig models." He added that published accounts of Fender having unfinished bodies and necks in stock do *not* demonstrate actual production runs (we can almost hear the *harrumph*), and he specified in his book that "the first production run of the Stratocaster (with tremolo) was in the month of October 1954, to fill Purchase Order #242 (for 100 units) from Fender Sales, dated October 13,

1954." Moreover, although that very first ad specified that the Strat was "available with or without 'Tremolo' Action," the first non-trem Strats were actually a year away. Forrest White: "The first production run for non-tremolo Stratocasters was in April 1955 … (for 25 units)…."

But reputable collectors have authenticated several Strats pre-dating October '54. Keep in mind that Fender Sales, Inc. and the factory were two different operations. Richard Smith: "Forrest was the production supervisor, so from his viewpoint, the first Stratocasters that fulfilled official orders from Fender Sales were put through late in '54. But other production Stratocasters were out there before then. Some might have been salesman samples. The salesmen would take guitars out on the road and show them to dealers. When they finished their trip, they wouldn't bring the guitar back to the factory. They'd sell it. My own Strat is an authentic April '54. It's not a prototype at all, in terms of being experimental or anything like that. Forrest might have called it a 'prototype,' but only in the sense that it was made before the first full order from Fender Sales.

"Another thing was tooling. Forrest might have considered the first true production guitars to be the ones manufactured with the final tooling, even though identical guitars could have left the factory with parts tooled in a different way."

The "Bigsby Problem" and Gibson's Les Paul

From sales director Don Randall's point of view, the decision to design a new guitar was market driven, period. No one disagrees. Fullerton, Randall and Fender all recalled that one of the earliest motivations in designing the Strat was to react to the success of Paul Bigsby's popular vibrato attachment. Leo said his response to "this Bigsby problem" was under way before he met Tavares — even before he met Carson. (On tracks 2 and 3 of the CD that accompanies this book, Mr. Fender discussed the influence of the Bigsby vibrato on his own designs.)

Randall explained that the new Fender was *also* intended as a response to Gibson's Les Paul, which appeared in mid 1952. This may indicate that Randall's requests, not surprisingly, covered a period of months — stressing the need for the vibrato early on (prior to Leo's meeting Bill Carson), and later mandating a fancier guitar after the impressive new Gibson provided one more reason to upgrade the line.

The fabulous "Tremolo Action" ad of 1954, complete with its the-future-is-now atomic symbol. The claims that the Stratocaster was new, revolutionary, thrilling, and "designed to be part of the player" were unremarkable except for one thing. They were all true.

Multiple Influences

Despite disagreements over details, most parties agree the Strat was the result of overlapping influences extending across a period of about two years: Leo's setting his sights on the new model early on by working on improvements to the Telecaster; his responding to Don Randall's ongoing requests for a vibrato-equipped, three-pickup guitar and later for a fancy upgrade; his early (and continuing) exchanges with local and traveling musicians like Rex Gallion and Bill Carson; his in-house consultations with George Fullerton and later Freddie Tavares; and his never-ending, sometimes solitary experiments with pickups, hardware, and circuitry.

Where's The Big Picture?

Now let's step back for a moment. Fixating on these details can distort the big picture. To pick one example, let's assume for purposes of discussion that Mr. Fender was accurate in his recollection that Rex Gallion suggested the contoured body before Bill Carson did. Such an assumption would point up Gallion's creativity but wouldn't diminish Carson's importance or even prove that Gallion's input was more influential. Hearing Gallion's suggestion confirmed by a player of Carson's high regard might have been just the impetus Leo needed to commit to the idea.

After all, Carson not only suggested the contoured body, but as we'll see in the next chapter, he also took a hacksaw to his Telecaster to prove his point. He continued to work on the project while out on the road and almost got himself fired after showing up on the bandstand with sawdust on his stage outfit. He was so valuable and spent so much time at the factory that Fender put him on the payroll. Leo called him his "favorite guinea pig for the Strat"; Forrest called him "the 'suspected father' of the thing."

Also, we should not let our focus on the contributions of Leo's advisers lead us to mistake Mr. Fender's own role as merely some sort of conduit for the ideas of others. An idea is not a functioning product; sometimes years of trial and error and piles of junked prototypes separate the two. It's one thing to say, it'd be swell to have an improved vibrato, quite another to work out the physics, the mechanics, the woodwork, the metalwork, the cost effectiveness, and all the rest. From Don Randall's point of view: "The players were invaluable. They provided feedback, and that mattered a great deal, but that doesn't make them 'designers.'"

It would be fascinating if we could specify the exact sequence of experiments (successful and fruitless) and know the details of the prototypes, first-vibrato guitars, and early second-vibrato guitars. It would be useful to review Freddie Tavares' drawings. It would interest some people to document the dates on which Leo received feedback from every musician, colleague, and salesman, and which suggestions were original, which ones Leo had already heard (perhaps repeatedly), which ones reinforced decisions he'd already made anyway, and which ones were discounted.

But none of that would change what we do know. As George Fullerton wrote, "Leo Fender had the final word. Leo did not use any idea regardless of whose it might be until he carefully and thoughtfully examined every part of it and then added his own ideas to it." Forrest White put it this way: "Even though he could not play or even tune a guitar, he was the one with the ability to accept those ideas offered to him, add his own innovations, and come up with a masterpiece like the Stratocaster."

Thus it is no more realistic to apportion a precise degree of credit to every individual who offered a suggestion than it is to pick a date when "refining the Tele" shifted to "designing the Strat." While the Stratocaster was the culmination of an ongoing process — entailing "a world of suggestions from many people," as Fullerton put it — more than anything else it was the result of one man's vision. George Fullerton: "They were Leo's designs, and the people who helped, why, we'd all just look at it and make suggestions and eventually we'd accomplish what

A pair of metal-pickguard Fenders. The unusual Strat is similar to one owned by George Fullerton and pictured in his book *Guitar Legends*. Fullerton's 1954 guitar has several variations, but its nonstock metal top plate and control layout are identical to this guitar's features. George Fullerton: "One reason Leo asked me to work for him was I played a lot of guitar. I liked to mute with my palm and I've got big hands, and that volume knob was too close to the bridge for me, so I moved it a bit on the guitar I built for myself. I made a template for that metal plate, and later on, in about 1955, someone at the factory must have liked my guitar because they used my template to build this one. There are only those two, so far as I know."

Perry A. Margouleff: "The Tele has a very unusual but stock chromium-plated pickguard. Looking at the wear patterns, I think this is an experimental pickguard that's been on this Tele since the day it was built."

we set out to do. We tried lots of things, and we didn't have specific parts that this person or that person was responsible for."

More than the sum of its parts

One pitfall of fixating on individual Stratocaster innovations is that it undervalues the Strat's continuation of Fender hallmarks such as the Telecaster's solid ash body, bolt-on maple neck, six-on-a-side tuners, non-angled peghead, straight string pull over the nut, 25½" scale, bright sounding single-coil pickups, and 3-way switch, not to mention the Precision Bass' elongated, double-cutaway body horns. It also provides a disjointed picture of the Strat's origin — Fullerton gets credit for the output jack, Gallion and Carson for the contouring, Randall for the name and the sunburst finish — which loses sight of the uncanny synergy of elements so indispensable to the essence of the Strat.

One Perspective

We'll never know every detail. My own take on the origin of the Stratocaster is this: With his eye on a new model, Mr. Fender continued his never-ending work on improving "the Fender guitar" after the Broadcaster/Telecaster's introduction in mid 1950. Before long, Don Randall was pressuring him for a vibrato-equipped guitar, echoing the salesmen's opinions that Fender needed a line, not just a model. Once the Precision Bass had been introduced in late '51, Mr. Fender could devote more time to his new guitar (even though he had his hands nearly full with meeting demands for Teles, Esquires, Precision Basses, steel guitars, and a growing line of amplifiers).

During 1952, listening closely to several musicians, Mr. Fender devised "Telecaster improvements" that over time evolved into features of a new guitar. In the summer of that year (no later than autumn), Randall's list of requests had grown to include a fancier model that could compete with the new Les Paul.

In 1953, Leo Fender and Freddie Tavares worked together to give shape and focus to a new project whose roots now traced back at least a year, perhaps a year and a half. For the new guitar's body shape, Leo drew from his own twin-horned Precision Bass of 1951. He consulted Freddie on refining that shape, on fine-tuning the individual-saddles idea that Carson and others had championed, and on designing the second vibrato, the one that worked. Given the delay caused by the failed first vibrato (six months to one year), accounts that the Strat's development "required less than a year" seem to make sense only if we exclude Mr. Fender's preliminary design work on essential components.

The Stratocaster appeared at last in 1954, having been designed by Leo Fender, long requested (and christened) by Don Randall, and bearing contributions or reflecting feedback from Randall, George Fullerton, Rex Gallion, Bill Carson, Freddie Tavares, and other musicians and salesmen.

Freddie Tavares is fondly remembered not only for his musicianship, engineering skills and amiability but also for his integrity. I once asked him whether, given that several people contributed ideas, the Strat was "essentially Leo's design." Without hesitation he said,

"All of the guitars were essentially Leo's design."

See the next chapter for comments on the origin of the Stratocaster from Leo Fender, Don Randall, George Fullerton, Freddie Tavares, Bill Carson, and Forrest White.

CHAPTER 2

IN THEIR OWN WORDS

An Imaginary Roundtable

Key participants discuss Leo Fender's one-of-a-kind, pretty good guitar

The following comments are from parties involved in the Stratocaster's conception and early production. I interviewed Leo Fender, Freddie Tavares, Forrest White, Don Randall, George Fullerton, and Bill Carson, some of them repeatedly over a period of 25 years. About ninety percent of the comments below are excerpted from those conversations. Documentary videographer Dennis Baxter discovered a previously unpublished interview with Forrest White, and he also interviewed Don Randall and George Fullerton; a few quotes from those interviews are interspersed below, as are additional comments from Mr. Tavares from a July '79 *Guitar Player* article.

This not a true "roundtable." In a few cases the participants are responding to each other, but most of the time they are responding to an interviewer. In arranging these quotes, I have taken care to avoid distortions that can result from juxtaposing remarks in new contexts. I have introduced numerous but mild edits where necessary to minimize redundancy, to enhance clarity (e.g., replacing "he" with the person's name), or to group in one place an interviewee's scattered comments on a single topic.

The following summary of viewpoints is necessarily incomplete, although I hope it is fair and reasonably comprehensive. Please see the previous chapter, "Perspectives on the Origin of the Strat," which serves as an introduction to the following exchanges. You can hear additional comments in Mr. Fender's own voice on the accompanying CD; those statements are referenced throughout this and other sections. My own remarks are in italics. Additional opinions may be found in books by Carson, Fullerton, and White; see Chapter 10.

— Tom Wheeler

Forrest White: There's some controversy on how Leo happened to make the Stratocaster in the first place. Some people say it was made for a particular musician, but I worked with Leo all those years and the first time I heard that was after Leo passed away! The Stratocaster was *not* designed for any particular person. It was designed to broaden the line. Fender had quite a few salesmen at that time, and they had to have something to sell. They had the Telecaster but they needed to broaden the line.

George Fullerton: A lot of people take credit for things sometimes — some people like to get involved with something after it gets successful — but I don't know that you can say that any particular person was responsible for this feature or that one, except Leo Fender.

Don Randall: A lot of these guys who claim credit for the Stratocaster didn't have a damn thing to do with it. I don't mean to put any of them down, but the salesmen and I — we were the ones who knew the business, knew the competition, and we knew what we needed. There were at least half a dozen professional players, and we'd give them prototypes. I wasn't just one player, or two. They'd *all* come back with ideas — put the volume knob over here, that sort of thing. We used those players a lot. Leo was the designer, principally, but he depended on those players. The guys at the factory were putting nuts and bolts on the guitars. They didn't know about the business, and that's not a criticism — it wasn't their job to know the business. It was their job to build guitars and they did a very fine job. A decision like adding a guitar to the line would have come from Leo and from me. He and I were working very closely at that time.

Bill Carson: Don Randall was pushing Leo to add another guitar to the line.

Don Randall: It was market driven. We had a very plain jane Telecaster. Gibson came out with the Les Paul. It was a nice looking instrument. It was pretty, and we needed an upgrade in our own instrument. And we prevailed on Leo to say we've got to make the next step up. So we eventually developed the Stratocaster guitar.

Was there a sense of urgency?

Don Randall: Not with Leo [*laughs*]. He didn't see the emergency. If it had taken five years, that would have been okay with him. He was a very clever man, but I had to pound on him — just *constantly* — to get the thing designed and ready for the market.

Was the vibrato the first departure from the Telecaster, the first step toward the new model?

George Fullerton: Yes, I think so. It wasn't long after the Telecaster came out that people were asking us all the time — say, when are you guys going to have a guitar with a vibrato, like the Merle Travis guitars with a Bigsby? And three pickups — they wanted that, too, but we had no idea how to go about building a three-pickup guitar, or a vibrato.

Leo Fender: All the salesmen were asking for a vibrato, and so the [Stratocaster] was begun.

Bill Carson: Steel guitars were very prominent then, and if a standard guitar player could use a volume pedal in conjunction with a vibrato, he could be more in demand and make more money because he could play steel effects as well as standard guitar things.

George Fullerton: We gave Bill a lot of the pickups to work on, to take out and try. The pickup we finally decided to use for the Stratocaster was the one Bill

thought was the best. We built various models, and he selected one.

Bill Carson: I liked the pickups that had the most hair on their chest. That was one of Leo's expressions.

George Fullerton: Rex Gallion was another player who used to press us hard to make some changes. Jimmy Bryant was another. That set the thing really rolling, because everybody wanted to play like Jimmy.

Forrest White: There are so many people who contributed ideas. Freddie [Tavares] contributed a lot of them, and Bill Carson … had a lot to do with the body contouring; same with Rex Gallion. Leo listened to *all* the musicians.

Bill Carson: Leo was receptive to a musician just walking in off the street to talk to him. He seemed to want to pick the head of every player who came around. He'd ask all kinds of questions and be very friendly and make you feel comfortable right away.

Given Leo's work on the pickups, vibrato, and so on, it seems the Strat came together over a fairly long period, with work progressing on several fronts, at different rates.

George Fullerton: We worked on it little by little, as best we could, but the company was booming, and we had the Tele and the Precision to keep up with, too.

Why have a three-way selector switch that is not intended to allow pickup combinations?

Leo Fender: Well, I don't think there were too many convenient styles of switches available then.

[*On the CD, track 5, Mr. Fender discussed the limitations of parts in the pre-miniaturization 1950s.*] It was a young industry then. They didn't have these specialty suppliers like they do now.

58

Disassembled 1961 Stratocaster. On the body, note the row of six holes for the tremolo base plate screws, and the slot where the trem's inertia bar drops in. Also note the shim in the body's neck pocket (for neck-pitch adjustment), the rosewood fingerboard, the nicely figured peghead, and gold plated hardware.

Below the rectangular white plastic spring cover and its six mounting screws we see the five tremolo springs next to the inertia bar, with the output jack at bottom. Below the two strap buttons and their mounting screws are the spring anchor plate (note solder point) and the two long screws that attach it to the forward wall of the body's rear cavity (see p. 75). Below that are the tremolo base plate, its six mounting screws, "ashtray" bridge cover, and trem bar. Between the tremolo's base plate and inertia bar are three screws that join those two pieces. Below the four neck mounting screws are the neck plate and the six individual saddles, with their six length-adjustment screws and springs to the left, their 12 height-adjustment allen screws to the right.

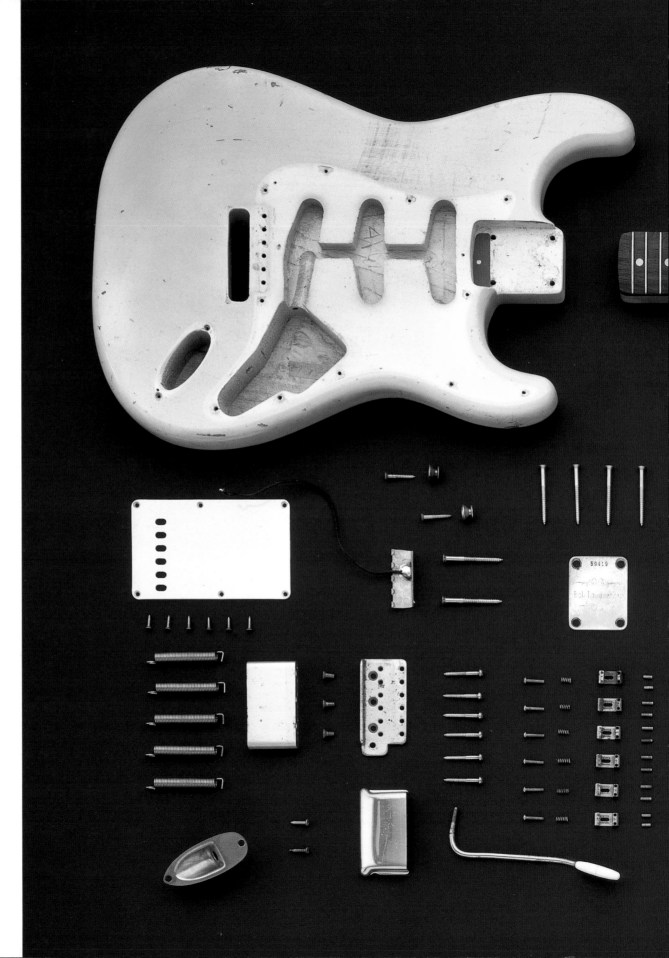

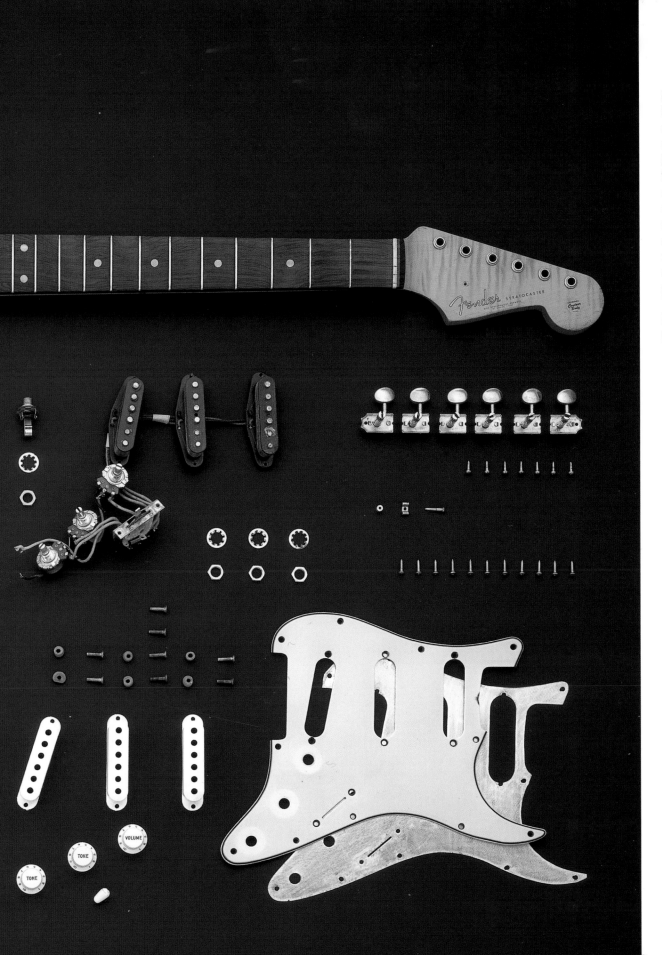

Note that the pickups, wiring harness, white plastic pickup covers, knobs, and selector switch tip are all aligned for installation; note the slant of the bridge pickup, its cover, and its body rout. Other details: six tuners with mounting screws, string tree with mounting screw and spacer, 11 pickguard screws, and (above the pickup covers) mounting screws for the pickups and selector switch. The metal shielding plate lies beneath the aged white/black/white laminated pickguard.

Did you ever consider changing the electrical layout in later years?

Leo Fender: Well, I think I would say yes, we did, but it's not necessarily so good to alter a model. [*On the CD, track 6, Mr. Fender explained the advantages of introducing a new model vs. altering an existing one.*] Now, about the three pickups, that was probably a combination of opinions. [*Note: Fender and Randall were no doubt aware of Gibson's three-pickup ES-5 of 1949.*] In the first place, the switch on the [Strat] had three positions, and that helped decide the third pickup, and then I think that Carson was agreeable that this would be a good idea; he played a part in that he confirmed our opinion. We respected his playing and leaned on him for advice. He was kind of our favorite guinea pig for the Strat, because we needed somebody who was dedicated to getting the job done.

Bill Carson: I wanted a whole bunch of pickups, four or five, but Leo said they wouldn't fit. I had played a Broadcaster up in the Oakland area, and it had a wonderful action, so I looked Leo up [on another occasion Mr. Carson recollected he met Mr. Fender in about September of 1951]. It was such a great guitar I wanted one like it. I got a Telecaster and a Pro amp from Leo, and the guitar worked out well except it dug into your ribs, so I sawed it off in the front and back.

You sawed it off?

Bill Carson: Yeah, with a hacksaw, a chunk in the front and a chunk in the back, and then I took sandpaper to it. It wasn't very pretty because the backside of the hacksaw starts hitting it, so you can't be artistic with it.

Did it work?

Bill Carson: Sure it did.

What did Mr. Fender think of your taking a hacksaw to a brand new Telecaster?

Bill Carson: Well, not much. He didn't think that was so good.

Leo Fender: When Bill first came out here we were already working on the Stratocaster — we had to because of this Bigsby problem [the popularity of Bigsby's vibrato]. We were going to have a new guitar anyway; we needed a new one. It wasn't just Bill who was suggesting it. Before he came out we'd been soliciting information from every musician we could find. We'd shown this instrument to Rex Gallion before Bill came out. The design of the Stratocaster, well, the body designed itself, sort of a product in conjunction with Rex Gallion. [*CD, track 1: Mr. Fender on Rex Gallion's suggestions regarding the Strat's body contours.*] We designed that guitar so it would feel good to hold.

George Fullerton: I was there from the start, and I wouldn't say it was one person. Bill Carson and Rex Gallion both made important suggestions in the body shape, the contours. I give them about equal credit on that. People that you don't always hear about may get involved in some of these things in some funny little way. On the head of the Stratocaster, it says *Original Contour Body*. My wife came up with that name for the body shape.

Forrest White: Freddie Tavares put the first lines on paper when he started with Leo.

Bill Carson: Freddie came on board [in March '53] and drew this instrument up. In my opinion he was the greatest man in both musical talent and personal integrity that I worked with at Fender.

Freddie Tavares: When I came to work for Leo in 1953, besides doing odd jobs, I helped him lay out the Stratocaster on the drawing board. I remember that

This January 1965 photo illustrates the polepiece array that Fender now calls the "vintage stagger": high G and D; low B.

we had a piece of paper with lines drawn on it: six lines for the strings, and two cross lines for the nut and the bridge. Then we drew a body on it, erasing here and there until we got the shape we liked. Remember, at that time Leo was the total owner of the place, which had some peculiar advantages. There was no stalling around when it was time to get something done. Leo would say, "That's the shape I like," or, "Let's put in three pickups — two is good, but three will kill 'em," and it would get done.

Bill Carson: That was another of Leo's expressions — *this'll kill 'em!*

George Fullerton: Don Randall was pressing Leo hard for precision drawings of the products — amp circuit boards as well as guitars. Leo never wanted to spend the effort on that sort of thing, the paperwork, so Freddie was brought in part-time [at first] to do drawings. The guitars were already completed, in the field. He still worked in the old building over on Pomona, which we kept for a while; our machine shop was over there. Leo and I were in the new building on Raymond and Valencia. Freddie wasn't so much a design person, although he was very talented, and he was certainly questioned on things for his opinions.

It seems a lot of work had been done on components before Freddie arrived, but he helped Leo put it all together into a cohesive, integrated whole.

Bill Carson: That's a fair statement. We did a lot of work in '52, and had prototypes and working instruments before Freddie drew it up. He was so talented. He never gets credit for the Bassman amplifier, by the way, which he had a lot to do with. Anyway, I also insisted that the instrument balance on me. So the horn on the top of the Stratocaster grew and grew in an effort to balance the guitar. And Freddie said it wouldn't look quite so ugly if you put a horn on the bottom, too, to give it a little bit of symmetry. And I sawed up the bridges [splitting each of the Tele's three saddles]. Leo didn't understand intonation until Freddie Tavares came on. Freddie was enough of an engineer — a very good engineer, I might add — and he got the physics across to Leo.

Leo Fender: Now about this six bridges business, I don't know what was on our first vibrato action, but the bass that we came out with in '51 did have individual bridges, one for each string. [*Note: To clarify Mr. Fender's comment, perhaps he was working on individual saddles for the Precision while also developing them for the Strat, but the production P Bass did not acquire them until several years after its introduction.*] So the idea wasn't new to us with the Stratocaster. You had to have them to get proper octave adjustments. See, the thing about strings is that they have cores of different elasticities, and when you fret a note on an elastic core, you won't increase the tension, thereby sharping the note, as much as you will on a stiff core, so you have to compensate with length adjustments for each string. Whether I'd seen a 6-string guitar with individual adjustments before the Stratocaster, I just can't tell you. I don't know.

By '53, other companies had individual length-adjustable bridges as well, on guitars. [*According to Tony Bacon & Paul Day's* The Gretsch Book, *the six-saddle Melita Synchro-Sonic was advertised in June 1952; it was adjustable for length, while the later Strat bridge was adjustable for both the length and height of each string.*]

Leo Fender: Most everything before that time was an acoustic guitar with that slanted bridge. On an acoustic you couldn't hear that accurately, because an acoustic puts out a rather broad tone, so you not only got the pitch you were after but a lot of others, too, and you didn't notice discrepancies as much. But on a solidbody, if something was a little off, you were in trouble. Eventually the competition — all the companies — switched over to the individual bridges, which they should have had a long time before.

Bill Carson: One of the early failures we had were the first pickups. They just didn't make it. I don't know what happened, but they seemed to lose a lot between when Leo made them at the shop and when I took them out on the job. The sound had a rapid decay and a somewhat banjo-like tone. One night I called Leo up at my first break and said, "This is not going to do it. I don't know what's wrong, but this is very bad." He was a little bit upset in that he had already committed some tooling to make that particular pickup and coil form fiber.

Leo Fender: The one that Bill was using was a prototype. Bill was a good musician, you know, and we were very interested in how the instrument suited him, as well as others. Well, we had problems with the entire vibrato action. It wouldn't sustain a tone too well. Bill thought it was the pickups, but it wasn't — they had no problems. But we had to completely retool the vibrato action.

Bill Carson: I hadn't realized how much effect the vibrato could have on sustain. Freddie had been experimenting with different metals and weights, and one that I tried was lighter, probably a little *too* light.

Why did you come up with the multi-spring vibrato, or "hand tremolo," in the first place?

Leo Fender: About 1950, maybe, Paul Bigsby was having a lot of success with his vibrato action on guitars, and that was kind of introduced largely by Merle Travis. So the sales force felt that we had to have a vibrato also, and so we developed a vibrato for the Stratocaster.

[CD, tracks 2 and 3: Mr. Fender on the problems with his first vibrato, the shortcomings of previous designs, and why he chose multiple springs for the Strat.] On our first vibrato, which we never produced for sale, we had to junk the tooling — about five thousand dollars down the drain, a lot of money, especially in those days. On that prototype Bill was using, there was a length of string between the bridge and the tailpiece, but the new one incorporated the bridge right into the vibrato unit.

What other changes did you make in order to perfect it?

George Fullerton: We had to fix the vibrations. The first one was too lightweight. See, you don't want something else to absorb those [string] vibrations. If anything else vibrates, it'll absorb that sound away and you get bad tone, not a strong enough signal. Leo used to say, you need this thing tied to an anvil.

Leo Fender: We had these little rollers, and they allowed lateral vibration. With a string, you can't have vibration in any direction at the bridge; it's got to be as solid as the Rock of Gibraltar. Today's Strat has six screws, one in front of each bridge section, and that gives you kind of an intimate relationship with the body, and that's necessary. Also, the bridge itself moves with the action, so you don't have the wrong kind of string motion at the bridge.

George Fullerton: We actually came up with quite a few different vibrato units, and finally got one we thought might work. They all denied it later, but

"The body shape is perfect. The pickguard, perfect. Control layout, perfect. I wish I'd thought of it. It's easy to make. The electronics drop in with a couple of solder joints; the neck bolts on. The scale length is about as long as you want to go, but it works, and that's part of the tone. It's a wonderful guitar to write songs on, you can play rhythm guitar all day on it, you can make a living on it, and the front pickup and in-between lead tones are musician standards. The Strat is part of our heritage. Someone once said that Leo was in a state of grace when he designed the Stratocaster. I can't argue with that."

– Paul Reed Smith

several of the players said the [first] vibrato was okay. [*As Bill Carson reports in his book, he pointed out to Leo that a prototype's satisfactory performance in the lab doesn't prove it will work in the field.*] I had my doubts, because it looked flimsy to me, but Leo put the first vibrato into production, along with bodies and necks. The vibrato was the new guitar's last piece [except for the flush-mounted plug receptacle]. We already had the body contouring, pickup design, third pickup, separate bridges, new headstock shape, the tooling — everything except that vibrato had already been accepted. We couldn't wait to get into the market. It was supposed to be all finished by the June '53 NAMM Show in Chicago. We started a hundred guitars through the line, a hundred sets of parts ready to go. Some of the bodies were already finished, and the metal parts were already chrome plated. But we didn't assemble many at all, just one as I recall. I couldn't wait that morning to get the first one off the line. I grabbed that one and tested it out, and it was terribly bad sounding.

You knew it was the vibrato?

George Fullerton: I thought it was. I rushed to the lab, Leo and I looked at it, and we called Freddie over to look at it. That vibrato sounded like a tin can. We all agreed it wasn't going to work, so we shut down the line. It was a sad day. It was then that Leo went back to the drawing board. We started completely from scratch. Freddie was very helpful with redesigning the vibrato, spent lots of time on it. It took us a year to get it back. We had to postpone until '54, and the guitar that we did finally come out with was the same design, except for the vibrato.

What did you do with all of those components?

George Fullerton: Cut 'em up, trashed all the metal parts, and the dies for making everything. Leo was kind of funny in this way — whenever a prototype didn't work, it went immediately to the band saw. We

couldn't save the bodies because they'd need different routings for a new vibrato. The necks were the only thing we saved.

The second vibrato was a vast improvement.

Bill Carson: Yeah, but he built it backwards. The plate [where the strings are anchored] was turned around, and you had to adjust it from the pickup side, underneath the strings. I was using it at the club, and I could tell if I ever broke a string I'd never get another one on there in time. I called [Leo] from the gig, during a break, and said it's all wrong. I took it back and he and Freddie changed the plate around and it's been that way ever since.

Once you were in production, the vibrato design remained fundamentally unchanged for decades.

Leo Fender: It's a deceptively simple vibrato that we have on the Strat, but it's effective. It's endowed with a lot of good features that we didn't even anticipate in the beginning. The action is made like a knife-edge scale balance. Any good fractional gram scale works with a knife edge as a fulcrum; this avoids the friction you get with bearings. Roller bearings, needle bearings, ball bearings, and bushings aren't good. Bearings tend to separate at the point of pressure from the axle. Friction's all right with a gasoline engine, where you have spare power, but if you want a delicate balance, you couldn't get it. That's why all fine scales use a knife edge — you don't have that friction.

How did you put the knife-edge idea into effect?

Leo Fender: There is a screw ahead of each bridge section [on what is now considered a vintage-style tremolo]; these screws hold the bridge against the body. We hardened those screws. The screw holes in the bridge plate were countersunk [from the bottom] to create the knife edge. So we're dealing with a knife edge against each screw body. [Note: The front edge of the bridge plate, or base plate, was beveled on the under-side so the bridge wouldn't hit the edge of the body.]

What was wrong with earlier designs?

Leo Fender: In all of the prior vibratos the bridge section would have to move with the vibrato, and I think this is bad, especially if there's much length of string between the bridge and the vibrato, because all of the strings stretch in different amounts, and they have to individually crawl over the bridges. Now, some players want that space between the bridge and tailpiece, especially if they have a vigorous picking style. They want that vibrato out of the way. It depends on the player. See, the Strat is sort of a one-of-a-kind guitar for people who like to play right in there kind of tight, with the little finger wrapped around the volume knob, and they're muting sometimes, and so on. Strat players seem to be tight operators, don't they?

You used multiple springs, while the Bigsby had one big one.

Leo Fender: If you had just one, then it would have to be pretty big and wouldn't fit inside — the profile would be wrong. It would also be difficult to concentrate all that energy in one spring, and since there would be so few links in it, it might not have the required latitude in its action. So it was a matter of profile, and a matter of having enough turns [in the spring] to get the latitude in adjustment — you can take out springs and change the action.

You said the vibrato had benefits you hadn't anticipated?

Leo Fender: Here's one thing — on a Stratocaster, when you flat a string, depressing the vibrato arm, the bridges not only move forward, they raise a little. Now, that is one big benefit, a hell of an advantage, because a loose, floppy string needs more space between it and the frets and the polepieces, in order to stay clear. So the vibrato compensates by raising

The Stratocaster was unveiled in 1954's jazzy looking brochure (after five pages of steel guitars). The copy promised that the new guitar delivered "that big professional tone so long sought after by critical players," and who can argue?

the bridges. And when you sharp a note [raising the arm], then the string doesn't flop as much as it does at rest, and with the vibrato pulled up, the string gets closer to the frets and to the polepieces. It's a balancing thing. It works to a benefit both ways. Another thing most people don't think of — those five springs act as an electrical shield underneath the pickups. We grounded them; the whole action was grounded.

The Strat's peghead was a significant departure.

George Fullerton: That Telecaster peghead was very small and people used to make fun of it — looks like a bare foot, and so on — but there was a reason for us doing that. Supplies were scarce in those days. We used to buy maple wood and a lot of pieces were fairly narrow, so we designed a way we could get two pieces out of it by having one end one way and the other going the other way [side by side, head to tail]. That wouldn't work with the wider Strat peghead, so we had to spend more money on it.

[*CD, track 7: how the inspiration for the Fender headstock came from Leo's seeing instruments played by visiting Croatian musicians.*]

How does the peghead design affect the vibrato action?

Leo Fender: Our peghead worked with the vibrato. See, the biggest problem isn't down at the vibrato; it's up at the nut. The strings crawl across the slots in the nut, and they can get hung up on their way back if you don't do those slots right, and this can give you tuning problems. Our peghead lines up all the strings in a straight line. I always felt that if you had three tuning keys on a side, rather than all six in a line like we had, then you'd have a problem with the strings going back and forth over the nut when the vibrato was operated.

Going one way, it'd make an angle in one direction, and coming back it'd tend to straighten out. This takes a toll in the string's accuracy after a while.

[*CD, track 8: more details on Leo Fender's preference for having the string lengths above the nut in a straight line rather than fanning out, as on typical "3&3" pegheads.*]

The flush-mounted plug receptacle was another distinctive feature.

George Fullerton: With the jack on the edge of the guitar, like on the Telecaster, you could set it down and if you had one of those long plugs you could damage the plug or the guitar. I had already worked on improving the jacks on our steel guitars, so I got to thinking about it and came up with the jack like you see on the Strat, and I presented it to Leo. [*Note: Bill Carson added that on one prototype, George's angled plug was hand-machined out of brass.*]

Leo Fender: Later on, why, we built our own right-angled plugs, small and compact, and we could mount the jack straight down. But for the Stratocaster we had the receptacle in the top, and the plug was protected in there, and it was pretty good. The whole guitar was pretty good.

The most recognizable headstock in the world has several functional advantages, as detailed by Mr. Fender on these pages and on the accompanying CD. This guitar is Brownie, Eric Clapton's "Layla" Strat.

The Stratocaster had Fender's first sunburst finish.

Don Randall: That was another market considera-tion. All of our competitors had one; we were the only ones who didn't. I thought a sunburst would make the Stratocaster a little more business-like, if you will — fancier.

Where did the name "Stratocaster" come from?

Don Randall: Well, I named all those guitars. "Stratocaster" sounded sort of like it was the next step up. We went from Broadcaster, up to Telecaster, and we wanted a name that kept the same theme, a similar ring to it. I wanted to reach up the ladder, so to speak, aim high. There were other products out on the market with "strato" in the name. People seemed to like "Stratocaster," so we stuck with it.

Was the Stratocaster initially as popular as the Telecaster?

Leo Fender: No, I don't think it took off quite so fast in the very beginning. The Telecaster was still so new, even when we came out with the Stratocaster, that the newness hadn't really worn off. Many players were sort of torn between which way to go. [*Note: Perhaps the Strat's slow start explains the delay between its appearance in the spring of '54 and Fender Sales' first order for an official production run six months later.*]

This 1954 letter may have been prema-ture in predicting initial shipments on May 15, but one sentence would prove to be prophetic: "You will undoubtedly experience a great deal of interest concerning this instrument . . . ."

What degree of success did you predict for the Stratocaster?

Leo Fender: You never know about those things. We knew it was good, and we were excited about it, but I just got this Japanese magazine. Almost the whole issue is devoted to all the Stratocaster copies made by everybody. I never thought it would be that popular.

ANNOUNCING THE NEW *Fender* **STRATOCASTER "COMFORT CONTOURED"**

ELECTRIC SPANISH GUITAR — WITH OR WITHOUT BUILT IN TREMOLO

Mr. Dealer:

The enclosed advertisement is a reproduction of the inside front cover of the April issue of the International Musician, which reaches approximately 220,000 musicians. This is just another of the many ways in which we, at Fender attempt to build sales for our dealers. You no doubt have already experienced some in-terest on the part of your local guitar players as a result of this ad.

Now, here are the facts concerning this extremely new and radically different spanish guitar. The Fender Stratocaster represents another "First for the Fender Company" with its "comfort contoured" body and its built-in tremolo. This guitar features a body which is shaped in such a way that, in reality, it becomes a part of the player and is the most comfortable instrument to play ever to be made. It features three highly improved pickups which are, in themselves, adjustable to insure proper tone balance. It has separate tone controls on two of the pickups and a three-position tone changing switch which gives instant response to any one of three pre-determined tone colorings.

The Stratocaster Guitar also features a surface mounted plug receptacle, which virtually ends the old hassle due to cord and plug interference. This feature alone, will be welcomed by all electric guitar players. Each string is in-dividually adjustable for action or height from the fret board and for length, which insures true fretting or pitch. This sectional bridge is a patented feature which no other guitar on the market today can duplicate.

Probably the foremost of the features of this new instrument is the built-in mechanical tremolo. This guitar is the first to appear on the market with its own built-in tremolo and while devices of this nature have been available in the past, as accessories, they have all been very weak in their effective-ness. The Fender tremolo provides easy action and a full tone change, both above and below the basic tuning, plus the fact that the guitar will remain in tune even after long playing with the tremolo, a feature which none of the other tremolo accessories, so far, have been able to duplicate. The tone of this instrument is extremely fine and variable within wide limits. Another feature which every qualified guitar player will recognize is this guitar's ability to sustain a note. Many instruments are very dead in this respect, which causes the player to have to work exceptionally hard to get the type of response he is seeking.

The price of the guitar with tremolo is $249.50. It is available without tremolo at $229.50. The case, which is of hardshell construction, crushed plush lined, with ample padding and covered in a grain hair seal simulated leather covering is available at $39.95.

You will undoubtedly experience a great deal of interest concerning this instrument, so place your orders now. Shipments are expected to begin May 15. When placing your orders for this guitar, do not forget that Fender Amplifiers are the standard by which all others are judged, so be sure to have a wide variety on hand at all times.

CHAPTER 3

THE STRATOCASTER ARRIVES

The Production Stratocaster of 1954

Announced in April 1954, Fender's new Stratocaster guitar was loaded with advantages readily apparent to anyone open-minded enough to give it a try. All six of its nickel-plated Kluson tuning machines were easy to reach, the straight string pull over the nut helped stabilize the tuning, and the twin cutaways facilitated upper fretboard access and helped balance the body, as they had on one structural predecessor, Fender's Precision Bass. The aptly named "Comfort Contour Body" was made of ash (typically two or three pieces glued edge to edge), and its highly original, torso-fitting shape beckoned players to cradle it like a curvy loved one.

The new guitar sported Fender's first stock sunburst, a shaded two-color nitrocellulose lacquer finish intended to appeal to players of more conventional — and upscale — models. Its white trim was another departure. The single-layer pickguard (affixed with eight screws), knobs, and pickup covers were made of a brittle plastic similar to Bakelite; in fact, it is often mislabeled Bakelite, a phenolic resin invented circa 1907 by Belgian scientist Dr. Leo Baekeland. Lab tests reveal that these parts were ABS (Acrylonitrile Butadiene Styrene) plastic, not Bakelite. Dan Smith: "The knobs, pickup covers and switch cap were all injection molded from the same compound mix while the pickguard was stamped from sheet stock of a different formulation. ABS was relatively new for injection molders and exhibited problems early on — the brittleness of the formulation used for the knobs, and also the fact that it didn't wear well, which explains the worn-through pickup covers on original Strats."

Thanks in part to its longer-than-Gibson's scale length of 25½" (647.7 mm), the Stratocaster had a bright tone — several tones, in fact, with three Alnico 3 pickups rather than the typical one or two, the heights of their polepieces staggered to better adapt to the inconsistent outputs of various string gauges (the B string's pole was the lowest). Among many departures from the Telecaster were new pickup covers made of plastic, intended to reduce microphonic feedback. The neck, middle, and bridge pickups were identified in Fender literature as the "Rhythm," "Normal Tone," and "Lead" pickups. The slanting of the bridge pickup lent an arty, almost Picassoesque touch, but its placement was rooted in the functional advantage of enhancing high frequencies on the treble strings.

George Blanda measured the polepiece diameters on an original 1954 Strat and found them to be .200", vs. the .187" or so they are today. Dan Smith speculates this might explain the longtime discrepancy between the size of the magnets and the polepiece holes in the pickup covers: "The larger holes were probably based on the fit of the original magnets, and apparently, no one ever changed them, even when the magnets got a little smaller." Bill Carson: "Many times, the original magnets were chipped on one end, so for cosmetic reasons the smooth, ground end was on the top side. The magnet was slightly over-sized for the die-punched fiber, and sometimes it sheared the inside diameter of the hole, leaving a burr of fiber on the bottom side. That's why we changed the size of the magnets. Dan is right in that the pickup cover was never remolded to another spec, to my knowledge."

A master volume knob and tone controls for the front and middle pickups — labeled *volume, tone, tone* — were mounted close to the bridge, within easy reach; all three were 250k potentiometers (helpful Fender literature explained, "Lead pickup does not require additional tone modification"). The 3-way switch was intended to allow a choice of one pickup at a time, period: "Forward position for deep soft rhythm work, middle position for straight rhythm work, rear position for lead work." Few advertising

From left: original-condition beauties from 1954, 1955, and 1956, with features typical of the period: ash bodies, maple fingerboards, single-layer pickguards, and spaghetti logos. The guitar in the center is a hardtail (non-trem) model, and the guitar at right has its bridge cover and tag intact. The hardtail, of course, has no fine-print "WITH SYNCHRONIZED TREMOLO" in the decal. Compare string trees, the varying effects of aging on the fingerboard colors, and knob profiles - the '54 has the earliest "miniskirt" knobs of brittle plastic.

promises would prove as prophetic as Fender's description of the brand new Stratocaster's sound: "as new and different as tomorrow."

Even the previously mundane output jack was elevated to a stylish detail. Mounted on the top and slanted at a rakish angle, the chrome-plated component may have looked like a teardrop ornament from a Buick Roadmaster, but once again the design reflected a functional advantage — protecting the guitar and the connecting cord's plug at the point where they meet.

The lacquer-sealed, 21-fret neck was the essence of simplicity: one piece of hard rock maple with no separate fingerboard, reinforced with an adjustable metal truss rod and attached to the body with four wood screws (or "bolts," in the common parlance) affixed through the corners of a steel plate. As on the Telecaster, the truss rod was installed from the rear, its rout filled with a "skunk stripe" of dark walnut. Other details included a mix of chrome plated parts (tremolo base plate) and nickel plated parts (tuners, strap buttons, saddles), the delicate "spaghetti" Fender logo in gold, black dot position markers, and a small, round string retainer for the treble E and B strings.

Dan Smith: "From everything we've seen, the fretboard radius was 7¼" on the early Strats. I'm told they did that procedure on a swing-arm sanding machine, and based on how the machine was adjusted on any given day, you'd get a little bit different radius. That's the nature of the way things were done in the early years."

The jewel in the crown was a vibrato system called the Synchronized Tremolo, a mechanical tour de force that made previous units seem clunky ("vibrato" would have been more technically correct than "tremolo," but Mr. Fender's use of "tremolo" has prevailed to this day). Its top-mounted, screw-in arm sported a snazzy white plastic tip.

Finally, the Strat's band-sawed body, pickguard-mounted electronic subassembly and screw-on neck all expedited manufacturing, as did producing the guitar in mass quantities on an assembly line. The brand new Stratocaster listed for $249.50, about 10% more than Gibson's gold-top Les Paul, and 30% less than its top-of-the-line Les Paul Custom.

Guitar buffs are quick to point out the many differences between an old Strat and a new one (during the 1970s, especially, the design strayed from its roots), but considering the half-century between them, the similarities are much more remarkable. We can still stand a classic '54 Strat next to a current model and marvel at the fact that here in the new millennium, the newer version is likely the world's most popular electric guitar. Concerning the vision of Leo Fender, little more need be said.

"There's something about the Strat's shape that is at once masculine and feminine. It fits everybody's body." — *Bonnie Raitt*

Advertisements for early electric guitars typically promised features that would enhance or facilitate the techniques of the day — whatever players were already doing. Don Randall believed the Stratocaster would deliver much more. A blurb in the May 1954 issue of *The Music Trades* revealed his almost preternatural foresight: "Mr. Randall believes this instrument will revolutionize the style of guitar playing."

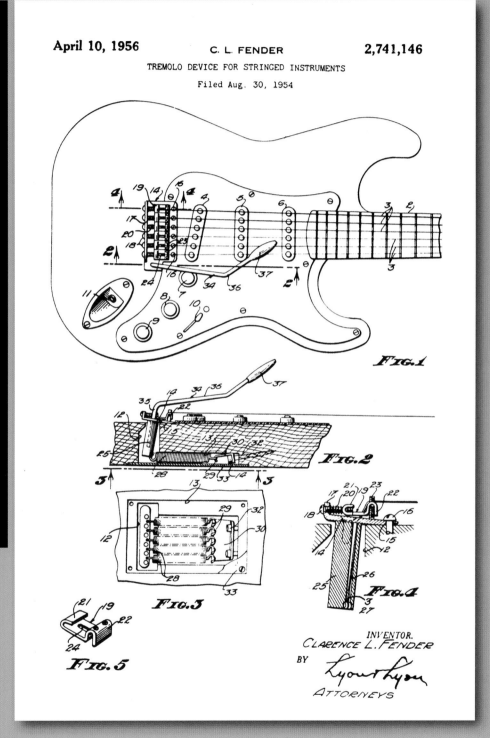

The Strat's patent diagram reveals the tremolo's fulcrum action. Note the orientation of the five interior springs, parallel to the strings. At lower right, the string (ball end at bottom) passes through the inertia bar and over the saddle mounted on the base plate; note base plate mounting screw. Lower left: saddle detail.

The road-worn Brownie has all five tremolo springs intact.

The Strat Tremolo — A "Real Mad Woggle"

In the Stratocaster's first catalog appearance, Fender called the Synchronized Tremolo "the newest and greatest of all recent Fender developments," and no wonder. As with so many of Leo Fender's designs, its simplicity was essential to its brilliance. As he explained in the Imaginary Roundtable (p. 56), Mr. Fender jettisoned the sustain-draining roller saddles of his pre-production vibrato, finding new inspiration in the design of a gram scale, which floats almost friction-free on a pivot point. He and Freddie Tavares fashioned a compact unit consisting of a relatively massive "inertia bar" of milled steel attached to a separate, flat base plate that was bent up in the back. Six nickel-plated steel bridge saddles were mounted on the base plate and held in place by screws running through the back edge. The entire unit pivoted against the six hardened screws that held it to the body's top surface.

Strings were drawn through round holes in the body's plastic back plate, then up through channels in the inertia bar and over the saddles. Instead of one big spring, the tremolo used five small ones concealed within the body and mounted parallel to the strings. Players could adjust the action by removing one or more springs or by adjusting the position of the spring's anchor plate, which was screwed into the tremolo cavity's forward wall.

Intonation adjustments could be effected for each string simply by turning its longitudinal screw one way or the other, increasing or decreasing the string's length. Adjustments to the action, or height, of each string could be made by using the tiny allen screws on top of each saddle. Some Gretsch guitars had featured the individually length-adjustable Melita bridge for two years or so, but the Strat unit was unprecedented in its versatility, offering individual adjustments for both length and height. This was a remarkable achievement in itself, even apart from the unit's pitch-changing vibrato action.

Players have experimented with tremolo adjustments since the Strat's inception. Jimmie Vaughan keeps the base plate flat against the body and, like Ronnie Earl, usually uses all five springs for maximum stiffness and tuning stability. Ritchie Blackmore uses four springs. David Gilmour uses three for light strings or four for heavier gauges, and he prefers a short whammy bar so, like Hank Marvin, he can hold it while picking. Yngwie Malmsteen uses four or five springs, as did Stevie Ray Vaughan. Jeff Beck uses three. All of these players have likely experimented with different spring configurations at various times.

Stevie Ray Vaughan: I started listening to people and noticed that when Otis Rush used [a vibrato bar] he had it on the top — he played upside-down. And Hendrix had the guitar upside-down, except he strung it regular. It seemed to me

The tremolo springs attach to holes in the inertia bar at one end, and to hooks on the anchor plate at the other. Note the ground wire, the ball ends of the strings, and the two screws for attaching and adjusting the anchor plate.

that the people who did that the best had it on top, so I moved mine. Sometimes it does get in the way. I've had it tear my sleeve halfway off.

So instead of working it with the little finger of your picking hand, it lays right in the middle of your palm.

Yeah, and I've got the springs set up so I couldn't move it with my little finger anyway. It's pretty tight, with four springs tightened all the way up. That's how I can do 'Third Stone From The Sun' and still be in tune. See, I have my old Strat set up where it won't go up at all. On my newer Strats, the vibrato handles are on the bottom, in the regular place."

Excerpt from an interview with Dan Forte, Guitar Player

Jeff Beck, on his Strat's whammy bar: "It's all there in my little friend. Sometimes I keep my hand on it while I play a whole line."[2]

"Few of us [in the 1950s] had heard of blues players like Albert King or B.B. King, and we'd never heard of finger vibrato apart from classical guitar. . . . I was overjoyed when I realized that not only could I give the tremolo bar a real mad woggle, but I could actually use it to produce a vibrato effect to help the notes sing more. I learned to play holding the vibrato bar in the palm of my hand while I picked so I could shake it while I was playing."

– Hank Marvin

Bodies await further sanding in the summer of '57.

Melodic Whammyisms, Track 19

Sound Aplenty: The "In Between" Tone

Three pickups, three basic tones. That's what Leo Fender intended for his Stratocaster to offer. Players had other ideas. They discovered that balancing the pickup selector in between the notched positions provided additional sounds, typically described as thin, delicate, honky, quacky, hollow, and especially funky. Many Strat aficionados made regular use of the two "new" positions, a prime example of players' fashioning innovative sounds or techniques from Stratquirks, to coin a term.

Contrary to a widespread assumption about the in-between positions, the pickups remain electrically in phase. Simply because they fall in different locations, any two pickups will respond differently to string vibrations, canceling certain frequencies when simultaneously activated. The location of the Strat's middle pickup accentuates the phenomenon.

Buddy Guy and Otis Rush were among the first in-betweeners. Rory Gallagher also liked the sound. For Eric Clapton, it's one of several favorite tones, while for Robert Cray it's his signature. Perhaps the best known exponent of recent decades is Mark Knopfler. Like Ike Turner, Eric Clapton, and Nils Lofgren, Knopfler likes the middle/bridge sound. In the early days, Buddy Guy preferred the neck/middle combo; Dick Dale's Signature Strat has a special switch providing that same setting.

For the Stratocaster's first 14 years on the market, the company officially ignored these tonal options, but the 1968 catalog advised, "Select any of three positions or even between the natural positions for sound aplenty." Finally, in 1977, Fender made the 5-position switch a standard feature.

"I've used the out of phase Strat sound all my life, but now it's become a cliché that you hear on Chevrolet adverts."

– *Richard Thompson*

"My first connection with a Strat is when a friend and I swapped guitars for a while. He got the Jaguar — 'the fancy one' — and I got the Strat, the 'working man's rig.' I was done with surf and just had to figure out how to get the sound that Hubert Sumlin got in Howlin Wolf's band. Only through word of mouth did I find out that you had to stick a matchbook cover in the switch to hold it in the 'in between' position, and then . . . magic! A very important thing for me was that the Strat always strung up softer than a Tele and made me play a more 'loosey goosey' style."

– *Bill Harkleroad, a.k.a. Zoot Horn Rollo*

"The most important inspiration is undoubtedly Zoot Horn Rollo's playing on Captain Beefheart's *Trout Mask Replica*. If I listen to it first thing in the morning, I am assured of a day of unbridled creativity."

– *John Frusciante*

And They Called It Rock And Roll

At the time of the Stratocaster guitar's first official production run in October 1954, the rock and roll phenomenon was only a year or so away, yet few music fans or even industry veterans saw it coming. The electric guitar was essential to the explosive new musical hybrid right from the beginning, although it shared a more or less equal co-billing with the saxophone for the first few years. Elvis Presley, Chuck Berry, Eddie Cochran, and most of the other first-generation rockers either played or were accompanied by flat-tops or hollowbody Gibsons or Gretsches; exceptions included Ricky Nelson, often seen on TV with the influential, Telecaster-wielding James Burton at his side.

Johnny Meeks, left, played lead guitar with rockabilly star Gene Vincent (center) and the Blue Caps in 1957 and 1958. Jimmie Vaughan, on his preference for maple necks: "I just always liked to look at the maple. It looks like Gene Vincent. You know that famous picture of the Blue Caps with all the Mary Kaye guitars? I look at that picture and go, 'Man! Look at that!'"

The few prominent Strat players included Buddy Holly, one of the first rockers to champion the new guitar; Ritchie Valens, who would perish with Holly in that February 3, 1959 plane crash; Johnny Meeks and Howard Reed, both of whom succeeded Cliff Gallup in Gene Vincent's Blue Caps; and the under-appreciated Ike Turner, whose blistering and sometimes reverb-drenched instrumentals were among the first to reveal the radical sonic potential of the Strat's tremolo bar.

Rock and roll burst across the sky like a meteor shower, then seemed to fade almost as quickly. By the dawn of the new decade several pioneers had died (Holly, Valens, Cochran), entered the clergy (Little Richard), been drafted (Presley), been scandalized (Jerry Lee Lewis, who married his 13-year-old cousin), or charged with crimes (Berry). Its leading lights snuffed out or dimmed, mainstream rock and roll devolved to bland pop after five short years or so — with a few welcome exceptions, including several chart-bustin', guitar-intensive instrumental hits. Meanwhile, the versatility of the Stratocaster was demonstrated by Buddy Merrill, who beginning in the summer of '55 regularly contributed jolts of electric guitar energy to a genteel TV show hosted by the Sultan of Schmaltz, bandleader Lawrence Welk.

The end of the '50s saw a boom in folk music that had little effect on electric guitars but helped spawn a folk-rock craze in the following decade that would indeed have lasting impact on electrics. Among the most influential players of the time were Chet Atkins (ostensibly a country guitarist but in reality a multi-faceted artist) and Les Paul, a mainstream pop superstar whose lightning runs and sonic experiments inspired youngsters who would become the guitar heroes of their generation.

The late Howard Reed replaced Johnny Meeks in the Blue Caps for a short stint in 1958. This is his historic '55, considered by some experts to be the first custom-ordered black Strat. Reed bought it from McCord Music in Dallas for $334.95, received a $140 credit for a trade-in, and paid $15.64 a month for nearly a year to pay it off.

Buffing painted bodies, 1957.

Buddy Merrill was only 19 when he began to bring Fender's new guitar to national attention on Lawrence Welk's "champagne music" television show on ABC.

The Strat Evolves

Changes in the Stratocaster's first incarnation, 1954 – 1959

Note: Some details regarding the 1959 Strat are included here, but most appear in a later section, which addresses the '59 - '65 Strat as a distinct model.

Body Wood

Early bodies often had somewhat of a primitive, handmade quality, lending both charm and quirks. Guitarist/historian Robb Lawrence: "Up through the end of '54, you sometimes see 'ribbing' on the back contour and in the cutaways of the horns, caused by the harder grain of the ash being raised up a bit compared to the softer, lighter wood in between the grain lines. George Fullerton told me they took care of the problem when they started using small wooden sanding blocks. Another interesting detail is that on some very early pegheads, the little walnut insert for the truss rod is a different shape, more elongated."

In mid 1956 the ash was generally replaced with alder, which was less costly, more consistent in appearance, and easier to work with. Ash continued to be used on blonde-finished models because its conspicuous and attractive grain patterns were highlighted by the finish's translucence.

Necks

The neck profiles on Stratocasters showed a great deal of variation in the early years, generally progressing from large rounded necks in 1954 to a more pointed "V" neck (or "boat neck") in 1955 - 1957. "V" necks had either "soft" or "hard" spines; the latter was sharper and more pronounced, and also considered by some experts to be the later version. There is also a "medium V." In 1958 and 1959 many necks were again rounder in back. Some were slimmer in front-to-back thickness; others returned to a bit of the "V" profile. Various rounded profiles over the years have been described as "C," "D," or "U" necks.

"I was always bad in school — I didn't like it … but I've got some of my books still, from when I was about 13. And there's just drawings of guitars … always trying to draw Fender Stratocasters."[3]

– *George Harrison*

Pop and country players were the Strat's intended market and its first endorsers. (Note the spectacular wide-figure ash on some of these guitar bodies.) Buddy Holly, Ritchie Valens, Johnny Meeks and others would use it for a new kind of music whose name, "rock and roll," had yet to be coined when the Strat was in development.

Purchasing Manager Joe Carducci joined Fender in November '73. One of his friends was Charlie Davis, who as a teenager had come to work in the '50s with Freddie Tavares and the factory crew. Joe recalled: "A so-called expert — who was really just some guy who got information through the rumor mill — was talking one day about the V necks. He had this grandiose vision of how they were some strategic design thing. When he left the room, Charlie Davis just snickered and told us the real story. At Fender we made necks by cutting the outer perimeter and then sanding them on a drum sander. You ever try to sand a neck on one of those things? I've worked in the shop on both bodies and necks, and drum-sanding is tricky. Well, the guy who normally sanded the necks was away for a few days, so they handed it to some guy who wasn't that familiar with it, had no idea there was a real skill to it.

"Next thing you know, they're having this big meeting — all these necks got sanded wrong! I asked Charlie how many, and he said hundreds. The quality control was so loose then. The question was, do we scrap them or use them?

 Early Strat champ Ritchie Valens, the first Hispanic rock star. He was only 17 when he perished in the tragic plane crash that also took Buddy Holly's life. His rollicking, guitar-intensive "La Bamba," sung entirely in Spanish, remains a timeless classic.

They let them go out in the field, and the rest is Fender lore now. They never got any complaints about them. This was around '57."

While this accident accounted for some of the V necks, it did not account for all of them, given that Fender made pre-CBS necks with "hard" or "soft" V profiles for a couple of years. Dan Smith recalled Freddie Tavares' explanation that some of Leo Fender's favorite musicians played Epiphones with somewhat V-profiled necks, which may have been one factor in Fender's temporary shift to that design.

Phantom Reds

In early or mid 1958, Fender changed the Strat's stock sunburst finish from two colors (yellow to brownish black) to three (yellow to red to brownish black). For a year or two, however, the paint used for the red tended to fade if exposed to the sun for prolonged periods. Bill Carson: "The chemists at the paint company couldn't understand why the sunlight through a showroom window would gobble up that red, so we took sections of alder wood about eight inches square, and we'd saw it out and sand it and fill it and paint it, the same as a body would be, and put maybe three different kinds of paint on there. We'd expose it to the sun, and we'd put strips of masking tape on part of it, so you'd get a contrast after the exposure. I'd have to get up on the damn ladder and get these blocks up and down to

Custom Shop 1957 reissue

Guitar Player speculated that this one-of-a-kind Lucite Strat may be "the most valuable non-celebrity solidbody Fender ever made." Originally billed as "the $1,000 guitar," this gape-worthy see-through was built as a promotional item for display at trade shows. According to Bill Carson, its construction began in 1957 and took years to complete. Weighing more than a hernia-poppin' 18 pounds, this anvil of a guitar was designed not for long nights on the bandstand but rather to grab your attention which, clearly, it does to this day.

Another showstopper trio, from left: a 2-color sunburst hardtail from early '57 (relatively late for an ash body), a 3-color '58 with tag, and a 3-color '59 that still has the maple neck and single-layer pickguard; later that year the Strat would go to the rosewood board and triple-ply pickguard.

In 1957, Fender built this unique guitar for one of its earliest Stratocaster endorsers, Eddie Cletro (photo, p. 83), of "Flyin' Saucer Boogie" fame. Note beige body and gold anodized pickguard. While "rosewood neck" is Fender slang for a maple neck with a rosewood fingerboard, the Cletro Strat has a one-piece neck of solid rosewood. Guitar courtesy Norm Harris.

the roof of number one building [at the Raymond & Valencia facility]. We figured out a good paint that wouldn't fade, and it was all right after that."

Plastic

The plastic used for the first production Strat's pickguard, pickup covers, and knobs proved to be brittle and impractical, in some cases accounting for worn parts (Buddy Holly's old '55 looked like he had Peggy Sue'd the ends of two pickup covers right off). In 1955 Fender began to substitute more durable plastics for these parts, although as late as 1957 some Strats were reportedly still mixing the newer pickguard and knobs and the older pseudo-Bakelite pickup covers. Note: The earliest knobs appeared in different profiles.

Serial Numbers

Serial numbers were relocated from the tremolo's back plate to the neck plate by the end of June '54. Extensive information on Strat serial numbers can be found in several books (see Chapter 10).

Miscellaneous

In early '55 the round string holes in the back plate disappeared and oval holes became the norm. By the fall of 1956, the peghead's round string retainer switched to a "butterfly" or "string tree" type with a half-tunnel guide for the B and treble E strings, and the pickup magnets had gradually switched from Alnico 3 to the newer Alnico 5.

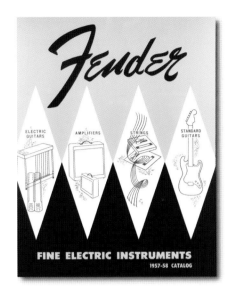

The 1957-'58 catalog continued to tout the Stratocaster's many "Fender Firsts."

May 1957: Positioning the "skunk stripe," which fills the slot after the neck rod is installed. Note adjustment mechanism at the end of the neck.

Buddy Holly's first album, 1957's *The "Chirping" Crickets*, was a debut of such potency and significance that *All Music Guide* compared it to *Elvis Presley* and *Meet The Beatles*. The photo inspired guitarists in the U.S. and the U.K. to check out the new-fangled Fender, its radical persona in sharp contrast here to the conventional hollowbody next to it.

Serial numbers appeared on the rear tremolo cover, as here, for only the first few months of production and were then relocated to the neck plate.

May 1957: As the new Fender company found out when it first tried to recreate the small headstock, one of the trickiest procedures was sanding the area where the "ball" joined the outside curve.

Mary Kaye

Among Fender fans, Mary Kaye is guitar royalty, the namesake (or nicknamesake) of Fender's elegant blonde Stratocaster guitar with 14-carat gold-plated hardware. It was announced in the February 1957 issue of *The Music Trades* and originally listed for $330 (sunbursts were $274.50). It turns out Ms. Kaye is royalty indeed, and not only figuratively. On her father's side she is related to Queen Liliuokalani, the last reigning monarch of Hawaii's centuries-old royal family and composer of perhaps the greatest Hawaiian song of them all, the lilting "Aloha Oe."

A Las Vegas institution in the '50s and '60s, the Mary Kaye Trio numbered Elvis Presley and Sammy Davis, Jr. among their most enthusiastic fans. Mary is credited with being one of the first women to hit the *Billboard* charts with a rock song, 1959's "You Can't Be True, Dear," and she has been inducted into several halls of fame. Meanwhile, the original Mary Kaye Strats continue to increase in value. Stan Jay of Mandolin Bros., Staten Island: "The original '54 sunburst might be catching up to it, but among vintage Strats, the Mary Kaye is the one."

Mary Kaye, 2003: "I was born Mary Ka'aihue in Detroit and grew up in St. Louis. No one could pronounce my name. They called me 'Mary K-something,' so we changed it to Mary Kaye. I started playing when I was nine years old, on ukulele and guitar. I'm a jazz singer. A lot of people compared me to Ella Fitzgerald, who was always number one to me. Mr. Louis P. Armstrong told me he listened to my recording of 'My Funny Valentine' every night before going onstage, because he said it did wonderful things for his spirit. He took me backstage because he wanted me to see my record on his record player. That was such a wonderful thing.

"I played jazz guitar — not solos, but pretty, symphonic chords a lot of players don't know. I used my thumb. One night Tal Farlow, who was a dear friend, and I played together, up at a club in Canada, and that was a thrill."

This photo ran for years in Fender literature, spawning the "Mary Kaye" nickname for gold-hardware Strats finished in blonde.

Mary Kaye's original Mary Kaye guitar, serial no. 09391. Owner Iain Hersey reported that the body is a January '56; the neck warped and was replaced at the factory with a neck dated 9/56. Mary Kaye's Mary Kaye belonged to Johnny Cucci, who got it from Don Randall at the Summer 1956 NAMM Show in New York after Mary had posed with it for the now-famous photo. Cucci recorded with steel guitarist Jody Carver, and this guitar appeared on the cover of their 1958 LP, *Hot Club Of America in Hi-Fi.* Iain Hersey: "It's blonde, of course, but actually a bit more of a cream color, a little darker around the edges, almost like a blonde sunburst. It's got the round string retainer, [pseudo] 'Bakelite' parts, and it plays like a dream."

Mary Kaye, 2003: "Fender gave me a special Stratocaster with a gold plate on the back that says, 'To Mary Kaye, from Your Friends at Fender,' and it has a certificate saying this is a special Mary Kaye, number one. I'm playing it now, and I'm very honored by the tribute."

be pleased to do that. The fellow who brought over the guitar didn't understand that Fender had told me I could keep it, and right after the photo, the guitar was gone. I used it for a movie [the Strat appeared in *Cha-Cha-Cha Boom*, released in 1956], and once again it went back to Fender. We were so busy working on the movie we didn't have time to pursue it, and I still had my D'Angelico so I was happy.

"The picture in the catalog went around the world and players were asking for a guitar like Mary Kaye's, but I didn't even know about all that until about four years ago. They told me my name was in all the magazines and books.

"I'm producing a musical in Las Vegas called *The Sounds of The 50s and 60s* with different people playing the Mary Kaye Trio. The production costs are about $40,000 a week. It's going to be sensational. The mayor has given us a proclamation that says January 9th, my birthday, is Mary Kaye Trio day. So I'm still here [*laughs*]."

"I was at the old Frontier Hotel in Las Vegas and Don Randall came to meet me. I was singing there with my trio, playing a guitar that John D'Angelico had made for me by hand. I told Mr. Randall, I'd be very pleased to play your amplifiers, but I couldn't give up my D'Angelico for anything. That was okay with Fender, but Mr. Randall asked me if I would be in a photo with the Stratocaster — the special one with the light white color and the gold fittings — and I said I'd

Set your dream machine for 1957: Custom Shop Mary Kaye Relic.

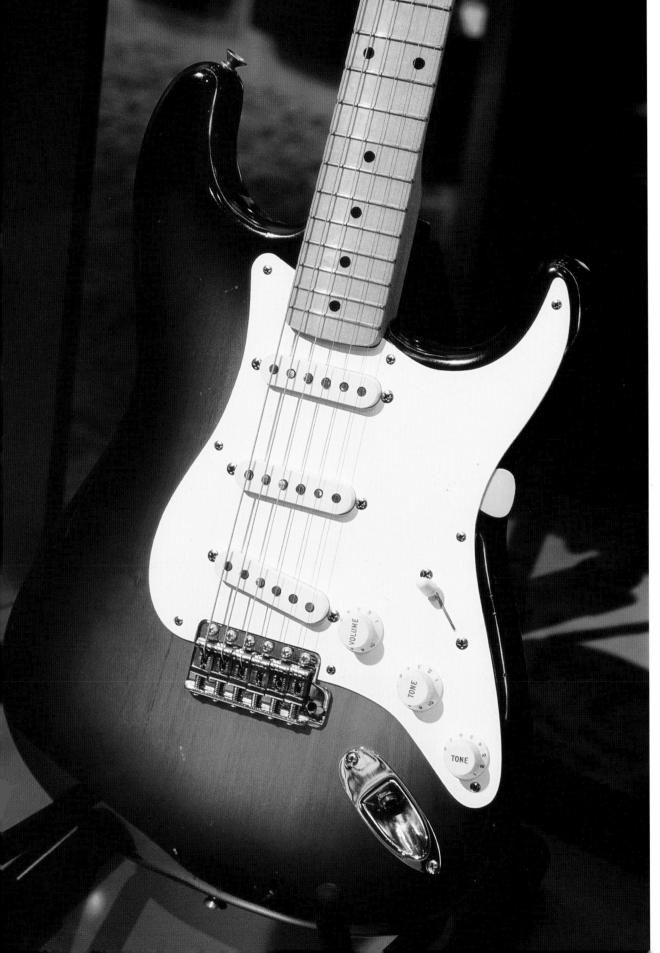

Buddy Holly played this '58 on the last night of his life. It was meticulously restored by John Page, who called the project one of the most meaningful experiences of his career. He discovered a white pick wedged underneath the pickguard, likely untouched since that fateful night in February 1959. The guitar is now on display at the Buddy Holly Center in Lubbock. Details include a penciled neck date of 4/58; serial no. 028228.

Finishes: Early 'bursts

Even before founding the Fender company, Leo Fender and his partner in K&F, Doc Kauffman, experimented with nitrocellulose lacquer, widely available in the furniture business. Leo continued using lacquers at Fender. According to the Custom Shop's Mark Kendrick: "On the earliest sunburst Strats, the colors were Canary Yellow, common in the furniture trade, and Dark Salem. Both were nitrocellulose lacquers. They'd get them wherever they could. They might walk across the street, literally, and pick up stuff from Fullerton Hardware. They used Fuller O'Brien, Old Quaker, Spartan — many manufacturers were around Orange County at that time."

Collector/researcher Clay Harrell has experience in both auto painting and guitar finishing (as we will see, these crafts are entwined). He has taken apart hundreds of old Fenders and documented many factory finish procedures and quirks. (On his website, Guitarhq.com, he credits author and former Custom Shop Master Builder Yasuhiko Iwanade for some of his research.) Clay Harrell: "Fender had to pore-fill the earliest Strat bodies because ash is an open-pore wood, and then they sprayed the whole sunburst — the yellow, then the brownish black. It's labor intensive and costly. In mid '56 they went to alder, a closed-pore wood, so they no longer had to pore-fill it. Also, instead of spraying the yellow, they started dipping bodies in yellow dye. Both changes were money savers. They still sprayed the brownish black. By mid-'58 when they added the red, they were dipping the yellow and spraying both the red and the brownish black.

"In about mid '64-ish they were still dipping the yellow, but they also started spraying yellow again. They did both, which is one reason a lot of those guitars have a less translucent yellow. Hiding the grain somewhat allowed them to use wood with minor flaws. Some sunbursts from that period have a 'targetburst' — separate, distinct rings of color instead of a gradual fade from one to the next. All three colors were now sprayed, and the less translucent coloring lends itself to the target look."

A worker draws wire from a spool and attaches it to a bobbin on the pickup winding machine, October 1966.

String installation.

Custom Colors on Pre-CBS Strats

The stock finish for Stratocaster guitars has been sunburst since the model's inception, but over the years Fender has offered dozens of other colors. A gold Strat was made for Texas Playboy Eldon Shamblin in the summer of 1954, the Stratocaster's first year. Other early Strats built for Bill Carson and bluesman Pee Wee Crayton were painted a solid color later called Dakota Red (Carson had called it "Cimarron" red). By 1956, available non-stock finishes were specified in Fender literature to be the "player's choice."

Soon after George Fullerton mixed up a batch of what came to be called Fiesta Red at a local paint store (in 1957, as best he could recall), Fender began to offer a somewhat more official array of "Custom Colors," plus blonde, for a 5% extra charge. (On the accompanying CD, track 9, Mr. Fullerton recounted the story of the development of the first official Custom Color.) For years the colors were available but never specified in catalogs or price lists. Finally, 14 paints were sampled on little rectangular chips on Fender's first color chart, which according to *Fender: The Sound Heard 'Round The World* was sent to dealers in 1961: Burgundy Mist metallic, Foam Green, Surf Green, Sherwood Green metallic, Lake Placid Blue metallic, Daphne Blue, Sonic Blue, Shoreline Gold metallic, Olympic White, Black, Inca Silver metallic, Shell Pink, Dakota Red, and Fiesta Red. Blonde (also spelled "Blond") remained in the line, bringing the total to 15.

The word "custom" typically connotes a one-of-a-kind product made to order for an individual, so Fender's "Custom Colors" might have been more precisely called "optional, extra-charge" colors. However, Fender did offer true custom finishes. If you wanted a Strat in, say, Desert Sand, Fender could provide it, even though Desert Sand didn't appear on the color charts. Also, the same color might be standard for one model but "custom" for another. For example, semi-transparent blonde is typical of Telecasters but rare on Stratocasters, while the Strat's standard sunburst was a special-order finish on early Teles. Additional confusion sometimes results from Fender's use of a color prior to its mention in the literature, or after its official discontinuation.

Except for blonde and Candy Apple Red, Fender's Custom Colors were originally formulated for the automobile industry. Their appearance on Strats and other Fenders generally paralleled their availability to the makers of Cadillac (Lake Placid Blue metallic, Daphne Blue, Olympic White, Dakota Red, Sonic Blue, etc.), Buick (Foam Green), Chevrolet (Surf Green), Oldsmobile (Burgundy Mist metallic), Pontiac (Shoreline Gold metallic), Corvette (Inca Silver metallic), and so on.

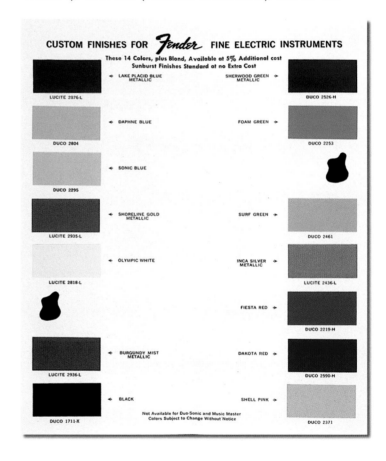

The first color chart specified 14 extra-cost finish options, plus blonde. Note that colors are often compressed on small samples such as these. For example, the Lake Placid Blue metallic at top left and Sherwood Green metallic at top right look almost black.

The guitar's silhouette has often been compared to the shape of a woman's body, but seldom so lyrically or lightheartedly as in this photo, depicting the curviest of all guitars. The Strat at left has a factory Desert Sand finish (stock on Duo-Sonics but almost unheard-of on a Strat) over a metallic silver undercoat. Regarding the middle guitar, owner Françoise Blasé pointed out, "This Mary Kaye is rare, yet much more common than the other two, and unlike the others it was cataloged as a separate guitar." The gorgeous gold Strat at right is a '56. Black spots along the edges reveal a sunburst undercoat. Joe Menza owns this guitar (and the Desert Sand Strat). He explained, "Like the other four or five gold maple-neck Strats I've seen, this one has gold metal parts. Usually the plating has been worn away by the player's sweat, but on this guitar it's in great shape."

Competition Colors

Fender wasn't the only company to depart from traditional blonde and sunburst finishes in the 1950s. Gibson introduced its gold-top Les Paul and all-gold ES-295 in 1952, and mid-'50s Gretsch literature pictured guitars in black, white, red, orange, gold sparkle, silver sparkle, Cadillac Green, and Jaguar Tan, among others.

A Multiplicity of Variables

For any Fender guitar, regardless of model, year, or type of finish, many factors can contribute to the overall look:

Body wood. As noted, Strat bodies were ash for the first two years and alder after that, with rare exceptions in poplar or mahogany. Different woods require different preparation processes and may then "take" identical finishes in different ways.

Preparation. Between sanding and painting, bodies were typically "prepped" by applying any of several types of sealers or other undercoats to stabilize the wood, increase moisture resistance, fill pores, and provide better adhesion for subsequent coats. Undercoats varied in their brand name (e.g., Sherwin-Williams, Fuller O'Brien), chemical composition, thickness, method of application (brushing, spraying, dipping), the order in which different types were applied, the number of coats — and even whether they were used at all. A guitar's color may be affected by these undercoats and their methods of application. One product was Sherwin-Williams' Homoclad, an oil-based sealer still used in the Custom Shop. Mark Kendrick: "Lacquer undercoats were used in conjunction with Homoclad as a sealer until the late '50s. Fender then began to use Fullerplast, from Fuller O'Brien."

Fullerplast is a clear, modified alkyd varnish known for its hardness, resistance to mars and abrasions, and production convenience. Norm Isaac is an employee of I.C.I., once the parent company of Fuller O'Brien, and also a guitar refinisher with 30 years'

A very rare combo – a factory stock gold finish on a left-handed, maple-neck Strat. Guitar: Buck Suker

experience. He believes Fender started using Fuller-plast a bit later, in the mid '60s. In any case, he added: "Fullerplast solved a lot of problems for Fender. It's clear, catalyzed, stable, and pretty impervious. It could be applied thicker, more easily, and in fewer coats, and it was chemically cured so you didn't have to wait for it to air-dry, all of which saved time, labor, and money. On some of the unpainted bodies, like those natural-finish ash Strats of the '70s, it's Fullerplast all the way through, from clear coat to base coat. Some necks and fingerboards are also sprayed with Fullerplast, but others have lacquer over the Fullerplast on the head-stock, and that lacquer can yellow. That's why you see mismatched aging on some necks."

Aside from being coated with pore fillers or sealers, some bodies were also dyed, stained, or both. Mark Kendrick: "Sometimes they'd have the bodies coming through there hanging on chains, sort of like an assembly-line laundry. They'd dunk one in a drum full of liquid and then raise it out. They also used what's called a base toner, on both ash and alder bodies but particularly on the alder, as early as late '55 or so and going through '73 or '74. It was translu-cent, and if you had a couple of boards that looked a little mismatched when glued side by side, the base toner helped to smooth out the look and give you a better blend. This base toner accounts for some of the really yellow sunbursts you see from that time."

Color coat. The same color of paint was sometimes provided by different manufacturers, which could account for slight variations in the paint's composi-tion and original appearance, and significant varia-tions in how it faded, thinned, or yellowed. For the most part, Fender used DuPont Duco nitrocellulose ("nitro") lacquers and DuPont Lucite acrylic lacquers on pre-CBS Custom Color guitars. Nitro and acrylic lacquers have different properties, but even within either category, different colors may have distinctive characteristics. For example, some colors are more light-sensitive than others, more likely to fade.

A quartet of blonde, ash-body pre-CBS Strats. The round string retainer on the guitar at left indicates it's from the first year or two. The middle and right guitars are Mary Kayes, a late '57 or early '58 with extensive neck wear, and a '59 with an early rosewood board and a beautifully figured peghead. Note the variations in finish translucence, visibility of the wood grain, and the yellowing effects of aging.

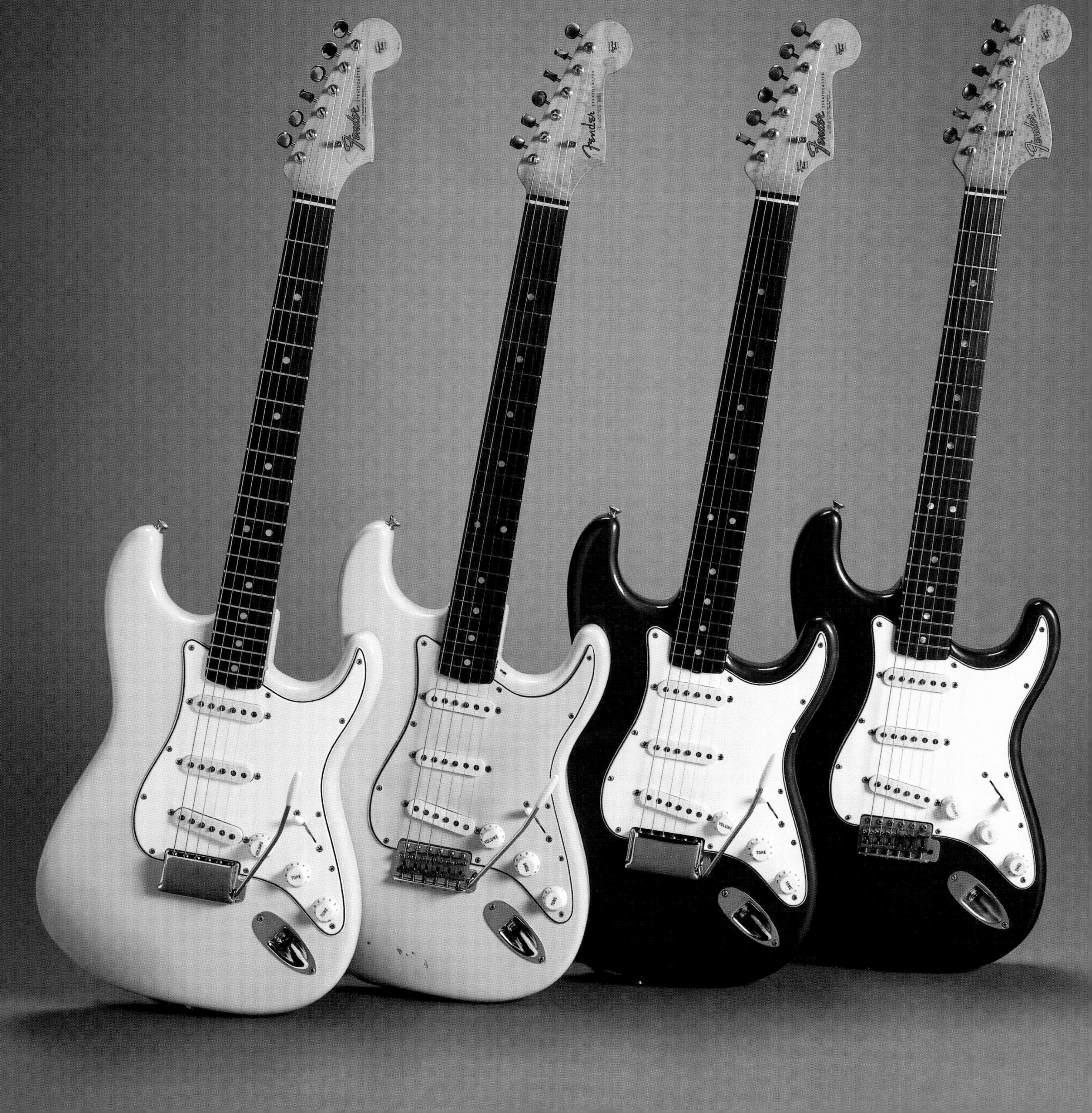

Thickness. Some Strats are practically embalmed in multiple layers of undercoats, paints, and a clear coat, their look owing more to flashy hot rods than traditional instruments. On others the finish is subtle, the result of a complex interaction of blended hues, transparency, wood grain, brightness, and other factors.

Clear coats. Clear, protective nitrocellulose lacquer coats were applied over pre-CBS sunbursts and sometimes over Custom Colors as well, especially the metallics. They varied in thickness and in their interaction with different color coats.

Masking & Cosmetic Makeup. While Fender Sales, rather than the factory, typically called the shots on which colors would be offered during a particular period, paints were sometimes selected by factory workers for reasons other than market demand or fulfilling individual orders — to hide glue joints or blemishes in the wood, for instance. An example of Leo Fender's legendary thrift is that a botched or flawed color coat could be used as an undercoat for a subsequent paint job; many custom colors were applied over a sunburst, silver, gold, or other color coat, with varying effects on the ultimate appearance. (Clay Harrell reported an original 1961 Strat that the Fender crew painted sunburst, then white primer, then Dakota Red, then Fiesta Red — "probably just a series of bad paint mistakes.")

«

From left, mid-'60s Strats in Sonic Blue, Daphne Blue, and Lake Placid Blue metallic; note the varying effects of aging on the plastic parts, and the oddball extra peghead decal on the Lake Placid Blue guitar. Perry A. Margouleff: "The green guitar at right might have been made up specially for someone. It's got a '66-era headstock, a highly figured bird's-eye maple neck, and gold hardware." Compare the brighter pearloid dots on the big-headstock green guitar to the clay dots on the earlier guitars.

Environmental factors. A guitar's exposure to sunlight, fluorescent lights, tobacco smoke, and even smog might affect how the finish ages. The yellowing of either a lacquer color coat or a clear top coat might change an original Lake Placid Blue metallic to an apparent Ocean Turquoise or Teal Green (in fact, the yellowed Lake Placid Blue may more closely approximate an unfaded Teal Green than does an actual, aged Teal Green). Such effects could also change an original Olympic White to an apparent Blonde, or a Sonic Blue to a light pea green.

Faded color coats cause additional confusion. For years, popular "Custom Colors" supposedly included salmon pink, also called coral pink, but Fender never applied that color (except perhaps on a one-off basis) and never used those names. Such finishes are typically faded Fiesta Reds. (Fender did offer a lighter color, Shell Pink.)

Expediency. The look of a particular Strat could be affected by additional variables that might come into play at every step, such as evolving production techniques, the temporary unavailability of a particular undercoat or paint, or pressure on the factory to increase output. Some guitars were rushed through without undercoats or clear coats. Among four Strats finished in, say, Dakota Red, one guitar might have one or more undercoats but no clear coat, the second might have a clear coat but no undercoats, the third might have both, and the fourth might have neither. Depending on the number, the colors, and the bleed-through of undercoats, the thickness and fading of color coats, the yellowing of clear coats, and other factors, it's conceivable that decades later only an expert could tell that all four guitars were once the same color.

Blues brothers: The hardtail on the left is a late '59 in Daphne Blue. Owner Joe Menza: "It hasn't faded, but it's worn away in places, and you can see that it was applied over a sunburst [note the exposed under-coat on the right body horn]. It's the only Daphne maple-neck Strat I've ever seen." This guitar is also an example of a transition model: By late '59, most Strats were fitted with the newer rosewood fingerboard and 11-screw, 3-ply pickguard.

The Strat at right is a '57 in a Lake Placid Blue metallic that was applied over Desert Sand. Joe Menza: "In the '60s, Lake Placid Blue became more common. This is the only one from the '50s I've seen, although I've heard of others."

Perry A. Margouleff: "This is one of the earliest Custom Color Strats I've turned up in all my years of collecting, a '55. It's unquestionably authentic and correct. Many years later the Tele turned up; it's from the same period, and looks like it was painted out of the same can of paint. I've heard this color referred to as Cimarron Red." By most accounts, the unofficial and very early Cimarron Red, a name coined by Bill Carson, evolved into Dakota Red; see p. 98. On this stunning Stratocaster, note how the lettering on the knobs has worn away.

Ted Ledbetter dresses frets in late '63. The stamp at the end of each neck reveals the date as well as the neck contour, in this case "B." Note the curved-bottom — or "round lam" – rosewood fingerboards.

ROSEWOOD BOARDS & CBS

The Dream Team

The early 1960s was an exhilarating era for everyone associated with Fender. The company was expanding — along with the rest of the instrument manufacturing industry, the record business, and pop radio — and its products were gaining broader acceptance. Thanks to photographer/designer Bob Perine's catalogs and ads, Fender guitar literature was elevated to an art form; thanks to Don Randall and highly motivated salesmen, the marketing of Fender products was also elevated to an art form of sorts. While Gibson brochures pictured men who looked like your dad, wearing business suits and playing elegant jazz instruments, Fender literature pictured guys who looked like you, playing rocketship guitars and hanging out at the beach with suntanned blondes in bikinis. Take your pick.

Never has any guitar company exceeded the potency of Fender's early-'60s dream team: Leo Fender and Freddie Tavares in the lab, plant manager Forrest White running a tight ship and keeping his hawk eye on quality control, skilled workers on the line, motivated salespeople in the field, Bob Perine behind the camera, and Don Randall assembling what Leo's old partner Doc Kauffman called "a sales distributorship like nobody had ever seen in the world." The arty shapes, functional innovations, and bright colors of early-'60s Fender instruments reflected the thrilling, all-systems-go technology of the space age, as well as the sunny California esthetic of souped-up convertibles and surf music and perhaps even the glamour and optimism of a Kennedy administration that came to be called "Camelot." From Fullerton, the future gleamed like the chrome trim on a Candy Apple Red Strat.

Leo Fender remembered, "We grew pretty fast, because in 1955 we had about 50 employees, but by the end of 1960 we were up to well over a hundred. We built more buildings, and we leased another 6,000 square feet in '60. Then we had a new warehouse and sales office — a 38,000-square-foot, one-story building with about 11,000 square feet of office space and a recording studio where musicians could come in and record for free on Ampex machines. By the end of 1964 we were occupying twenty-seven buildings. We were bursting at the seams in those days, with about five hundred employees in the manufacturing proper, and six hundred in all."

Bob Perine took this photo for the whimsical "You Won't Part With Yours Either" ads, which helped take the stuffiness out of guitar advertising and reinforced Fender's youth-oriented appeal.

The Fender look at the dawn of the '60s, as rendered by artist/photographer Bob Perine: arty, classic, colorful.

Dick Dale rocks Southern California at the dawn of the surf era. In May 1962, Dale and his Del-Tones unleashed "Miserlou." This song had everything: Dale's forearm-bustin' speed picking, a soaring Middle Eastern melody, and the noble machismo of the bullring (courtesy of mariachi horns), all punctuated with swirling piano arpeggios and cattle-drive whoops and hollers. Did instrumental rock ever get any better? The titles of Dale's later singles would conjure up the adrenaline and hot-asphalt energy of the culture coalescing around surfing and hot-rodding ("Mr. Eliminator," "Banzai Washout," etc.), while his ferocious concerts at the Rendezvous Ballroom in Balboa would enter into legend. Dick Dale: "For the particular sound you want – punch, power, a driving force of true rock and roll – you've got to play a Stratocaster."

Dick Dale Impales!, Track 15

Fender's three classic reds, from left: Candy Apple, Dakota, and Fiesta. Candy Apple was announced in November 1963. This example was sprayed over a silver undercoat in '65 – "right about the time they switched to gold undercoats," according to Joe Menza, who owns the left and center guitars. "The gold makes for a slightly warmer red that's not quite as bright as this one."

Compared to the orange/red Fiesta, Dakota Red is more of a fire-engine red (John Peden: "almost a barn red or brick red"). Joe Menza: "I've seen quite a few Dakotas with rosewood boards, but never another maple. Most Dakotas and Candy Apples hold their color pretty well. This one, a '58, hasn't faded a bit." The original hang tag specified the price, $301.

The Fiesta on the right is owned by Françoise Blasé, who observed: "Candy Apple is the most common of the reds, then Fiesta, then Dakota. But it's relative – they're all rare compared to sunbursts, and this one is very sweet. Sometimes Fiesta turns a little coral or salmon, but this one kept its color." In the lower right corner of the color chart, Fender's first, we see Fiesta on top, followed by Dakota and (at bottom) Shell Pink, which was replaced by Candy Apple Red on the late-'63 chart.

Strat II: Pre-CBS, Rosewood Fingerboard

The Strat's second incarnation ran from mid 1959 to late 1965. While it carried over some of the basic features from the first version — small headstock, nickel-plated Kluson tuners, 4-bolt neck, staggered-polepiece pickups, the tremolo with a separate base plate and inertia bar, nickel-plated steel saddles with the Fender stamp, etc. — it marked a significant departure in both cosmetics and production details. This '59 - '65 Strat was the "pre-CBS rosewood-neck" version, with the informal "rosewood neck" actually signifying a new rosewood fingerboard glued on top of Fender's standard one-piece maple neck (see A Word About Necks & Fingerboards, p. 114).

Aside from the fingerboard itself, the shift to rosewood entailed two other changes. The black dot markers were replaced on the new dark fingerboard with contrasting off-white, or "clay," dots. Bill Carson explained that the dots were fiberboard, similar in composition and thickness to the pickup coil-form tops. They were press-cut in a small punch press. Bill Carson: "I did some of these. Prior to fretting, we'd place a dot of glue in the pre-drilled positions, then press the markers in there with a light hand press. We used a neck oval sander to remove excess dot material after the glue dried, then fine-sanded it by hand with 600-grit sandpaper before the neck was sprayed with sealer." Bill added that aside from the color of the dots, the materials

and installation procedures for the original black markers and later "clay" markers were essentially the same. (Note: The Custom Shop has come close to duplicating the "clay" dots with an off-white phenolic.) Also, now that the truss rod was installed from the front, prior to attaching the fingerboard, the neck's rear skunk stripe and the peghead's "teardrop" plug were eliminated.

Fender's first rosewood fingerboard had appeared the previous year, on the new top-of-the-line Jazzmaster of 1958. The impetus for the change came from Don Randall and his marketing associates at Fender Sales. Like early Jazzmaster fingerboards, the rosewood boards first used on Strats in mid '59 were milled flat on the bottom to match the maple neck's top surface; this thicker type is nicknamed the "slab board." In the summer of '62, Fender began to use a thinner rosewood board that was curved on the bottom surface to match the convex top of the neck. About a year later, Fender switched to a rosewood board that was thinner still. Compared to the original one-piece maple neck, the rosewood board — whatever its thickness — is generally thought to impart a somewhat less bright or mellower tone.

The three-color sunburst finish with added red is typically associated with this second Strat incarnation, but remember that it actually appeared on the earlier maple-neck Strat in early or mid '58; thus the

Hank Marvin of the Shadows, at right, was the UK's first bona fide guitar hero, shown here with fellow Shadow Bruce Welch and pop star Cliff Richard. With their matching Fenders, Marvin and Welch ignited the Strat rage in the UK. Mark Knopfler, to *Guitar Player*'s Dan Forte: "A Strat was a thing of wonder. When I was 14 or 15 the Shadows were a big influence, and they had the first Strats that came to England."

From left, Strats from '60, '61, and '62, with three-ply pickguards, rosewood boards with clay dots, and no teardrop plugs on the pegheads. The '61 is an ash-body blonde. As is typical, the '60 has no patent numbers in its headstock decal, the '61 has two, and the '62 has three (according to A.R. Duchossoir, the third number appeared in Spring '62). The guitar at left may be a very late 2-color sunburst or a somewhat faded 3-color, while the guitar at right is a more conventional 3-color. Note the pickguards' slightly greenish tint, and the variation in fingerboard color.

three-color 'burst bridged the latter period of the maple-neck model and the dawn of the newer rosewood-board model. (While the three-color was firmly established by 1959, the older version was phased out over a couple of years, at least; collectors Ron Lira and Jim Werner reported stock two-color Strats as late as 1960.)

Aside from the new rosewood fingerboard and the carried-over three-color sunburst, another prominent feature of the second version was a shift from the old pickguard (8 screws, single layer, white) to an 11-screw, triple-laminated, white/black/white celluloid pickguard with a slightly greenish or "mint green" tint. (A few stock Strats had faux tortoiseshell guards of nitrocellulose.) Dan Smith: "The mint green was never intentional. Almost all the celluloid was coming from Italy at that time, and Fender got it from the distributor, Del Mar. The white color wasn't that solid. It had a little transparency to it, so part of the tint was from the black leaching through."

On many Strats of the time, a metal shielding plate was now positioned underneath the new 3-ply pickguard. Ritchie Fliegler: "The plate was the same size and shape as the pickguard, but sometimes the pickguard shrank over the years, and of course the plate didn't, so the pickguard screws got pulled around. Those '60s Strats with the lower pickguard tip broken off? The plastic shrinking over the metal plate — that's the reason." About the end of 1963, the left-side pickguard screw between the front and middle pickups was moved closer to the middle pickup.

Throughout its lifespan of six and a half-years, the first rosewood-board version showed less prominent top contouring than its maple-neck predecessor, as well as some inconsistencies in the rear contouring (the trough is generally shorter and shallower than on '50s Strats). Alder remained the standard body wood, with the same exception as before: Ash was used for blonde-finished guitars. A few oddball Strat bodies were built with mahogany, and a very few were made with poplar, thought to be more or less interchangeable with alder in most respects except for, on occasion, poplar's unappealing green stripes. On some sunburst Fenders of the period, the yellow paint is opaque instead of the normal translucent, most likely evidence of attempts to conceal the stripes on a poplar body.

A Word About Necks & Fingerboards

Fender players often say "neck" in reference to a fingerboard. A typical "rosewood-neck" Strat, like all regular factory Strats, has a maple neck but also a glued-on rosewood fingerboard; a more precise term would be "rosewood-board" Strat. (Fender's neck-plus-fingerboard arrangement is sometimes called a two-piece neck but is distinct from other manufacturers' use of two pieces for the neck alone.)

Most "maple-neck" Strats have no separate fingerboard at all; the "fingerboard" is simply the fretted surface of the one-piece neck. However, a few custom-ordered Strats of the mid '60s did have a third type of neck design, with a separate maple fingerboard glued onto the maple neck. According to Duchossoir's *The Fender Stratocaster*, this maple-on-maple arrangement, or "maple cap," became an advertised option in May 1967.

Suppose fingerboards were cut longitudinally from cylinders of wood. The outer curved surface of a fingerboard cut from a large-radius cylinder would be flatter than one of equal width cut from a small-radius cylinder, just as the surface of a beer mug is flatter than that of a shot glass. Fingerboards are cut from boards, not cylinders; still, "radius" has come to signify the fingerboard's relative arch or flatness. A 12" radius fingerboard would be much flatter than a 7¼", while a 9½" would be in between. Fender has used all three.

Transition Strats

The general model types sketched here are convenient for categorization but not perfectly distinct. Overlapping features resulted in "transition" models: As mentioned, the three-color sunburst was introduced in '58, toward the end of the maple-neck Strat's lifespan, and then became a hallmark of the first rosewood-board version ('59 – '65).

As was common at Fender, supplies of an older component were used up before any switch was made, so some Strats manufactured in the late summer of 1959 combined the old single-layer pickguard with the new rosewood fingerboard.

Many experts consider the gold "transition" logo, as it is called by collectors, to be a similar overlapping detail, in that reportedly in mid 1964 it began to replace the thinner "spaghetti" peghead decal and was carried over to the guitar's next incarnation, the first CBS-era Strat. However, in Richard Smith's view, that logo was not a transition at all but was instead introduced by CBS on guitars that left the factory in '65, having been assembled from parts fabricated and date-marked the previous year. Smith explained that photographer Bob Perine designed that logo, couldn't persuade Leo to adopt it, and finally convinced Don Randall to do so only after Leo had stepped down and CBS took over — all of which suggests that the question "When was this Fender made?" might be rephrased as "When were these parts assembled?" (The photo of three rosewood-board Strats on p. 118 shows a "later" guitar with an "earlier" decal, just one example of mixed or overlapping components.)

A '60s-era family portrait in green. The Strat is flanked by, from left, a Precision Bass; a top-of-the-line Jaguar; a block-marker, bound-neck Jazzmaster; and a Jazz Bass. Note variations in headstocks; some have matching Custom Colors (Strats with color-matched headstocks are extremely rare).

Are the body colors a mix of Surf Green and the slightly darker Foam Green? Perry A. Margouleff: "Good question. As these colors age, they shift, sometimes a lot. The Strat is a perfectly clean slab-board, and its color is unfaded. It does appear a little lighter than the others, and a couple of these might be Foam Green, but I'd be hard pressed to say so with certainty. When you pull the pickguards off these guitars and look at the unfaded areas underneath, the difference can be amazing. Sometimes two guitars that look different were actually the same color at one time. Look at these two natural headstocks, how differently they've aged."

Reverb Rules!

The Rise of Surf Music

Narrowly defined, surf music was a highly original, strictly instrumental genre that ignited in Southern California circa 1961. Popular stereotypes to the contrary, it was rooted not in some romanticized vision of a sandy, palm-tree paradise but rather in gritty late-'50s and early-'60s R&B, as well as the raucous guitar and sax instrumentals of Duane Eddy, Link Wray, the Fireballs, Johnny & the Hurricanes, and local hero Dick Dale. Had it been released two years later, Link Wray's slammin' "Raw-Hide" of 1959 might have been called "Banzai Rider," and Duane Eddy's yearning ballad "The Lonely One" would have made a perfect soundtrack for a scene where the teenage couple in silhouette against a coral pink sunset share their first beachside kiss.

Even after the emergence of the "surf" label, much of the early music continued to be performed by non-surfing musicians (the Ventures in Tacoma; the Astronauts, of "Baja" fame, in Boulder), and it had little or nothing to do with baggies, huarachi sandals or bushy bushy blonde hairdo's. Surfers dug it, that's all. Surf bands repeatedly covered instrumental hits whose titles referred not to surfing but rather to other themes: Western ("Rawhide," "[Ghost] Riders In The Sky"), south of the border ("Tequila," "The Lonely Bull," "El Rancho Rock"), space/sci-fi ("Telstar," "Out Of Limits"), or tough guy/loner ("Switch Blade," "Rebel Rouser," "Rumble"), all of which sat comfortably on track listings alongside "Wipe Out" and "Pipeline."

The flip side of the irony is that to the general public, surf music is best known for its association with culture totems that real surfers ridiculed (such as the popular *Beach Party* movies) and the "instrumentals only" purists excluded from the genre altogether (for example, the Beach Boys, who did, after all, sing).

In any case, a vital scene was already rockin' in Southern California's beach communities and less glamorous inland towns when Hollywood superimposed the kitschy stereotypes of *Beach Party* and its sequels — wriggling chicks in bikinis, knucklehead surfer dudes, clue-impaired black-leather motorcycle guys, and bongo beatniks modeled after TV's Maynard G. Krebs. The movies fostered a featherweight Frankie & Annette image that for some observers obscured the fact that along with "girl groups" and proto-Motown, surf music was the best thing in pop music between the decline of the first-generation rockers and the arrival of the Beatles and Bob Dylan.

1962-63 CATALOG

Fender

FINE ELECTRIC INSTRUMENTS

The cover of the '62-'63 catalog featured the first of a series of modern/impressionistic paintings used to good effect in Fender literature. The message: Fender products are for players of all ages, all styles, both sexes – anyone who wants to have fun with music.

On the bright side, the "surf music" label benefited many musicians, including otherwise little known California bands with rabid local followings, as well as national hitmakers for whom the surfing tag was a reasonable marketing convenience or, in some cases, mere schtick. While *Beach Party* and its sequels packed no more punch than a gentle spray of Pacific foam, these fun, silly movies were not inconsequential. Most surf music fans were teenage boys in Wichita Falls, Atlanta, Denver, and every other landlocked city and town in America. Few ever took up surfing, but many took up the electric guitar. Amazingly, Dick Dale's singles never cracked *Billboard*'s Top 40, but thanks in part to *Beach Party* and *Muscle Beach Party*, music fans knew who he was, and they knew what kind of guitar he played.

The Beach Boys made the charts a dozen times in their first two years, most of their singles with surf or hotrodding themes. While it later became clear the "surf" label was too narrow to characterize the brilliance of Brian Wilson and his cohorts, back in 1962 and '63 they dominated the genre as it was more broadly defined in pop radio. In 1964, the Beach Boys released their engaging and extraordinarily professional *Concert* album. The Fender gear pictured on its cover, and on the cover of *The Surfaris Play Wipe Out* and other LPs from 1963 to 1965, indelibly linked Fender to the look as well as the sound of surf guitar (the cover of the Astronauts' *Everything is A-OK!* — color-matched guitars, amps, and sport coats — looked like it could have been

The shirts looked like they were borrowed from the Kingston Trio's wardrobe trunk, but the guitars were all electric, all California, all Fender.

orchestrated by Don Randall). Dan Smith: "Where I grew up, if you showed up to an audition without a Fender, they might not even let you play. It was all because of the photo on the cover of *The Ventures*."

Many surf guitarists favored Jaguars or Jazzmasters, officially up the ladder a rung or two from the Stratocaster. Still, Strats appeared on those Beach Boys, Ventures, and Surfaris album covers and most famously in the hands of The Man, Dick Dale himself, undisputed King of The Surf Guitar. While it was not yet the Age of Strat (that would come two decades later), surf music was of enormous benefit to Fender amps, reverb kits, and instruments — all of them. Never has a style of pop music been more closely associated with a particular brand of electric guitars.

"I'd get a real thrill seeing a genuine Fender guitar in the music store window ... I feel really fortunate because I have a Stratocaster which was the first one Fender made; not the prototype, but the first production model. It's a wonderful guitar."   – *Carl Wilson*

"I wish I had a dollar for every time I've played 'Walk— Don't Run.'"   – *Don Wilson*

"From '63 to '67 it was the surf guys who really pushed the rock guitar envelope."   – *Miles Corbin, The Aqua Velvets*

 Strats on a Surfboard, Track 17

The last of the Leo-era Stratocasters, from left: '63, '64, and '65, all beautiful 3-tone sunbursts with typical and subtle variations in body color and pickguard tint. The hardtail's decal not only lacks a reference to the tremolo, as you would expect, but also lacks patent numbers. The '65 has an earlier style decal than the "transition" logo on the '64, likely due to Fender's sometimes using leftover decals or parts.

After testing, a brand new 1960 Stratocaster gets a final polish before packing and shipping.

Joe Walsh, to *Guitar Player*'s Jas Obrecht:

"A lot of people ended up playing guitar because of 'Walk-Don't Run.'

We used to look at the album cover of *The Ventures*, and nobody could believe that there was a Fender Jazzmaster and a Fender Strat and a perfect Precision. That band and that particular song really paved the way for a whole new approach to instrumentals, and lead guitar became so much more important in the song."

The Sale of Fender to CBS, 1965

Aside from the introductions of its classic instruments and amps, the sale of Fender to CBS was the watershed event of the company's first four decades. Negotiations were conducted through much of 1964, and the sale took effect on January 5, 1965. Mr. Fender did some consulting with the new owners, established an R&D lab called CLF Research, and later went on to productive associations with Music Man and G&L. When asked why he sold his successful, world-famous company, Leo replied:

> I was sick. On a vacation in '55 through Yellowstone and across the Rio Grande and all around, somewhere I picked up a strep infection, and I had a bad fever, and it stayed with me for years and years, off and on, until about 1967 …. [After treatment] I felt better, and I've felt okay since. To tell you the truth, back in '63 or '64, I thought I wouldn't last but a couple of years more, so I thought I would make arrangements to get out and wrap up my personal affairs. I thought I'd be out in the daisy patch in a couple years. I was in bad shape. If I hadn't had that sickness, I probably never would have gotten out.

Additional perspective was provided by Mr. Fender's old friend and colleague Freddie Tavares, whose insights had been crucial to the Stratocaster's design: "Leo told me later that we were into the solid-state age, and he knew it was better to sell, and that it was a golden opportunity. He's been working too hard all his life anyway. He didn't know how to relax, how to play. All he knew was work."

Leo approached Don Randall and asked if he would buy Leo's interest. "I could have done it," Randall told videographer Dennis Baxter. "I gave it some thought. Baldwin piano came along and they

"Curtis amazes me. He's so original. His is one of the great electric guitar styles. It's very subtle, very lyrical. . . . The way he uses the instrument for counterpoint to his voice is genius. There's a caressing sound he got out of that Stratocaster. To me, the Stratocaster is a very unforgiving instrument. Curtis was the first guy I heard who could make it pretty and soulful."
– Ry Cooder

The incomparable Curtis Mayfield with the Impressions at the historic Regal Theater in Chicago, 1964. Mayfield tuned his guitars F♯ A♯ C♯ F♯ A♯ F♯ (low to high), liked medium-gauge flatwounds, and often selected the middle pickup. "You don't practice making love; every time it's fresh to explore, to find, to comfort, to pamper, and to discover. Such is my way with my axe."

"Hendrix might have created 'Voodoo Chile' or 'Purple Haze' without Mayfield's influence, but probably not 'Little Wing,' 'Castles Made of Sand,' or 'Bold as Love.' In fact, the title track of *Electric Ladyland* is a virtual Mayfield tribute, down to the churchy progressions and falsetto vocals."
– Joe Gore, *Guitar Player*

"The obvious thing you start hitting is the soul licks. I thought to myself: Curtis Mayfield. Curtis is the king of that."
– Keith Richards, on playing "Almost Hear You Sigh" and "Beast of Burden"

Mayfield's Soulful Rhythm Method, Track 21

were very interested … but I didn't like the way they had structured the deal. [CBS contacted us] and finally we came to an agreement that I thought would be adequate. I called Leo [and gave him a figure] and said, how does this sound, and Leo said you've got to be kidding, and I said no, we've got a deal on this thing, and he just couldn't believe it. He wanted to sell the company for a million and a half bucks. We closed the deal [for thirteen million dollars]. I consulted with Leo … but basically, he had little or nothing to do with the sale. He wouldn't even go back to New York and pick up his check … he was busy working at Fender."

The sale came as a surprise to Fender workers, even those closest to Leo, such as George Fullerton and Freddie Tavares. Mr. Tavares remembered, "There was no prior mention to us down on the production line about the sale to CBS. They sold it out from under us without saying a thing. There was just an announcement that day."

Mr. Randall later defended the new owners' stewardship of Fender and downplayed reports of declining quality control: "The attempt was always to improve the product whenever possible, to put a better finish on it, use better hardware, improve the performance. We built a beautiful new building with 120,000 square feet and modern equipment [in 1965, located adjacent to the previous facility]. We had a completely dust-free environment … and it was really a nice plant. Any large corporation would likely have the same problems of immediately trying to understand a unique process like guitar manufacture. They thought, well, you ought to be able to stick in a plank here and have the neck come out there. But they caught on … as long as I was there, which is five years [after the sale] … as far as the instruments go, I don't think they deteriorated that much; I think this is a figment of somebody's imagination."

When asked if the instruments declined in quality, Mr. Fender said, "I really don't think so; they weren't trying to cheapen the instrument. Maybe they tried to

Don Randall in his office at Fender Sales, October 1966.

accelerate production, but it was natural for them to do that, because on one instrument alone — I think it was the Mustang — we were back ordered something like 150,000 units. Well, on a back order of that size — and there were others, too — you can't just sit around. But whether or not the instruments were lower in quality, I really don't have any comment on that. I was over here at CLF at that time, working on guitars."

Mid-'60s Strats pose with Bass VI's.

Many Fender employees, dealers, and players have long contended that the CBS era's factory modernization and impressive growth in both dollar-volume sales and output were more than offset by a demoralizing shift in the work environment and production blunders with costly, long-lasting consequences. For starters, CBS blanketed Fender in layer after layer of paperwork. Employees found their simple but reasonably efficient procedures under close scrutiny by systems analysts. Many employees were confused, and resentful of the new institutional attitude. Freddie Tavares recalled, "[CBS] didn't understand that a guitar is something you cradle next to you, and you take it out into the spotlight and make music, try to make your living with it. They looked at things the corporate way. They came in and said, oh, you make electric guitars, with wires and electronics? Then do you also make radios? You make guitar bodies out of wood? Then do you also make furniture? All they talked about was productivity, quotas, budgets…."

Bill Carson: "CBS, like a lot of large corporations, was strung out in so many different directions they didn't really know they were doing Fender any harm. They had no quick strike capability; they couldn't react to things in time. We'd need some capital expenditures in order to launch a product, but by the time you could float that through a dozen committees, the need had come and gone. Plus we had the burden of all the overhead, and supporting sister CBS companies that were failing."

Dale Hyatt told Tony Bacon and Paul Day that by 1968 or so, "it got to the point where I did not enjoy going to any store anywhere, because every time I walked in I found myself defending some poor piece of workmanship. They got very sloppy with the finish, with far too many bad spots, and the neck sockets were being cut way over size."

Tom Wheeler, 1978:
Did you ever regret selling to CBS?

Leo Fender: No, I don't think so. A company like we had was a sure a big job, I'll tell you. It was so big. And then we had so damn many doors to lock up each night. Jesus, George [Fullerton] had a career just to lock up at night. By the time we sold, we had 27 buildings spread all over. We finally got some security people, but for a long time there we'd have to check all the doors ourselves. We were so darn strung out. I wouldn't want the company back now as a gift. It was just too much, too much trouble. Hell, we used to have a lot of trouble with the juice going off. The power just wasn't adequate in those days, and we'd have interruptions. When the juice went off, you would pretty nearly have heart failure. You didn't know if it was going to be off for two minutes or three hours. I wouldn't want a company that big again, I just wouldn't.

The earliest Strats came in flat-sided "Form-fit" cases like the one in front. The lid is facing us, and the guitar would be upside down, its shorter horn and knobs near the handle. Perry A. Margouleff estimates that this type was used only through the first few months: "By the end of '54, we see the earliest tweeds. The Form-fits weren't sturdy, and they vanished right away." In back, from left: the earliest tweed case (red lining, center pocket, "crystal" handle), then the later tweed case with a leather handle and orange lining, then the standard brown, off-white, and black cases.

July 25, 1965, The Day Dylan Went Electric. At the Newport Folk Festival – a veritable convocation of traditional folkies – Bob Dylan astonished the assembled multitude and his acoustic-purist fellow troubadours by stepping onstage with that most electric of guitars, a Fender Strat.

The CBS Era, Part I

CBS & The Strat

Restructuring a huge corporation is like making a U turn with an aircraft carrier. It doesn't happen quickly. The guitars built in the first weeks after the sale to CBS were for the most part made with previously fabricated components and assembled by veteran workers using pre-CBS methods. However, by the end of the first year, the Stratocaster had undergone several changes, and the keenest observers did indeed perceive a deterioration in the quality of its sound and workmanship. Based upon detailed accounts of former employees, it is fair to say that some products — both guitars and amplifiers — suffered a loss in quality, the Strat among them. Author/collector/retailer George Gruhn has carefully examined thousands of guitars. He said, "I remember very well comparing several 1966 Teles and Strats to some early-1965, pre-CBS models, and the 65's were a whole lot better. It's no myth — CBS really cheapened the quality."

In 1965, there were no Internet chat rooms, of course, and no guitar magazines or other forums for a nationwide discussion of these events. Word spread slowly, and for every confirmed fact passed among dealers and players there were several unsubstantiated rumors. But eventually, as guitarists and retailers examined enough instruments to make reasonable generalizations, the changes introduced by CBS came to signify the decline of the Stratocaster and other Fenders. Forrest White left the company on December 6, 1966, after defying his new supervisors and refusing to sign off on transistor amplifiers that "were not worthy of Leo Fender's name." Indeed, the tinny-sounding and failure-prone solid-state amps helped foster CBS Fender's image of a stumbling corporate giant increasingly out of touch with its roots. The stigma would linger for decades.

STRAT III: The First CBS Version, late '65 – mid '71

The 4-bolt neck, rosewood fingerboard, tremolo with a separate base plate and inertia bar, 11-screw laminated pickguard, and staggered-polepiece pickups of the '59 - '65 Stratocaster were carried over into the early days of CBS as standard features. During 1965, CBS introduced a new neck plate that featured an oversized F, a detail that author A.R. Duchossoir called "an adequate symbol of the CBS invasion." An even more significant alteration was the enlarged headstock, made official on December 19, 1965, according to *Gruhn's Guide*. The Stratocaster was now truly a CBS Fender instrument.

Fender began using thicker polyester undercoats in the late '60s. The new finish not only looked different but also aged differently than previous finishes. In some cases, polyester was also sprayed on the rosewood fingerboards. According to the Custom Shop's Mark Kendrick, "1967 was pretty much the transition year, although Fender had experimented with polyesters as early as 1963. Polyester is catalyzed with a methyl-ethyl ketone peroxide, which is a hardener, and whereas lacquer was air-cured, the polyester is chemical cured, which is much more convenient in terms of production. It fills quicker, sands easier, dries quicker, fluffs up nice, and doesn't 'load' the sandpaper as quickly. The color coats and top coats were still lacquer at this time, up until 1983 [see pp. 145, 188]."

Mirror-image Fiesta Reds meet mirror-image Burgundy Mists, from left: a '63 Fiesta, '62 slab-board Burgundy, lefty '65 Fiesta, and lefty '64 Burgundy, all in drool-worthy condition. Among the complications of identifying Custom Colors in publications are the realities of photography and printing. Perry A. Margouleff: "Here, the red guitars look almost like Dakotas, but they are actually Fiesta Reds."

Jimi Hendrix made his American major-venue debut at the Monterey International Pop Festival during 1967's "Summer of Love." Following his historic, mind-blowing set, he further stunned the crowd by squirting lighter fluid on his hand-painted '65 Fiesta Red Strat and setting it aflame, inspiring journalists to wax eloquent about everything from antimaterialist destruction as concept art to ritual voodoo sacrifice.

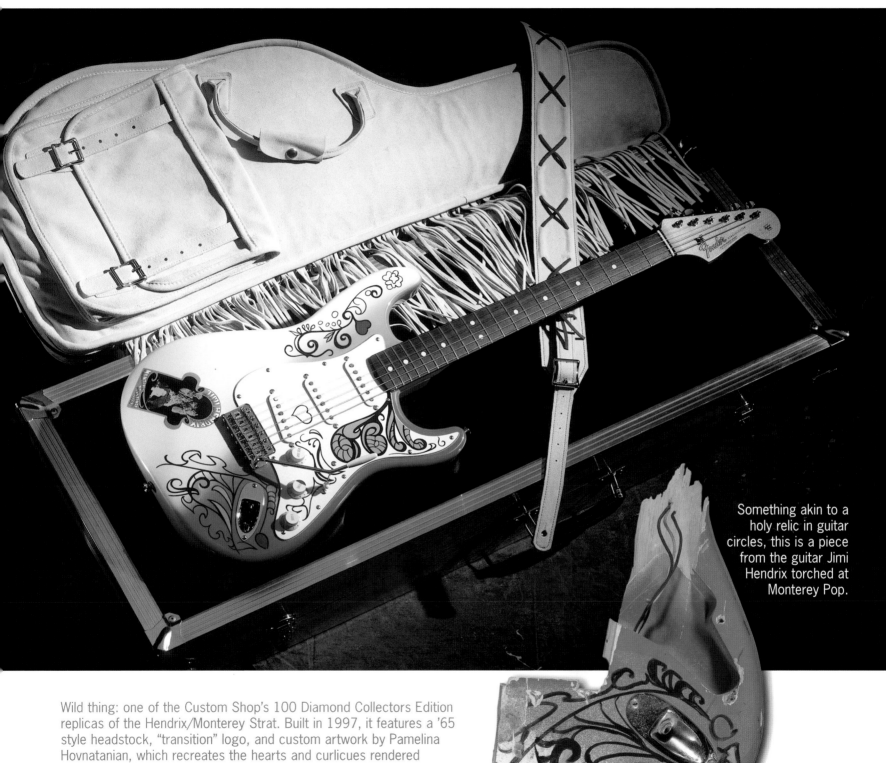

Something akin to a holy relic in guitar circles, this is a piece from the guitar Jimi Hendrix torched at Monterey Pop.

Wild thing: one of the Custom Shop's 100 Diamond Collectors Edition replicas of the Hendrix/Monterey Strat. Built in 1997, it features a '65 style headstock, "transition" logo, and custom artwork by Pamelina Hovnatanian, which recreates the hearts and curlicues rendered in Jimi's hand. The extra image on the top is a commemorative "backstage pass" with Ed Caraeff's famous photo of the original event.

Other details from the lifespan of the first CBS Strat:

- The "clay" markers were replaced with pearloid dots in late '64 or early '65; some fingerboards mixed pearl top markers with leftover "clay" side markers.
- The somewhat greenish-white celluloid pickguard material of the early '60s (reportedly highly flammable and dangerous to store) was replaced on most guitars during 1965 with an untinted white vinyl. Fender continued to use both vinyl and celluloid until about 1969, after which the newer vinyl was used consistently for white guards. Fender still used celluloid for tortoiseshell guards.
- In mid 1967, a "maple cap" neck was offered, with a separate maple fingerboard glued onto the maple neck; this type had been made in small quantities for years and was a favorite of Jimi Hendrix, but it was much less common than the rosewood board. As with rosewood-board necks built through the late '70s, the maple-cap necks have top-mounted truss rods and no skunk stripe.
- The supposedly pre-CBS gold "transition" Fender logo (see p. 115) was replaced in about mid '68 with the thicker "CBS" version in black.
- A few Strats with white neck binding were released in '65, '66, and '67; examples were pictured in the '66-'67 catalog.
- In 1967, the nickel-plated Klusons were replaced with Fender keys that were plated with chrome and stamped on the back with the F logo.
- As was the case with early-'60s Strats, the body contouring in the late '60s continued to be inconsistent and generally shallower or less pronounced than on '50s models (compared to late-'60s Strats, the back contour on '50s Strats often begins closer to the upper body horn and extends further along the back's upper edge).
- After 1967, Fender dropped the gold hardware option.
- Stratocaster necks varied in almost every dimension — width at the nut, depth at the low end of the fingerboard, depth in the treble registers, etc. Some were particularly deep and rounded. The 1968 catalog specified the official width as 1⅝"; available on special order: 1½", 1¾", and 1⅞".

- In 1960, the list price of the sunburst, trem-equipped Strat was hiked from its late-'50s figure of $274.50 to $289.50, where it stayed through the sale to CBS. Oddly enough, CBS *lowered* the price to $281 in the summer of '65, the same time it announced the Marauder, a new top-of-the-line, what-were-they-thinking model with four pickups all concealed beneath the pickguard. At $479, the lovely but doomed newcomer was slated to cost a whopping 70% more than the Strat, but it was never put into production and vanished after the December 1965 price list. By the end of the decade, the Strat was up to $349.50.

Michael Indelicato thought he'd found the "Lost Rosewood Hendrix Strat," but no, this one is that elusive guitar's mate. He reported: "Fender made two, the presentation guitar [hand-built for Jimi Hendrix in 1968 by Philip Kubicki] and also a prototype for a new model that never went into production. Jimi never did take possession of his guitar, and it's never been accounted for. This is the other one, the prototype." Tipping the scales at just over a whopping 11 pounds, its details include a large CBS-style headstock, a fingerboard cap and neck of solid rosewood, and a maple veneer in the middle of the body.

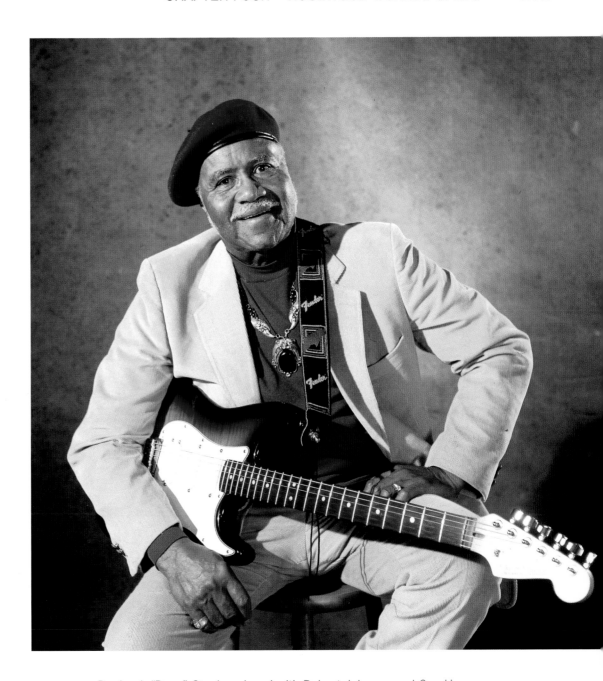

Roebuck "Pops" Staples played with Robert Johnson and Son House and was the patriarch of the Staple Singers, the revered gospel group. He died in 2000 at the age of 85. "I was the first artist with a singing group to take a guitar into the church. They didn't allow it, but they had faith and believed in Pops Staples enough. We weren't trying to pull off no stunts for money. We were singing because we love God's word and we love God. The ministers could see that, and they let us come in with the guitar. That was a new thing – the guitar!"[4]

Fender Looks Back: The Telecaster Bass

The Telecaster Bass of 1968 was an odd duck in some ways and yet historic all the same. It was Fender's first-ever reissue — sort of. Actually, Fender had never made a Telecaster Bass before. The new model was in fact a vaguely authentic recreation of the early Precision Bass of 1951-1954. While the original was dissimilar in a few respects, it did have several features that were recreated on the newcomer, including through-body stringing, two strings per saddle, and a bare-bones, slab-body Telecaster vibe. (Fender wasn't the only company looking back. That same year, Gibson reintroduced its single-cutaway Les Pauls and has been offering remakes of its 1950s designs ever since.)

Giving the instrument an utterly new model name — instead of calling it, say, the Heritage Precision or the Precision Classic — was only one of several confusing moves. Brochures "explained" that its ancestor "was originally introduced before 1950" (the P Bass appeared in late '51) and was "dropped from the line" because its many advantages were underappreciated (the P Bass was redesigned but never discontinued). CBS' inability to accurately document pre-CBS Fenders resulted in full-page advertisements picturing the "1948" Telecaster (the Tele and its predecessors date to 1950; in fairness to CBS, let's note that much of this misinformation came from the fallible memory of Leo Fender).

While the Telecaster Bass was hardly "vintage correct" by today's electron-microscope standards of authenticity, it did mark the reappearance of a 17-year-old design, and it demonstrated that way back in the third year of the CBS regime, some sort of nascent vintage consciousness was already brewing in the boardroom. Previously, in designing and marketing its instruments, Fender had only looked to the future. Now, it offered an instrument that was supposedly "brought back by popular demand," a concept that would resonate forcefully in years to come.

The large, bullet-rod headstock and extra string tree of the paisley Strat identify it as a '70s-era guitar, likely built as a one-off promo item. Perry A. Margouleff: "This appeared in *American Guitars* and came from the John Entwistle collection. The guitar on the left has just a bit of a green tint, but under the pickguard it looks like an original Inca Silver. The gold one is a little too dark, too brown, to be Shoreline." The gold finish is likely Firemist Gold metallic, which replaced Shoreline Gold in '65. The near-perfect Candy Apple Red is a '69 (note enlarged decal), and the guitar at far right is painted Charcoal Frost metallic, which appeared in 1965. While the two guitars at left are both small-headstock Strats, compare the earlier, smaller logo at far left to the gold guitar's larger "transition" version, designed by Bob Perine.

"You have to stick with it. Sometimes you are going to be so frustrated you want to give up the guitar. You'll hate the guitar. But all of this is just a part of learning, because if you stick with it, you're going to be rewarded."

— Jimi Hendrix

Jimi in the garden, his long, graceful fingers holding one of his many Strats. This photo appears on the cover of *The Inner World of Jimi Hendrix*, a book by his fiancée, Monika Dannemann.

"My brothers bought Jimi his first Strat. I would have been about 10 or 11. They had heard there was this player in the Village that was better than anybody. I was like, yeah, right. They track him down and say, 'You wanna play with the Isley Brothers?' And he was like, 'Yeah!' He was unemployed and broke. They said, 'Play me something,' and he said, 'I can't – my guitar's in the pawn shop.' So they go and get the guitar. [After auditioning] they said, 'You got the job. You can come to New Jersey and rehearse.' Jimi says, 'I can't; I don't have a place to stay.' So he stayed at our house. That guitar he's playing is pretty ratty looking. 'If you're going to play with us, we need to get you a new guitar. Which one do you want?' And he says,

'Are you kidding me? ... I want a white Strat.'

The thing about Jimi is the difference between the human being and the icon ... He played very well, he was quiet and introspective, polite, minded his business and played all the time – before, during, and after every practice. The night the Beatles performed on Ed Sullivan, he was in our house. I was sitting next to him."
– Ernie Isley

 *Jimi's Univibe Diatribe, Track 29*

"I was performing with Paul Butterfield and I was the hotshot guitarist on the block — I thought I was *it*. I'd never heard of Hendrix. Then someone said, 'You've got to see the guitar player with John Hammond.' I was at the Cafe Au Go Go and he was at the Night Owl or the Cafe Wha? I went across the street and saw him. Hendrix knew who I was, and that day, in front of my eyes, he burned me to death. I didn't even get my guitar out. H-bombs were going off. Guided missiles were flying. I can't tell you the sounds he was getting out of his instrument. He was getting every sound I was ever to hear him get right there in that room with a Stratocaster, a Twin, a Maestro Fuzztone, and that was all ... I didn't even want to pick up a guitar for the next year.

He had no favorite guitar. They were all expendable. Buddy Miles has some of his Strats, and all the ones that I've tried are hard to play — heavy strings and heavy action. I'm amazed that he could play them as facilely as he did."

– Michael Bloomfield

Rhythm & Octavia Tones of Doom, Track 23

"I saw him put 25

"I remember anxiously waiting to see Jimi play his guitar up close because ... I thought he might have a magical something or other built into his guitar to help give him the incredible sounds he achieved. I soon discovered that he played a regular old Stratocaster through Marshall amps. He did have some gadgets ... but these items were available for anyone. The magic obviously came from Hendrix' own fingers."

– Harvey Mandel

ears on the guitar in five years.

Some people thought he was crazy because they couldn't understand why a man would constantly be playing a guitar all the time. But basically what he was doing was making this instrument an extension of his body."

– Billy Cox

of god. He's just an ordinary guy. I mean, he's just like a nice, loving, sweet person. That's all. He's just like one of your friends, you know? He wasn't pretentious or anything. He was just a guitar player. That's all he was. That's all he ever wanted to be."

– John McLaughlin

This gear all belonged to Jimi Hendrix. Richard Friedman is a third-generation music merchant and collector of memorabilia. He reported: "Jimi's ownership of the Strat was authenticated by people at Manny's who have the receipts, and by several of Jimi's closest friends, including Noel Redding, who autographed the back. Jimi played it at a party at Electric Lady studio, and at one time it belonged to one of his girlfriends. The shirt is one he wore in Sweden." This big-headstock, pre-bullet rod Strat has a stock maple fingerboard, unusual for the period. Its big decal with two patent numbers suggest it was manufactured from mid-'68 to mid-'70 (the serial number, 274200, is in keeping with a date of 1969, but serial numbers aren't definitive). Jimi Hendrix died on September 18, 1970, scarcely four years after forming the Jimi Hendrix Experience.

Guitar Player: "Your tastes seem broader than the typical rock and roll fan or listener."

Jimi Hendrix: "This is all I can play when I'm playing. I'd like to get something together, like with Handel, and Bach, and Muddy Waters, flamenco type of thing [*laughs*]. If I can get that sound. If I could get that sound, I'd be happy."

Jimi's Blues-o-rama, Track 25

A Brother's Memoir
Dónal Gallagher reminisces about his late brother Rory and his beloved Stratocaster

My big brother Rory had made great strides in learning the guitar, so much so that by the tender age of fifteen he had joined a professional "showband" whilst still at school. To improve his abilities he required a better instrument than his Rosette "Solid Seven," so when he spotted the '61 sunburst Stratocaster in the window of the only music store in Cork, he unwittingly got me to come see it with him. On viewing the guitar it felt like Buddy Holly's craft had landed, as I stared at the contoured beauty.

Rory had already entered the shop and opened up negotiations with the owner, Michael Crowley. The secondhand price of the guitar was an unaffordable £100 (then $300). Rory had turned in his Solid Seven, taking £20, and readjusted the existing purchase agreement which had been signed by our mother. "Your mother is agreeable to these changes in the purchase contract?", Michael asked Rory, who with innocent face looked to me to confirm the dubious transaction. I nodded my answer.

The guitar was taken home to our bedroom and hidden beneath my bed and I became its guardian. Rory would practice in the bedroom while I sat guard on the staircase looking out for stray adults. The worst episode was when the guitar was stolen from the van in '67. Rory was bereaved. Ireland had only one TV station at that time, so when the police crime programme kindly announced the guitar's loss it was soon found abandoned, too hot to handle.

Today, the orphaned Strat's in my company. It has had a good hard working life, evidenced by the wear of its coat, this occurrence not through disregard but due to the alkaline in my brother's blood which had an acidic effect on the guitar, coupled with the enormous amount of gigs Rory played, with sets that would last for two to four hours. Whilst it is difficult to see Rory's mistress in the hands another, I have and will make exceptions. There's talk of the guitar going back out on tour, among the company of Fender's top ten Stratocasters (Holly, Clapton, Marvin, etc.). With the combined DNA of these instruments, I only wish I could eavesdrop on their conversations.

– Dónal Gallagher

DARK CLOUDS, SHIFTING TIDES

Bullets Over Fullerton, The 3-Bolt Neck

Leo Fender's association with the company that bears his name didn't end with the sale to CBS in 1965. Part of the deal was that he would be a consultant to the new owners and would not compete with them during a specified period. One of the challenges he tackled from his independent lab at CLF Research entailed a tricky aspect of guitar construction: attaining the proper angle, or "pitch," of the neck relative to the body. Another task was to improve methods for correcting neck warping caused by string tension or changes in temperature or humidity.

From the Stratocaster's inception its neck had been reinforced with a metal truss rod that could be adjusted at the body end of the neck. It worked well enough, but the other problem, neck pitch, entailed loosening the neck, inserting flat shims in the neck pocket, tightening the neck, testing it, and possibly repeating the hassle all over again.

In 1970 Mr. Fender came up with a system he called the "tiltable guitar neck incorporating thrust absorbing pivot and locking element" — the "tilt-neck" or "Micro Tilt" for short. The neck angle could be adjusted by means of an allen wrench inserted into a newly designed neck plate; loosening and re-tightening the neck were no longer required. The truss rod was now adjusted at a bullet-shaped knob protruding above the nut at the peghead. One more detail: The 4-bolt neck attachment featured on the Strat since its introduction was replaced with a 3-bolt setup. In 1971 the new system was installed on the Stratocaster guitar.

 Perry A. Margouleff: "This is about a '63, and you can see that it isn't the typical alder or ash body. It's mahogany, like the Tele behind it, but it might have gone unnoticed had the guitar not had the scraped-away area on the horn. I've learned that apparently Fender got a batch of mahogany, maybe to make those rare mahogany Teles. I think some Strats were made out of leftover mahogany, although I would guess that most were covered up with Custom Colors instead of a sunburst like this one. You know what's interesting about both guitars? They're two of the best sounding Fenders I've ever heard, very warm."

Hubert Sumlin to *Guitar Player*'s Dan Forte, on *The London Howlin' Wolf Sessions*, with Eric Clapton: "We recorded two numbers before we even reached over and made names together. He said, 'My name's Eric,' and I said, 'My name's Hubert.' And he said, 'I know about you,' and I said, 'Well, man, I heard about you, too.' So we got to talking and he invited me to dinner. I went outside and he had a Rolls Royce out there with a chauffeur. We went way up from London in some woods. Man, it was a big old place . . . . The first thing he did was take me down in the basement and show me his guitars. 'Have one,' he said. I picked out a Fender Stratocaster."

Ernie Isley. One highlight of his 30-year career was his soloing on the Isley Brothers' 1973 smash "Who's That Lady," which channeled the spirit and the whooshy/phased sound of Jimi Hendrix.

Full CBS: The Stratocaster of the '70s

The Stratocaster of 1971 – 1981 had the general body shape, three pickups, and one-piece maple neck of the original Strats of the mid and late '50s, plus the rosewood fingerboard of the second Leo-era Strat of '59 – '65. A slew of details from the first CBS Strat of '65 – '71 were also carried over, including the enlarged headstock with the black logo, Fender tuners with the F stamp, and the thick, hard-looking polyester-undercoat finish.

On top of all that, the '70s Strat sported several all-new features:

- the tilt-neck adjustment
- 3-bolt neck attachment
- bullet truss rod adjustment
- a new tremolo construction in which the base plate and inertia bar were die-cast as a single piece; it was made of an inferior metal, and replaced the steel version of 1954 – 1970, which had a separate inertia bar attached to the base plate. (Die-casting entails pouring a molten metal, or slurry, into a metal mold. Fender's Dan Smith explained that the resulting "pot metal" is a mixture of zinc, aluminum, and other metals.)
- cheaper die-cast bridge saddles, replacing the original pressed steel units
- two string trees (for two strings each, high E through D) instead of one

The original one-piece maple neck (no separate fingerboard), stock from 1954 until 1959, again became available in early 1970, this time as an option.

The staggered-polepiece pickups, standard on the Strat for 20 years, were replaced by one-height-straight-across, flush-pole pickups by late 1974.

The distinctive white pickguard, knobs, and tremolo bar tip were replaced by black versions in 1975; generally, the black pickguard appeared first (sometimes with white knobs and pickups covers), followed by an all-black color scheme.

Toward the end of the 1960s, Fender's nitrocellulose lacquer finish had been modified to include an undercoat of more durable and production-friendly polyester. By the mid-'70s, Fender's once lavish array of Custom Colors had been reduced to a few forgettable hues, and the trend toward a harder, plastic appearance intensified with the new "Thick-Skin" finish, entailing the application of about a dozen polyester undercoats. Mark Kendrick: "They just blew a tsunami of polyester on there [laughs], because it was easy in production and filled very quickly, it was chemically hardened, and it was very forgiving in that you could sand off as much as you wanted and not hit the wood. I've seen some guitars with between 50 and a hundred thousandths [of an inch] glopped on there. Encapsulating the guitar in a cocoon of plastic like that is going to dampen the sound." Guitar bodies continued to be sprayed with nitrocellulose lacquer color coats and top coats. Sometimes the peghead facings and necks aged differently because the pegheads were sprayed with lacquer after the decal was applied, while the necks were sprayed with polyester.

A sensible upgrade appeared in 1977: Following the lead of small accessories suppliers, Fender offered a 5-way switch to replace the limited 3-way unit. No longer would players have to balance the switch in one of the two precarious in-between positions to get that delicate "Bell Bottom Blues" solo tone.

At the end of the decade, Fender began installing *all* truss rods from the rear; now, both rosewood-board necks and one-piece maple necks had skunk stripes.

The late Rory Gallagher was revered for his impassioned solos and all-out marathon concerts. His '61 Stratocaster, its "ex-sunburst" finish worn down to raw alder, was reportedly the first Strat to arrive in his native Ireland. It's been called the most battered playable guitar in history. Rory Gallagher once said, "I like a good bright tone, and I like the out-of-phase sound you can get with the switch set between the normal positions. It's comfortable, the scale seems right, and I like having the machine heads on one side . . . the Strat is ideal because you can easily reach the volume and tone controls to get that crying sound."

 Slide Summit, Track 53

Microphonic Pickups

One complaint about some CBS-era Fenders was that their pickups were squealy and microphonic. The wire coils were dipped in wax to avoid the problem, but the wax was rendered ineffective in some cases because of changes in the way lacquer was applied to the coils. Fender's Dan Smith spoke to several of the workers who wound pickups in the '50s. He discovered that the wires were lacquered after a few winds, to keep them neat. Somewhere along the way, in the late '60s and into the '70s, the lacquer was sometimes put on much later in the process, after *many* winds were on the coil. When the wax was applied, it couldn't get through that outer layer of lacquer, so it couldn't do its job, and some of the pickups howled and squealed. Beginning in the early '80s, the lacquering process was revised to alleviate the problem.

During the Strat's first decade and a half, the tremolo base plate (which holds the saddles) and the perpendicular inertia bar were separate pieces. CBS changed the design to an inferior one-piece, die-cast unit. Dan Smith and his associates changed it back.

Goin' Down: The Strat's Reputation for Quality

CBS' first remake of the Strat (particularly its large-head-stock incarnation) was almost universally considered a step in the wrong direction, and with a couple of welcome exceptions such as the 5-way switch, the '70s "updates" only made things worse. Going beyond cosmetic changes such as the enlarged headstock, new decal, and untinted pickguard, CBS had now altered the Strat's basic structure. Unfortunately, the 3-bolt, tilt-neck arrangement of the '70s confirmed the suspicions of the late '60s: New Strats couldn't measure up to the old ones.

The tilt-neck concept itself is valid. After all, Mr. Fender put it to good use in his later, post-Fender designs, and Fender uses it to this day on dozens of acclaimed guitars. Was the culprit the 3-bolt attachment, assumed by many players to be weaker? Given that production reportedly reached almost 500 instruments a day by the end of the decade, the problem was more likely in execution than design. A decline of quality control may have been the inevitable consequence of corporate pressure to stoke up the assembly line and maximize short-term profits.

Fender's Mike Lewis: "The tilt-neck is a great feature, with a proven track record. It just wasn't executed very well in the '70s. Our American Series and American Deluxe Series all have it. The American Standard had it, the Strat Plus, the Strat Ultra — generally, it's a stock feature on all the American stuff, except the vintage-correct reissues of guitars that predated the tilt-neck. We also make a '70s style reissue in Mexico that has the 3-bolt neck. All these guitars are fine, solid as a rock. On those Strats of the '70s, those necks move around because the slot [or neck 'pocket'] in the body was too big."

Dan Smith: "The slot had to be enlarged so they could mount the neck. The problem was, the neck mounting screw goes into a threaded hole in a little disc in the pocket. The disc was a punched part, and if it was punched crooked, it would be misaligned when they threaded the hole. Then, when they mounted the neck, it would pull to one side. Because they didn't

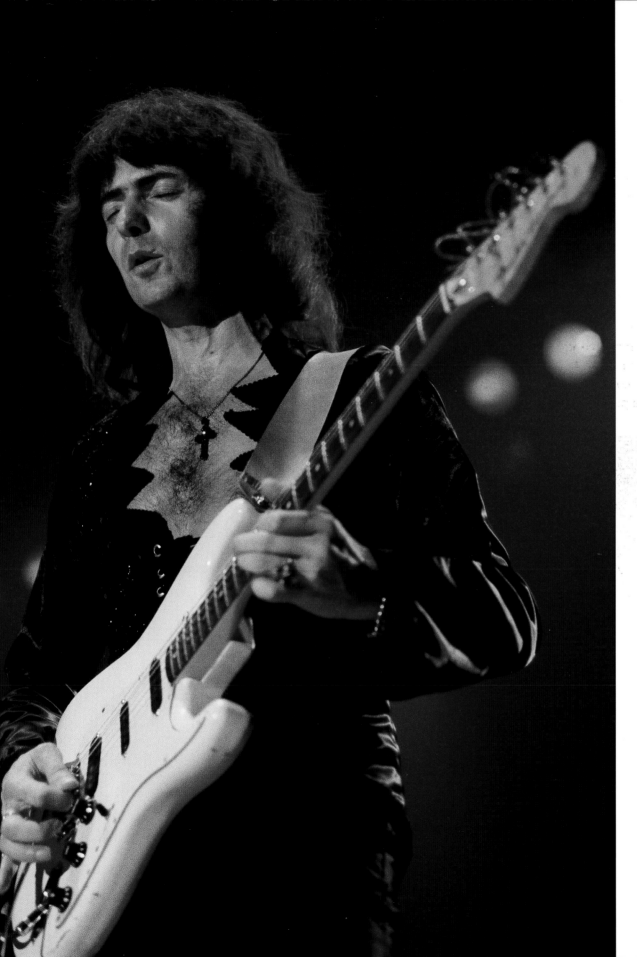

Ritchie Blackmore became enamored of the Strat after playing one that Eric Clapton gave him. "I found great difficulty in using it the first two years. With a Gibson you just race up and down, but with a Fender you have to make every note count — you have to make the note sing or otherwise it won't work. It's more rewarding . . . . I put the middle pickup all the way down because it gets in the way of the pick. I only use the straight bass and treble positions. It wouldn't do me any good trying to use any of the special middle positions on the selector switch because the way I play, I'd just be knocking it out of position constantly."

 Blackmore Riffery, Track 43

David Gilmour, shown here in 1973 with Pink Floyd, has crafted lyrical solos of almost operatic sweep and power for 30 years. His compelling, vocal-like vibrato comes from regular use of the trem bar. "When I was a lad, I always wanted a Fender, because the people that I saw and dug were playing Fenders."

understand what the problem was, they'd take a hand-held router, which isn't the most precise kind of tool, and enlarge the pocket.

"There's this misconception that the tilt-neck was all CBS, but it was already in the works and the patent was in Leo's name. To vintage guys, the 3-bolt neck is like the cross to Dracula [*laughs*] — they think it's the worst. So when I got to Fender [in 1981] the first thing we did was get rid of the 3-bolt. Then 20 years later we wanted to recreate it for a reissue CBS-era guitar, because to some of the 20-year-old guys, that's a vintage guitar, so we had to put the authentic 3-bolt on there, but by then we'd figured out how to fix it, and the reissue 3-bolt necks fit perfectly. Also, the bullet truss rod was a way to make it easier to access.

Gilmore Delay Madness and Lickery, Track 39

James Young of Styx, power ballad/arena rock stars of the '70s and early '80s.

from New York — which is really where the company was being run from — and they needed the numbers. The mindset was, let's ship them out to dealers, and we'll fix them in the field. Just that day, 50 or 60 guitars went out like that. When I was a kid, I had a paper route so I could buy my first Fender, you know? And now here I was working at the factory, but this was not a proud moment to be in quality control. You were supposed to inspect a minimum of 200 guitars a day, five days a week, so there were a lot of shenanigans going on just to move them out."

Bob Hipp worked at Fender for 38 years, many of them in sales. He remembered, "Sometimes when they painted the bodies, a little ball of paint would build up on the neck area that would make a pivot, and if you did not clean that off during assembly, with only three bolts the neck would move around. Another thing was the weight of that larger headstock. Sometimes just setting the guitar down in the case was enough to move the neck to where the E string would be off the edge. It was very easy to adjust — you could just put it up against your chest and pull it back a little bit, but the salesmen were told never to do it in front of anybody [*laughs*]. You had to do it behind your back."

The real and perceived shortcomings of the new Stratocaster weren't limited to poor production tolerances at the neck/body joint. Once the epitome of sleek, the Strat's body was now less sculpted — likely another result of CBS' crank-'em-out attitude on the assembly line as well as its reportedly less meticulous wood-buying practices. Even the upper-horn strap button, mounted on early Strats in such a way as to continue the horn's outline, was now sometimes attached in a haphazard way that interrupted the horn's natural curve. The popularity of the slightly tinted, see-through natural finish was at its peak (it looked great with your

So a lot of those things were done for good reasons, but they didn't look like the instruments from the '50s and '60s, which suddenly started to become popular."

Purchasing Manager Joe Carducci: "I was in quality control back then. Behind where the inspectors worked was a large steel rack where you put finished guitars for shipping. One time somebody took a picture, and in the general area were 50 or 60 guitars that had been rejected for finish cracks, or bone nuts that were cut way too low so the string was resting right on the fretboard, or necks that were bowed way too far to fix with the truss rod — grotesque stuff.

"They rearranged the racks for this photo. I went to lunch and came back and all those guitars were *gone* — boxed up and shipped. My boss said, well, I got a call

flowered bellbottoms, suede vest, and shaggy 'do), and Fender's natural-finish Strats were made of ash; the extra heft of many ash bodies made some of the '70s Strats even clunkier.

The bullet rod was convenient, but some people thought it looked ungainly. Others longed for the smaller headstocks, familiar logos, and softer finishes of the good old days. Then there was that pot-metal base plate and inertia bar (or "spring block"), now die-cast as a one-piece unit. The "knife-edge" parts of the tremolo were less sturdy, and the die-cast saddles were blamed for a loss of sustain and a thinner tone. Dan Smith explained that on some die-cast components, the hardest surface was actually the plating, and once that flaked or broke, the part could wear out rather quickly. The fact that the new flush-pole pickups didn't seem to sound as good as the originals didn't help the new Strat's reputation, either. George Gruhn's blunt assessment is typical: "The 3-bolt necks didn't stay in tune as well, and some of those guitars weighed like boat anchors and didn't sound as good."

A 2003 Classic Series '70s style reissue: big headstock, two string trees, bullet rod, big decal.

"I play inhumanly hot licks on my Stratocaster," said the Caterpillar, "and back myself with everything else."

Alice in Fenderland. The fact-packed ads of the '50s and '60s were replaced in the '70s by positively trippy concept ads like this one.

The Rise of the Vintage Market

The gobbling up of storied guitar companies by monolithic corporations had been the dominant industry trend of the late 1960s. Fender had been acquired by CBS in '65, Guild by Avnet in '66, Gretsch by Baldwin in '67, Ampeg by Unimusic in '67, and Gibson by ECL/Norlin in '69. The quotes from Fender workers about the dispiriting effects of new management were echoed almost verbatim in the laments of employees at other companies who also faced new bosses who had little experience in musical instruments — guys who were moved over from the refrigerators division and were now in charge of guitar quality control.

The seeds of a boom in vintage instruments were planted during this age of corporate takeovers, stoked-up production, corner-cutting, and ill-conceived changes to popular models. As new guitars began to look less cool, old guitars looked cooler than ever. As with other trends, the vintage boom was stimulated by influential players. George Gruhn: "The electric vintage guitar market kicked in precisely the moment Michael Bloomfield joined the Butterfield Blues band [Bloomfield played slide on 1965's *The Paul Butterfield Blues Band* and regular electric on *East-West*, Butterfield's groundbreaking LP of 1966]. Before that, there was no interest whatever in old electric guitars. At first the market seemed to be whatever Bloomfield played; that's what was popular — Teles, then gold-top Les Pauls, then sunburst Les Pauls. Before then, you could get Les Pauls for $75. They went to about $600 almost overnight."

By the early 1970s, rumors of declining quality at Fender and other companies had gained strength, and these misgivings were confirmed by another trend too flagrant to ignore: Influential guitarists seemed to be following Mike Bloomfield's lead and playing old guitars, not new ones. Consumers found themselves reconsidering assumptions that were essential to America's post-war economic boom and long taken for granted — such as, leading companies know best; they can be trusted to innovate, to continually improve their products, to show the way. How could such faith be sustained when some of the most admired and presumably most knowledgeable players were recording and performing with *used guitars*? Whatever had made those old guitars better was subject to some confusion, but one thing was all too clear: You couldn't get them anymore — at least, not from the manufacturers.

cont'd, p. 156

Rick Derringer's *All American Boy* yielded "Rock and Roll Hoochie Koo," now entering its fourth decade as a radio staple. According to *Vintage Guitar*, this '59 slab-board Candy Apple Red Strat was on loan from Johnny Winter. Once a sunburst, it acquired the new finish in the early '70s, along with a matching red headstock, a conversion from trem to hardtail, and Tele style knobs.

 *Riff Medley, Track 37*

With his classical orchestrations, scathing satire, synth experiments, highly original guitar soloing, and insanely prolific output, the late Frank Zappa could have been half as accomplished and still be in a class by himself. He is shown here with the charred 1963 Strat he acquired from one of Jimi Hendrix' roadies. "If I miss a note, I'm not going to commit suicide over it ... what have I got to lose? I'm not famous; I'm an unknown guitar player. Nobody's going to punch my score-card the wrong way, or give me brown stars if I screw up. Big deal. I'll take the chances."

Steve Hillage worked in a butcher shop to pay for his first Strat. Sometimes compared to Robert Fripp and David Gilmour, he experimented with electronic sounds in the mid '70s and was a member of the European avant-garde band Gong. "With a Fender, you have to work a bit harder, and so most of the guitarists who play Fenders have a more distinctive sound. And I, personally, find it more expressive."

After helping to start crazes for Telecasters, gold-top Les Pauls and sunburst Les Pauls, soulful bluesman Michael Bloomfield took up the Strat and played it for the rest of his career. He once said, "Without a guitar, I'm a poet with no hands." His untimely death came in 1981.

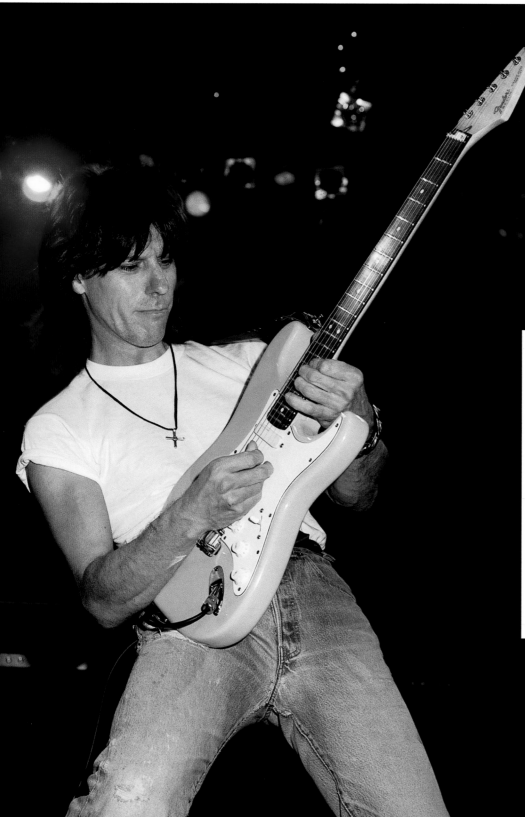

"I've got my guitar. It's a '50s Strat. It's just terrible, but it looks at me and challenges me every day, and I challenge it back. It has the vibrato, and it's difficult to play, it goes out of tune and all that, but when you use it properly, it sings to you."[5]

– *Jeff Beck*

1976's *Wired* was an exhilarating follow-up to the landmark *Blow By Blow*. It signaled Jeff Beck's return to the Stratocaster. These days, Beck is rarely seen onstage without his Jeff Beck Signature Strat.

 Jeff Beckian Stew, Track 47

"When he's on, he's probably the best there is."

– Jimmy Page

Jimmy Page, Eric Clapton and Jeff Beck share the stage during the ARMS benefit tour, 1983.

Eric Clapton: "At the time of the ARMS shows, and for many months afterwards, I began to think of Jeff as probably the finest guitar player I'd ever seen."[6]

Jeff Beck: "You can't imagine how that makes me feel. For him to say that, it really means a lot. It sort of blows me away."[7]

Jeff Beck's *Guitar Shop*: "The work of a player who has integrated technique, emotion, spontaneity and attitude so completely that you can't begin to separate them. It's a superb rock instrumental record, one of the best ever. This album will remind you of everything that's soulful, cool and honest about our instrument."

– Joe Gore, Guitar Player

Steve Miller was one of several Hendrix-inspired players who reversed the stringing on left-handed Strats.

It dawned on players that a golden age might have slipped away, that the guitar's best years might lie in the past rather than the present or the future. As this unsettling suspicion sank in, the electric guitars of the 1950s increasingly seemed bathed in a warm glow of romance and perfection, and players' attitudes toward manufacturers underwent a revolutionary shift. A kind of product nostalgia was borrowed from other categories (Detroit autos, kitchen appliances, tube hi-fi gear), ascribed for the first time to electric guitars, and invoked with sighs and regrets: They don't make 'em like they used to. Even Fender, once the essence of cool, had lost its luster.

A new consciousness arose, first among a small, well-informed elite who knew each other and bought and sold guitars that were once called "used" but were now described as "vintage," like a wire-wheeled Aston Martin or a rare cabernet. The lexicon of nicknames invented by these collectors would filter out to the larger community: P bass and stack-knob, soapbar and PAF, Tele and Strat. (One of the earliest buzzwords: "pre-CBS.") The scene was awash in rumors, but in the early '70s the word-of-mouth network was

supplemented with articles in *Guitar Player* (founded in 1967) and informative stock lists published by specialty retailers. Over time, the sharing of observations refined the knowledge of vintage dealers, some of whom had graduated from trading out of their station wagons to opening stores with national and then international clienteles.

Most vintage guitar aficionados reveled in the glories of the past, real or imagined. In a turn of events that left Leo Fender shaking his head in bewilderment, players began to value his older designs more than his new ones, and to buy guitars not only to play them but also to trade them, to put them in glass cases or vaults, or simply to round out their collections. Some buyers saw old Teles and Strats as investments, like soy futures or South African Krugerrands. A few sophisticates refined the sort of aesthetic criteria that characterize collectibles markets in Tiffany lamps or Fabergé eggs. Plenty of vintage buffs simply wanted a great guitar to play and couldn't find one among new models.

This multifaceted vintage scene gathered momentum throughout the '70s, fueled by undeniable declines in the quality of several companies' new guitars, as well as the romantic yet reasonable notion that faceless corporate managers in business suits were poor substitutes for fabled inventors in lab coats. Our usual motivations of sounding great, looking cool, and playing our heroes' guitars were supplemented with a genuine yearning for authenticity, a longing to preserve the heritage of the guitars we grew up with, even if — *especially* if — the companies who built them had lost their way.

Throughout the decade, this devotion to vintage instruments spread beyond the scattered elites as the larger community of players picked up the torch. Ultimately, the manufacturers would catch on, and the guitar market would never be the same.

≪

One of the first Dallas guitar shows, 1980. To see under one roof so many classic vintage guitars, many in excellent condition, was nothing less than astonishing.

 Riff Medley, Track 37

Only rock and roll, indeed: Ron Wood hams it up with Mick Jagger on tour with the Stones. Alan Rogan: "Ronnie's had plenty of Strats over the years, good ones, originals from the '50s, but he's not a collector. He's a guitar player. He buys them to use them, not just to have them."

Some people put a lot of importance on tiny details in old guitars, like a particular wire that was used for a time. But in one sense, manufacturing has never changed. It's always a matter of, what can we do with what we have? If you run out of a part, you don't shut down the factory. You go get a different part to do the job, a substitute bolt or component or whatever. In the old days, production was changing all the time. Some of the changes were intended to be design improvements, but many were accidents that never got fixed, or they ran out of parts, or somebody screwed up and instead of throwing it away they used it.

– Mike Lewis

New Life for Old Strats: E.C. Was Here

Eric Clapton recorded dozens of famous solos on various Gibsons, but in the late '60s he began using Strats on sessions with various artists and then on albums such as 1970's epochal *Layla and Other Assorted Love Songs* and 1973's *Derek & The Dominos In Concert*. Retailer/author George Gruhn: "There was *no* market for old Strats before Eric Clapton. People talk about how much Jimi Hendrix influenced everything, but he played CBS Strats. It was Clapton who sparked the market for *vintage* Strats. Before Clapton, I remember very well buying a mint maple-neck Strat with a black finish and gold hardware: seventy-five dollars. These days, a maple-neck, pre-CBS Strat in original condition can easily bring $20,000, probably more like $25,000. Then again, you don't see many clean ones anymore. Among the rosewood-board pre-CBS Strats, the early ones with slab boards tend to bring more. A late-'59 would bring less than a maple-neck but easily $10,000, and more for a Custom Color."

Stan Jay, of Mandolin Bros., Staten Island: "Guitars that people wouldn't touch with a 10-foot pole back in 1965 are now embraced, but that happens in every genre. People used to say early-'70s Martins weren't worth owning; now they look back and say, gee, those guitars were good! That effect is especially dramatic with Strats because they were once inexpensive, and now they're so dear to us. It's a much bigger jump than with most of the guitars. You know, the stock market goes down and people reevaluate what's important. We realize, that wealth we might have had on paper didn't mean so much, but the things we have and hold, that's what really matters."

Little Feat's slide wizard Lowell George often tuned his guitar to open-A and used a Sears Craftsman 11/16" socket on his pinkie. Note nonstock output jack. Biographer Mark Brend, in *Rock And Roll Doctor*: "He said he favored Stratocasters mainly because he found that the intonation high up the neck was more accurate than any other guitars he used." Bonnie Raitt: "He was the best singer, songwriter, and guitar player I have ever heard, hands down, in my life."

 Slide Summit, Track 53

The Anniversary Strat

In the summer of 1979 Fender introduced the Anniversary Strat to commemorate the model's 25th year. Although not acclaimed for its innovation, the model was successful at the time and historically significant for at least three reasons. For the first time since the dawn of the decade, Fender jettisoned the 3-bolt/tilt-neck/bullet-rod combo of the regular production Stratocaster and went back to the 4-bolt neck and the old truss rod of the Strats of yore.

Second, it marked an early effort on the part of CBS to acknowledge Fender's historic past, not just with advertising slogans but with a new model bearing at least a couple of old features. Finally, its advertisements acknowledged the growing influence of the Strat on other makers ("It spawned 20 imitations"), a phenomenon that would explode in the next five or six years.

No one pretended the Anniversary was a reissue. Like the 1968 Telecaster Bass or the 1970 reintroduction of the one-piece maple neck (as an option), it was little more than a nod to the past. It's a matter of speculation whether Fender's return to the old neck joint was an admission of the tilt-neck's tainted reputation or simply a way to include at least one vintage feature in keeping with the anniversary theme. Perhaps it was a bit of both, but the fact is, with the exception of later reissues of 3-bolt models, Fender never went back to the 3-bolt neck.

At first, the new model seemed star-crossed, as if the guitar gods had deemed it blasphemous to invoke the Strat's hallowed past with a large-headstock CBS guitar with all-black plastic trim. Its water-based pearlescent finish was prone to cracking, which left some of the bodies with a parched, Death Valley lakebed look and CBS with yet another image problem. (Bill Carson recalled that the paint was a type used on Schwinn bicycles.) Now a Senior Vice President, Larry Moudy joined Fender in March '75 and was a district sales manager at the time the Anniversary was introduced. He reported: "It was supposed to be

Robin Trower: "The first thing I'd do would be to use as high an action as possible on the Stratocaster. It's the only way to get a good sound out of it. When I used to buy a Strat, old or new, I would go through them all and listen to them acoustically. . . . If it doesn't sound good without an amp, it'll never sound great with one. With strings, use only as light a gauge as you have to. The heavier the string, the bigger the sound."

Trower Power!, Track 41

silver all along, but there were a couple of colors to be mixed, and in the first run the proportions were reversed, so instead of silver we got this sort of frost white. After the finish started cracking and in some cases actually falling off, they got it right. We ended up selling every piece in the production run."

Aside from the large headstock, 4-bolt neck, older truss rod design, and silver color, details included: a special neck plate marked *1954 – 1979 25th Anniversary*, Sperzel non-locking tuners, two string trees, a 6-digit serial number beginning with 25, and the word *Anniversary* in black on the upper horn. Fender asserted that about 10,000 Anniversary Strats were shipped in the model's two-year lifespan of 1979 and 1980.

Robbie Robertson: "Having a pickup in the middle is no good for me. My fingerpicks cling to the magnets, and I can't do the harmonics right because the middle pickup is in the way. . . . So I had the middle and bridge pickup coupled together, which turns them into a humbucking pickup."

As on many others, the finish on this first-run 25th Anniversary Strat is flaking away (note lower rim). Later versions had different paint formulas and sold well.

Eddie Hazel of Funkadelic, after acquiring a '54 Strat: "Overnight something happened. I started stretching out, grabbing new ideas. Suddenly I was capable of soloing in ways I'd only dreamed of before. It was unbelievable what that guitar did to me. It gave me such a vision. It talked back to me. I could feel it, just like I feel my heart pulse."

"Funkadelic is my favorite band. Rock, funk, whatever you want to call it, they were one of the greatest. Eddie Hazel is right up there with Jimi Hendrix."

– *Flea*

Hot Rod Guitars & Groovy Brass Parts

Aside from the expansion of the vintage guitar market, another trend of the '70s that would ultimately affect the production and marketing of Fender instruments was the customizing of stock guitars with accessories or replacement parts purchased from specialty suppliers. The Stratocaster's growing popularity and modular construction made it certainly the most modified guitar of the decade (and every decade since). From tuners to tremolo bar tips, from nuts to knobs, you could take a factory-stock guitar and make it your own with little skill and few tools. In fact, you could order everything you needed to assemble an entire non-Fender SLO (Strat-Like Object) from the ground up — pre-routed bodies, pre-fretted necks, pre-wired circuits, the works.

As former industry giants struggled to maintain their reputations, smaller outfits stepped in. Pickup companies like Seymour Duncan or DiMarzio couldn't have succeeded unless players believed the stock pickups on their new guitars weren't as good as they could have been. And if you're replacing your pickups, why not replace your frets, strap holders, or output jack while you're at it?

Another trend, small but significant: big bucks for limited-production instruments. Alembic was loosely organized in 1969 (more formally in 1970), and its exquisite guitars and basses were unlike anything musicians had yet seen. Expensive and dazzling, these multi-laminated, neck-through instruments featured extravagant sculpting, exotic woods, high-tech components, sometimes exuberantly complex circuitry, and a level of inlay, marquetry, and other ornamentation rarely seen even on custom instruments and never on anything from Fullerton or Kalamazoo. Alembic didn't sell enough guitars — or "move enough product," in the parlance of the boardroom — to threaten major manufacturers like CBS Fender, but like B.C. Rich ("the Alembic of heavy metal," as author Jim Roberts called it), they nurtured the notion that new ideas and exciting guitars were no longer the exclusive domain of Gibson, Fender, and the other well known brands.

Sustain was the holy grail of tone in the '70s, and one answer, supposedly, was brass (another: heavy bodies and necks). There seemed to be no end to the parts rendered in brass — string nuts, bridges, tailpieces, knobs, strap buttons, tremolo bars, even solid brass blocks that did nothing but fill holes in your guitar's body, presumably providing even more sustain. In the early '80s, Fender would respond to the trend with its own Brass Master series of replacement components.

"For me the most striking and inspiring thing about Richard Thompson is how diligently he works to improve himself. To this day he continues to expand himself as guitarist, singer, songwriter, and performer. The scary thing is that he was one of the best of each of these to begin with!"
— *Henry Kaiser*

Asked why he plays a Strat, the ingenious and absurdly under-recognized Richard Thompson (here in a 1970s photo) scribbled this note: "Great ergonomic shape from a non-playing designer, single-coil pickups with unintended groovy out-of-phase sounds. A plank with wires strung across, in the best possible sense, but Leo was the one to get to the basics. Magic Sam was playing a Strat at the Albert Hall in London, in '68 or '69. Sounded superb. Tommy Allsup did the nifty bits on the Buddy Holly records — great tone, great player. Hank B. Marvin, Strat, Vox AC-30, a Binson Echorec Baby — such tone!"

"Upgrading the quality of the Fender Product has been the most important beneficial result of the acquisition of the company by CBS ….we once used cotton push-back electrical wiring on all solid-body instruments … this type of wire is quite prone to signal leakage and noise. Currently, and for the past several years, we've used a much more costly, higher quality wire with non-conductive shielding; the end result is a much better signal to noise ratio….

"In the early years of Fender, we used (and still do) cabinet ash for Telecaster and some Stratocaster bodies. (Alder was also used on some Strat models.) Ash can have extreme density variables; one end of the board can be balsa weight, the other end heavy as lead (with all the variations in between).… In the pre-CBS days, there was a broad range of body weights and mass resulting in a fairly wide spectrum of sound and sustain between instruments. Since that time we have alleviated the problem by upgrading the materials used for all of our guitar and bass bodies. From the Mustang models up, we now use only ash and maintain an average body weight of 5.6 lbs. For the unfinished Stratocaster bodies . . . this provides a much more consistent product with respect to tone and sustain characteristics. Many of the older instrument bodies made pre-CBS were of lighter weight ash or even alder wood and were inferior sounding … so 'vintage' does not necessarily mean 'best.'

"Perhaps the fairest conclusion to the pre-CBS and post-CBS discussion is to simply look at the record: Fender sales are growing every year and have now reached the point where our customers are supporting us at levels two to three times higher than previously!"
— Director of Marketing David L. Gupton, in the June 1977 *Musician's News*

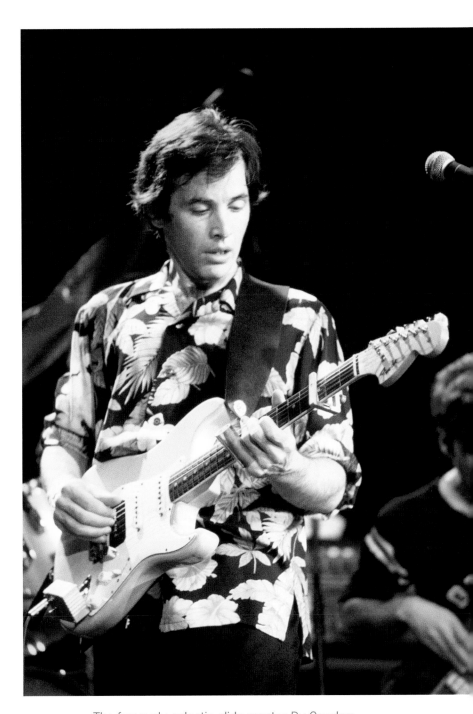

The famously eclectic slide master Ry Cooder: "Somebody gave me a Strat a long time ago. I didn't play it very well, because I hadn't been reared on electrics. I didn't understand it, but I came to like the chunky, fat sound, especially for bottleneck."

 Slide Summit, Track 53

Challenge & Irony at the End of the Dismal Decade

Despite the somewhat tarnished reputation of late-'70s Fender guitars as well as various misgivings about the long-term future of the company, Fender was doing just fine at the end of the decade, at least from a bottom-line point of view. Dan Smith: "1979 might have been the best year in Fender's history. That may sound weird, given all that was going on, but we were selling an incredible amount of guitars overseas in the late '70s and early '80s. It actually got out of whack so that about 55% or 60% or sometimes 65% of the sales were going offshore. In 1979 they did something like 72,000 guitars and basses out of that factory."

Given the Stratocaster's prominence among Fender guitars, not to mention its impact on the entire industry, it's easy to forget that until the modern era, the Strat was Fender's top-of-the-line model for only its first four years. It was relegated to the number-two spot by the more expensive Jazzmaster in 1958, and bumped further down the price list with 1962's introduction of the new top dog, the Jaguar. But the Jag was dropped in 1975, the Jazzmaster in 1980, making official what had already become apparent on sales ledgers and bandstands everywhere: The Stratocaster was Fender's premier guitar.

Several CBS "improvements" to the Strat's design were ill conceived, poorly executed, or both, while additional cosmetic changes put even more distance between the new models and the pre-CBS guitars whose status by now had been elevated from "used" to "vintage." Ironically, it was during this same period that more and more prominent players were seen with Strats in hand, including influential artists such as Eric Clapton, George Harrison, and Ritchie Blackmore. Fender found itself facing both a tantalizing opportunity and a frustrating irony, because many of those newly popular Strats were vintage instruments. Fender had decades of experience marketing its products against those of Gibson and other manufacturers. Now it faced competing with its own legacy. As one executive said at the time, "Some of the biggest competitors for new Strats are old Strats." Fender's response to this paradox would shape its strategies for decades to come.

Richard Lloyd, at far right with Television at CBGB, New York City: "A Stratocaster is a guitar you can make a fist around. A Strat asks you to play a certain way; it demands a certain grasp. It's just the way the neck is shaped, I guess. That kind of neck is really conducive to a certain kind of string-bending that you can't get on most guitars."

The Imperfect Science of Dating Old Strats

Regarding the Stratocaster's structural evolution, you'll find plenty of dates here, but as with other books, most are approximate. Much of my research over the past three decades has involved interviewing retailers who handle hundreds or thousands of guitars a year. They are the experts; they've seen enough Strats to make observations (or at least informed guesses) about what happened when. But even experts sometimes disagree, and even well researched books and web sites contain numerous (if usually minor) discrepancies. These are inevitable, given Fender's lack of in-house documentation as well as production methods that reflected the market needs, tooling limitations, unpredictable availability of parts, and other challenges of day-to-day guitar building rather than the convenience of future historians.

Let's remember, Fender is a business. Vice President Dan Smith: "We're trying to make a good product, and trying to send our people home with a paycheck. Like any business, we're not concerned with documenting every little thing. If Leo Fender and those guys ran out of a part, they wouldn't halt production. They'd go down to the hardware store, see what was available, and make it work."

Fender's regular production guitars are put together from components stored on shelves or in bins. In the early years, some parts might have been fabricated months before assembly; some were stamped with serial numbers or penciled with dates well in advance of their coming together in a finished instrument. There was no particular necessity for a system by which guitars would be completed in the order in which their components were built. As noted, the question "When was this Fender made?" might be more precisely framed as, "When were these parts assembled?"

Transition Guitars. Another factor was Leo Fender's legendary thrift. He abhorred waste, and nothing short of a California earthquake would stop him from building guitars — certainly nothing so minor as a mismatch of old and new parts. (Not even the lack of a model name would halt production. Between the discontinuation of *Broadcaster* and the adoption of *Telecaster*, Leo or his associates simply snipped the model name off the *Fender* decals and stuck them on guitars now nicknamed "Nocasters.")

New parts were introduced gradually. If Leo or his successors devised a new neck shape, it would go without saying that old necks would be used up. Not surprisingly, we see both rounded and V-shaped necks coming out of the factory during the same period. We see '57 Strats that mix leftover Bakelite-like parts with newer plastic parts; '58 Strats that mix older maple necks with newer three-color sunbursts; '59 Strats that mix old single-layer pickguards with newer rosewood fingerboards; 1965 Strats with new CBS decals but pre-CBS components; '64-'65 fingerboards with "clay" dots on the top and sides, or "pearl" dots on the top but clay dots on the sides, or pearl dots on both the top and sides. We see '75 Strats with older white knobs but newer black pickguards, and '76 Strats with older white pickup covers but newer black knobs. These sorts of overlaps are common not only on Strats but on other Fenders as well; some Precision Basses were assembled with slab bodies up to three years after the introduction of the beveled body.

Senior Vice President Ritchie Fliegler: "If you go back and compare a '57 Strat and a '59 Strat, there's almost nothing in common. There are more differences than between an American Standard and an American Series. The company and the consumers are all more market savvy than they used to be, but it was a more naïve time back then, and they just did it, they made the changes — maple to rosewood neck, different neck shape, the pickguard, pickups, colors, on and on. You didn't have historians going back and looking at every detail, alleging these 'blasphemous' changes." Vice President Mike Lewis: "The Strat was so new. The whole electric guitar market was still young, and the spirit of discovery was raging. There wasn't so much history, and players weren't thinking about history anyway. It was all about the new, and it was all being invented as they went, so if you ordered a Strat, then it just came with the three-color sunburst or the rosewood fingerboard or whatever the new thing was."

Catalogs are one source of information, but their usefulness is mostly in revealing how Fender perceived its instruments and its relationship with potential customers, rather than in documenting minor alterations in design. Even during the quarter-century when Fender offered only one Strat at a time, virtually every detail of the guitar was repeatedly altered — not just bodies, necks, and pickups but also string trees, tuning keys, strap buttons, and pick-guard screws. Some modifications are visible only by disassembling the guitar, and most were never noted in catalogs. Except for acknowledging momentous changes such as the shift to the rosewood finger-board, the same catalog copy was sometimes repeated year after year. Even the details deemed worthy of mention in catalogs sometimes appeared in print years after their actual introduction (Fender produced Strats with one-off finishes from the very beginning, a year or two before listing Custom Colors as official options).

Given a general familiarity with the evolution of a few Stratocaster features (the material used in plastic parts, for example), plus a combination of other clues (serial numbers, pencilled markings on bodies and necks, date codes on potentiometers, etc.), it is certainly possible to approximate, if not pinpoint, the time when a particular guitar left the factory. Details can be found in any number of useful books; see Chapter 10.

"You can't beat that Strat and those old pickups they had on it – I don't care what you say."[8]

– *George Harrison*

 Harrison Melodious Sliding, Track 51

CHAPTER 6

TOWARD MAKING THINGS RIGHT

The Early '80s: Transitions

Bending with the winds of change

The trends of the 1970s reflected the willingness of players and new, small companies to take upon themselves the quest for innovation previously accorded the big manufacturers. The new attitude among players was, in a sense, *we know better*. (Sometimes we did indeed know better; other times we loaded up our guitars with brass parts, or routed out our old Fenders for humbuckings.) With the tainted reps of some of the big companies, with the new reverence for old guitars, with instruments from Alembic, B.C. Rich, Veillette-Citron, Travis Bean, Hamer, and others challenging the conventions of design and marketing, and with almost every part of popular guitars subject to upgrades or replacement, players were liberated from the old choices of a few models and familiar brands. The question for Fender was, what are we going to do about it?

Enter "The Strat"

There was a time when Stratocasters were called Stratocasters. The model was around for more than a decade before acquiring its now inescapable nickname, *Strat*. The word came not from Fender but from the street — from collectors, dealers, and players who were hearing it, reading it in *Guitar Player*, and repeating it. "Strat" is so ubiquitous now it's hard to imagine a time when your use of the word signified you were something of an insider. In any case, Fender execs thought it was high time to get in on the action (and high time to squelch the application of the word to non-Fender copies), so on June 28, 1976, they filed a claim with the U.S. government to protect the name "Strat." On February 8th of the following year, the name was duly registered.

Now, what better way to proclaim Fender's ownership of the word "Strat" than to put it on a new model for all to see (in can't-miss capital letters, no less)? Accordingly, Fender introduced "The Strat" in 1980; it listed for $995, compared to $870 for the regular model with either the maple neck or rosewood board. Like the recent Anniversary, the new guitar was significant not because it marked a permanent redesign but because it hinted at new strategies. Aside from laying claim to the "Strat" nickname, it reflected Fender's intent to invoke the past, at least a bit, and also demonstrated that the company was catching up to trends that had been brewing for years. The new model's advertising slogan — "looks like yesterday, sounds like tomorrow" — captured Fender's evolving strategy of blending vintage pride and cutting-edge R&D.

Most important of all, The Strat wasn't merely an excuse to glam up the same old guitar with new options or a snazzy paint job. It was a separate model on its own, a full-fledged "regular" member of the line (unlike the Anniversary, intended from the outset to be a short-term, limited edition model). In its own way, The Strat was a milestone: For the first time — but hardly the last — Fender's line now included more than one regular production Stratocaster guitar.

As a response to the replacement-parts trend, The Strat was Fender's way of asking, why hot-rod your guitar when the factory can do it for you? It had an extra-hot "X-1" pickup in the bridge position and an intricate circuit offering nine tone settings instead of the stock five (one of the knobs was now a rotary mode selector; the new options included pickup combinations in both series and parallel). Details included a heavy brass bridge/tailpiece and brass knobs, and 22k gold electroplated parts — except for the tuners; one of several quirky things about The Strat was its mismatch of plated parts. According to Bill Carson, many components were left over from Fender's fizzled foray into the replacement parts aftermarket.

Dan Armstrong, highly respected in repair and design circles, was consulted on The Strat's wiring and switching. Aside from the versatile circuit itself, the fact that CBS brought in a "name" outsider was further evidence that it recognized the need to try something new.

 Thumbin' it a la Knopfler, Track 49

Among players with recognizable Strat sounds and styles, Mark Knopfler was the foremost guitarist to emerge in the pub-rock/New Wave era of the late '70s/early '80s. The emotion and the lilting in-between tone of "Sultans of Swing" and subsequent hits by Dire Straits probably influenced more players to take up the Strat than any event since the conversion of Clapton. Knopfler told *Guitar Player*'s Dan Forte: "I like to play all kinds of guitars, not just Strats, but I wasn't getting the sound I really wanted until I got a Stratocaster."

Fender caught up to various trends with 1980's "The Strat." Note color-matched peghead, gold hardware, and metal trem bar tip.

Along with its trendy brass parts and flexible switching, The Strat offered two features that recalled the pre-CBS era. The first was a small headstock. Although indeed smaller than the recent CBS-era headstock, it didn't look like the original. (Some observers wondered why Fender would go so far as to recreate the old shape, but not far enough to do it right.) The other "old" feature was a welcome return to the 4-bolt neck, a detail shared with the Anniversary Strat of 1979 and 1980. A commercial success, The Strat was available in Candy Apple Red, Lake Placid Blue, and later Arctic White.

Dan Smith: "The Strat had that misguided smaller headstock. I don't know where they got the shape; maybe the template was from the Lead I and II [introduced in 1979]. That switching system had a gazillion connections underneath the pickguard."

George Blanda: "It was important, though, because it was the first [unlimited-production] Fender in all those years to go back to the 4-bolt neck and the vintage type truss rod. It did have some weird features. Brass was trendy, and The Strat reflected all that. The smaller headcap wasn't right, but it was the best they could do at the time. The idea behind the guitar was important. It sent a message about Fender returning to roots while at the same time incorporating improvements."

Let Jimi Take Over

Ten years after the death of the Strat's foremost disciple, Fender built a few Jimi Hendrix-inspired guitars with an extra body scoop on the top, as well as a reverse headstock that vaguely recalled the look of Jimi's upside-down, right-handed CBS-era Strats. A generally overlooked guitar, it dated to 1980. How many were made? Some reports put the number at about 25; Dan Smith thinks it was more like a dozen. While it was the first of many Stratocaster models to be more or less officially associated with an individual artist, it had nothing to do with Fender's "signature" guitars, introduced years later and now a major component of the line.

1981: The Arrival of Bill Schultz

Dwindling public interest in guitars, foreign and domestic competition, the cumulative 15-year effects of the "CBS Fender" stigma, and a debilitating home-front recession all combined to force CBS execs to look outside the company for a visionary manager who could take charge, shake up the place, and stave off potential disaster.

They found him. A year into the new decade, CBS hired away two executives from Yamaha. One was William Schultz. As Fender's new president, the no-nonsense newcomer possessed the business savvy and street smarts he would need to streamline and refocus a once revered but now bloated music industry institution. Equally important, he could talk to people, even inspire them. He would guide his new company through the unprecedented complexities of manufacturing instruments in a global economy, ultimately restructuring Fender from the ground up, reinvigorating the production, sales, and marketing teams, and rebuilding Fender's reputation for quality and innovation. He would become the most important person in the history of the company since the days of Leo Fender and Don Randall. Bill Carson wrote: "I honestly believe that if Bill Schultz hadn't joined the Fender operation when he did, there would be no Fender company today."

William Schultz told videographer Dennis Baxter: "Fender was being used as a cash cow for the rest of the CBS musical instruments division. They took the money out of Fender and put it into other companies and kept pressing Fender for more and more. It was a disaster. After we were here for five or six weeks, we made a trip to CBS and laid all the cards on the table. They appropriated money to retool and to rebuild the company."

John Page: "It was pretty bad before Bill got there. One example, CBS sent a guy to an overseas factory to negotiate manufacturing details, and he knew *nothing* about guitars. He came back and said, 'They told me they could knock another 20 percent off the

New president Bill Schultz regularly visited the production line to rally the troops. John Page: "Bill changed everything."

cost if it didn't matter how high the strings were off the metal things on the neck.' I mean, this guy didn't know what action was. Another time I got called down to the factory floor because the tremolo arms were bending. Management had told purchasing to disregard whatever engineering or R&D told them and just do whatever they could to save money, so they were using cold-rolled steel, and they eliminated the heat treating on the arms. Bill found out about all this sort of stuff. I was this young, freaky, long-haired Mohawk-lookin' dude [*laughs*], and Bill Schultz is asking me how to improve things. And he listened."

Joe Carducci: "I was working on the guitar line, and before Bill arrived, *very* rarely would you see anyone from the front office come down there. The attitude was employees vs. management, not harmonious at all. You know, a guitar is something you hold against your body, and you express your soul, but for the people in New York we might as well have been making toasters. It was a powerful moment when Bill got involved, and he'd walk down the line and talk to the employees who were tune-testing or boxing the guitars, the girls who were winding the pickups: 'Hey, how's it going? What do you think? How can we do this better?' That had a huge impact, and finally a sense of harmony started to happen."

John Page: "Bill changed everything. He talked to us as musicians, like Leo Fender had done. He said, 'Hey guys, you're out there, you're building these things, what's wrong?' We said, 'Gee, they're not good guitars, Bill.' He said, 'Well, let's *change* it. Tell me what you need.' Boom — that was it."

Making Things Right:
The "De-CBS" Standard Strat of 1981 – 1983

The updates of the early 1980s — versatile switching, brass parts, fancy finishes, etc. — were all well and good, but if Schultz & Co. were to rebuild Fender's reputation, they knew they had to offer more than trendy brass doodads or extra switches. In fact, the Stratocaster's functional details would have to be reconsidered from top to bottom, a task that would intimidate many designers.

Not Dan Smith. Another Yamaha veteran recruited by Bill Schultz, Smith was a designer, musician, and repairman who arrived at CBS Fender in August 1981. He would be Fender's chief guitar designer for the next 20 years, although like Leo Fender before him, he would benefit from input from many players, his colleagues in marketing, and talented co-designers such as George Blanda.

In the summer of 1980, Fender had added the extra-hot X-1 pickup to the standard Stratocaster, but otherwise the early-'80s guitar was basically the '70s version, encumbered with the big headstock, the tilt-neck, and the bad rep. Dan Smith: "At Yamaha, I had made trips out to dealers all the time and heard about what was wrong with Gibsons, Fenders — everybody's guitars. So I had a good idea of what needed to be changed. CBS was building the Strat they'd been making throughout the '70s — 3-bolt neck, Micro Tilt, bullet truss rod, big headstock, pot-metal bridge, crappy tuning keys. It didn't take a brain surgeon to figure out the 3-bolt neck and bullet had to go. They weren't bad ideas. In fact, Leo figured out how to do it later at G&L, but it didn't matter because the bullet was ugly and Fender customers just didn't like it."

In late 1981 Smith redesigned the basic Strat, which now had a 4-bolt neck with the adjustment at the body end again, which was relatively easy to do because Fender was already building The Strat that way. It also had a smaller headstock, more authentic than The Strat's but still not perfect. The bullet was gone.

Dan Smith: "The idea was to make things right, to take the U.S. Stratocaster back to the way it used to be. It still had the crappy bridge, to be frank, but we knew it was only a transition piece. We just called it the Standard. There was so much going on at the Fullerton factory at that time, all the transition stuff with Bill Schultz reorganizing everything, we didn't end up making very many of them. I call it the 'first

Eric Clapton and Brownie, in concert with Derek and the Dominos, October 1970.

Brownie's appearance on the back cover of *Layla and Other Assorted Love Songs* became an iconic guitar image of the '70s and helped stimulate a new interest in Strats.

"Clapton — I thought, now *here's* a guy, here's a *rock star*. Boy, did he play. I thought, if I could only do what he could do. I thought he had taken the blues just absolutely as far as it could go."
— Mike Bloomfield

"The center of Eric Clapton's music, to me, is obviously the blues. But he has another plus — he's very lyrical . . . . We did a show at Nassau Coliseum where John McLaughlin jammed with us. Clapton waited for John to say his thing and for me to say my thing, and then he came out with a *switchblade*, man. . . . he gets inside the note."[9]
— Carlos Santana

"Clapton was unbelievable, just so sparkling and fluid. He was what turned me away from the Shadows' style and sent me back to listening to B.B. King, Bo Diddley, and all those people. I didn't realize the depth or emotion there was in their music until I saw Eric Clapton doing it."
— Brian May

"I love Eric. I love the touch he has on his guitar. When he comes over to play on my songs, he doesn't bring an amplifier or a guitar. He says, 'Oh, you've got a good Strat.' He knows I've got one because he gave it to me [*laughs*]."[10]
— George Harrison

"He can play anything he wants to play, but he plays blues with the feeling - you know it's blues when he plays it."[11]
– B.B. King

"I know every solo he's ever played, note for note."

– Eddie Van Halen

Clapton's Signature
Strat Tones, Track 35

round' of the Standard Strat, because we would use that name again later."

This "de-CBS" version of the Standard, nicknamed the Smith Strat, was made only through 1982. Details included several carryovers from the previous version, such as the black *Fender* headstock logo with "STRATOCASTER" in huge capital letters, F-stamped tuners, one-piece die-cast tremolo unit, and flush-pole pickups.

 Late-'70s Clap-Tone, Track 33

Portrait of a man and his guitar, 1980. Eric Clapton recalled assembling Blackie in 1969 or 1970. By mid-decade it was his main guitar, and he used it on many tours, jams, benefit gigs, and recordings through the mid '80s.

Gilding The Lily:
Strats in Walnut and Gold

In the summer of 1981 Fender introduced two variations on the Stratocaster theme. The Walnut Strat was a top-of-the-line version of The Strat, while the Gold Stratocaster was a gussied-up Standard. They borrowed features common to their kin, including the not-quite-right smaller headstock and the 4-bolt, non-tilt neck of the pre-CBS era. (Fender catalogs began to show close-ups of the neck plate, as if to say: *See? No more 3-bolt necks!*)

The Walnut Strat had The Strat's elaborate switching system, "STRAT" peghead decal, and gold-plated brass hardware. Its body and neck were made of hefty American black walnut, reflecting the trend in exotic woods and also acknowledging the common if unconfirmed notion that heavier guitars sustained better. Cosmetically, it had sort of a Gretsch Country Gentleman vibe: rich brown woods and black plastic parts set off with gleaming gold-plated hardware. The costliest Stratocaster to date, it retailed for $1,195.

The Gold Stratocaster ($975) featured standard pickups and pickguard, a one-piece maple neck/fingerboard, gold-plated hardware, and a metallic gold finish later deemed prohibitively expensive for production purposes.

Fender Japan

By the early 1980s, imported guitars had been a big part of American instrument retailing for years. Early on, they were targeted at the student market, and the best that could be said about, say, a typical Japanese import was that it was "a good guitar for the money." Stateside, the perception was, these guitars might compete with budget instruments by Kay or Harmony, but Gibson, Guild, Gretsch, Martin, and Fender had little cause for concern. CBS Fender Vice President Dave Gupton told *Guitar Player* in 1978 that Fender was "not adversely affected by the Japanese copies. . . ." A very different realization would sink in soon enough.

By the mid '70s and certainly the early '80s, many Japanese guitars weren't just good guitars for the money; they were good guitars, period. The problem was, more and more of them were copies of Strats and other Fenders. Fender's own export business, which had accounted for a significant part of its revenues for 20 years, was taking a beating in Japan and other markets.

William Schultz' solution was, in effect, to engage the competition on their own turf. With international trademark protection being haphazard, to say the least, it was difficult for Fender to protect its designs against foreign competition, so Schultz decided to make real Fenders in Japan to compete with the copies. In March 1982 CBS Fender established Fender Japan Co., Ltd., partnering with manufacturer Fuji Gen-Gakki (makers of Ibanez guitars, well known in the U.S.) and distributors Kanda Shokai and Yamano Music. Strats, Teles, and other familiar designs would be licensed by CBS Fender, manufactured by Fuji Gen-Gakki, and sold in Europe as well as Japan.

Because of Dan Smith's background as a builder, player, and repairman, he had much more input than would typically be expected of a marketing director. He interfaced with Fender Japan's R&D department,

keeping a close watch on design details and quality control. The guitars would be made in Japan, but Dan Smith would be "driving the bus" in Fullerton.

Forward Into The Past

At the dawn of the '80s more guitarists seemed to be playing Strats, and CBS could hardly fail to see an opportunity for growth — but how to capitalize on it? So far, strategies had included designing deluxe Strats like the Walnut and Gold models, a trendy hot rod version (The Strat), and an upgraded mainstream production guitar (the Standard of '81 and '82).

Leo Fender had always responded to the practical needs of musicians, and yet his products were revolutionary, ahead of the curve. In the '70s and early '80s, however, the company seemed to be following rather than leading, catching up to trends in brass parts, specialized pickups, more versatile switching, and cosmetic upgrades. (The 5-way switch, an obvious improvement, had been introduced by others by the time Fender offered it in '77.) Bill Schultz, Dan Smith, and their colleagues recognized the need to acknowledge those trends, but they also knew that Leo Fender hadn't put their company on the map by following others. They were tired of following. It was time to lead.

Nils Lofgren has several favorite late-'50s and early-'60s Strats, including this stripped-finish '61 with a hand-made pickguard of oak. He likes a higher than average action and doesn't mind wrestling with the guitar a bit to get a fatter sound. He avoided the bridge pickup (too "bitey") until he had his Strats rewired to allow blending in the neck pickup.

With the bare-knuckles sound of the Blasters, Dave Alvin managed to appeal to punks while also helping to kickstart early-'80s revivals in roots rock and rockabilly.

They mapped out an ambitious campaign to reorganize the design, production, and marketing of Fender guitars. For one thing, they would rethink their response to another major trend of the '70s, the vintage boom. While CBS' previous attempts to invoke the company's heritage had recognized the widespread reverence for the Fenders of the '50s and '60s, those efforts were scattered and sometimes half-hearted. There was the quirky, new/old Telecaster Bass back in '68. Then in 1972, CBS Fender pictured Leo Fender in its "This man started a revolution" advertisements; prior to that time, few people outside the company knew anything about Mr.

Fender. Typical players of Fender guitars had never heard of him. Knowing the names behind the guitars you played simply was not part of the accumulated lore of the day (industry giant Ted McCarty, directly or indirectly responsible for Gibson's best known electric guitars, was, like Mr. Fender, unknown to the vast majority of players).

In the 1970s and early 1980s the "1948" Telecaster was spotlighted in Fender literature that, while inaccurate (the Tele's predecessor had actually appeared in 1950) at least revealed a modicum of "vintage awareness" at the company. The Anniversary Strat of 1979 and other models' reversions to the 4-bolt neck and smaller headstock all were part of the same, evolving philosophy: If we are going to move forward, we have to look back.

But Smith and the others also knew that inept efforts like The Strat's so-called "vintage" headstock wouldn't cut it. If Fender were going to remake "vintage" guitars, they'd have to get serious. Along with a rededication to innovation, and the Stratocaster's morphing from a model into an entire line, this new approach to Fender's own heritage would form the cornerstone of Strat design and marketing up to the present day.

Milestones: '57 and '62 Reissues
In early 1982, Fender reissued the maple-neck 1957 and rosewood-board 1962 Strats. Officially called Vintage Stratocasters, the new models' serial numbers began with a special "V" designation. Fender called them "virtually perfect reproductions," but neither was an exact replica. To cite a few examples, the '62 reissue's pickguard had no greenish tint, and its fingerboard markers weren't the "clay" type. Other discrepancies could be detected in neck profiles, string guides, the spacing of the 12th-fret dots, pickup wire, finish undercoats, etc.

Still, both reissues were remarkably accurate for the time and bore the prominent features of their ancestors: The '57 had a two-color nitrocellulose lacquer sunburst finish, single-layer pickguard, and maple neck; the '62 had a three-color nitrocellulose lacquer sunburst finish, laminated guard, and rosewood board. Both models' staggered-polepiece pickups, smaller headstocks, and generally vintage-style hardware were crucial steps toward the authenticity of later reissues. Moreover, their seemingly innocuous advertising slogan was in fact the most conspicuous acknowledgement to date of Fender's coming to terms with its own legacy: "We brought back the good old days." Nostalgia's expensive; both guitars retailed for $995.

It may seem ironic that a pair of "old" designs were among the most important instruments ever made by a manufacturer renowned for innovation, but the new models' response to what Fender called "the continued demand for vintage instruments" was only one aspect of their significance. Even more important, the reissues of '82 proved that Fender could once again build world-class guitars, and they did so at a time when the company's reputation needed a boost.

George Blanda: "The people I knew thought the reissues were incredible. It was the first time since CBS bought the company back in '65 that Fender proved they could build great guitars. They were the first good U.S.-made Fenders in a long, long time."

Richard McDonald: "I remember thinking, everyone else is embracing our history, and we weren't. If you wanted a really cool vintage Strat copy, Tokai made a nice one. A lot of people were making copies, and some were pretty good. Then suddenly everyone was saying, hey, Fender's making cool guitars in California again! That was the hue and cry. That's what got me into the music store to buy my '62 reissue Strat. It was the biggest news."

≫

Trevor Rabin is perhaps best known for his solo in 1983's "Owner of a Lonely Heart" by Yes. The song has a dated, '80s vibe, yet the solo sounds inventive to this day. Rabin's favorite guitar is a road-weathered '62 Stratocaster. "I use an old Strat 80 or 90% of the time. It's basically a '62, but it's got totally different insides."

Catalog pages for The Strat and Walnut Strat.

'57 Vintage reissue.

Catalog pages for the '82 reissues.

A conversation with Dan Smith, project manager for the '57 and '62 reissues

Fender had already introduced the Vintage Tele prior to your arrival.

Yes, and it was clear we also needed to do a vintage Strat. So I started that, and we came up with the '57 and the '62. We had prototypes at the end of '81, and they were introduced at the January '82 trade show. Both came out in the '82 catalog. We built them in the Fullerton plant.

How did you research their design?

John Page and I flew all over the country and took apart vintage guitars. We measured every dimension, every detail. We found that those old Strats had a lot of variation from guitar to guitar, even if they were supposedly the "same" vintage, but it gave us what we needed.

Where did you find the guitars you ended up using as models?

Ax-In-Hand Music, DeKalb, Illinois. That's Larry Henrikson's store, and he was a friend from my days at Yamaha, so John Page and I flew there in the winter of 1981. It was in the middle of an ice storm, the coldest day in local history or something, and the only car at the airport that would start was a Gremlin. They had to use a blowtorch on the transmission to get it going [*laughs*]. Anyway, Larry had a huge collection of old guitars and was real nice about letting us go through them. We checked out probably 200 Fenders — took the necks off, took pictures, measured everything. For the '62 we actually picked two parts, a body and a neck. One part was about December 1960, and the other was about May '61. I forget which was which.

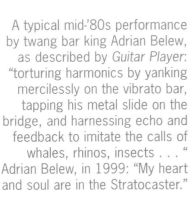

A typical mid-'80s performance by twang bar king Adrian Belew, as described by *Guitar Player*: "torturing harmonics by yanking mercilessly on the vibrato bar, tapping his metal slide on the bridge, and harnessing echo and feedback to imitate the calls of whales, rhinos, insects . . . " Adrian Belew, in 1999: "My heart and soul are in the Stratocaster."

So why call the reissue a '62?

When I picked '57 and '62, it had nothing to do with those being the greatest years of the Stratocaster or anything like that. 1962 was just a good year in general. People had good memories of it. The other reason was that 1962 was the year of the transition from the thicker, slab rosewood fretboard to the thinner, curved one. People think the thin one is a veneer, but it's not. They start with a solid block of wood and use shaper cutters to hollow it out. The result is what we call the round lam fretboard.

Why did Leo Fender switch from the slab boards to the round lams on the originals?

Because of the way he cut fret slots, and the difference in the coefficient of expansion between rosewood and maple. On most slab boards, slots are cut straight across, parallel to the flat back. They go almost all the way through, so instead of a solid hunk of wood, the effect is to have a bunch of little blocks. When the weather changes, and the rosewood and maple expand or contract at different rates, they can twist or warp. It's not a big problem with deep slots, because the fingerboard is more flexible and there's some "give." But Leo used a swing-arm fret slot cutter, and the slots were curved on top and not as deep, so he had this thick beam of rosewood running down the neck, and it could twist or bend with shifts in the weather; it didn't "give." He didn't want to change the way he cut slots, so he went with a thinner, curved piece of rosewood. The vintage guys wanted the slab boards for the reissues. My thinking was, if we started doing the slab and had the same problems Leo had, we could switch to the round lam at some point and still call it an authentic '62. So that was a bail-out option.

For the other reissue, why pick 1957 as opposed to, say, '56?

'56 Strats are great. 1957 was just a cool *year.* When people talk about cars, for example, look at 1957 — the coolest. Seven's a cool number.

Like the original Strat of 1954, the reissues of 1982 were delayed by almost a year. Were the problems with the guitars, or with the manufacturing process?

It's all tied together. There were so many things in the factory to fix, we won our battles one inch at a time. See, we weren't just designing reissue Strats; we were reorganizing the whole factory. Every rock we turned over, we'd find 50 snakes, and we

1982

Fender

THE SOUND THAT CREATES LEGENDS

After the travails of the '70s, the 1982 catalog embodied the reborn Fender's renewed vigor and pride.

Yngwie Malmsteen lights it up with a mix of post-Blackmore metal, Bach, Paganini, and virtuoso shred rock. Maligned by some for his over-the-top speedfests, he can also render melodies of lyricism and grace. His main guitars in the mid '80s included a 1969 cream colored maple-neck Strat and a left-handed sunburst that he played right handed in sort of a reverse Hendrix approach. Some of his old guitars have scalloped fingerboards and brass string nuts, as does his Signature Series Strat. "In terms of feel, sound, and looks, there's nothing like a Strat."

went through a lot of pain to get all that stuff right. Like the '70s headstock was so much easier to sand, because on a vintage headstock, where the ball at the top meets the French curve, it's a tight radius in there, very hard to sand. And that was just one challenge on the reissues.

Did it take a while to get it right, or were they good guitars from the outset?

Both. They were *very* good guitars right from the beginning, and yet they didn't have every vintage-purist detail correct at first. It took us till '84 to get up to full production and get things running smoothly — ironically right about the time CBS decided to sell the company. There were so many idiosyncrasies to get authentic. Some details we've fine-tuned only in the last few years. Those first guitars could have been closer to the originals, but they just weren't, for a variety of reasons. It would have taken too long, and they had been delayed long enough. Another reason

Ode to Yngwie, Track 63

was the limitations of the tooling; you can only do what your equipment lets you do. We can do so much more now, but back then we were stuck with what we had.

The original '57s and '62s were different in neck profile, but for the reissues you used a generic neck common to both guitars.
It was just something we had to do to get them done. The other thing is, most players had not played a '50s Strat, and that V neck isn't comfortable for a lot of guys, especially if they play with their thumb on the

center of the back. So back in '82, playability was more important than total vintage authenticity. Remember, we didn't have a Standard series that we had that much confidence in, so the reissues had to be practical. We picked more of a '60 or '61 type neck that would be comfortable.

Those reissues of '82 took a big step toward re-establishing your credibility.
Absolutely, no question. The reissue aspect was just a part of it. We had to prove to everybody that we hadn't lost sight of what made Fender what it was, that we could still do it right. Look, we basically had to relearn how to make Fender guitars. In '81 and early '82 we were still making them pretty much with the same processes as CBS had done for a while, and yet every week there were little changes we'd make. The *major* ways of building guitars didn't start to change until mid or late '82.

Was that when you introduced CNC [Computer-Numeric Controlled systems, in which computers control the cutting of bodies and other components]?
That's when we improved it. CBS had used CNC before, albeit pretty archaic CNC, which was one reason why the body shapes weren't right on some of the late-'70s and very early-'80s Strats, and especially on the Tele's upper left body, the little curve at the neck joint. The body perimeters had been changed to accommodate the failings of those routing systems. Programming CNC computers was more complicated in the late '70s, and they made compromises to get it done. So when we did the reissues, we were actually pin-routing those bodies at first, because we couldn't get the shapes right otherwise. The equipment continued to improve toward the end of '83 and into '84.

American Vintage '57 reissue. Note "ashtray" bridge cover, and beveled Alnico 5 magnets with vintage stagger.

The Squier Series

Fender purchased string manufacturer V.C. Squier back in 1965 and found a convenient new application for the brand name in 1982. Less expensive versions of the reissues were made by Fender Japan for overseas markets, and these bore an extra *Squier Series* peghead decal to distinguish them from the American-made reissues. Later, the Fender logo was replaced altogether with an enlarged *Squier* logo, to differentiate the country of origin more vividly. The quality of the Squier reissues was so high that it actually set the standard for builders back in Fullerton, where Leo Fender and his crew had designed and built the originals in 1957 and 1962. The irony was lost on no one.

3-bolt Strat, Slight Return

Although the Squiers were initially intended only for overseas markets, it became clear that given the reorganization of the Fullerton factory (and the resulting reduction in guitar building), some sort of import would be necessary to meet domestic demands. On the other hand, the last thing Fender wanted was to further confuse an already complicated situation (Fender guitars were labeled *Fender*, or *Squier*, or *Fender* and *Squier*) or to harm the market for its own U.S.-built guitars. The solution: an imported Stratocaster that could be distinguished a mile away from the made-in-America guitars. Yep, it was back to the '70s-style Strat, complete with a big headstock, 3-bolt neck, and a bullet truss rod. Fender Japan's well-made version demonstrated that the 3-bolt neck and bullet rod were inherently valid, and it also helped erase once and for all any remaining stigma of the "made in Japan" label.

This 1983 experiment had neck-through construction with an ebony fingerboard and American black walnut body "wings," two humbuckers, and decorative brass pickup housings. None of its unique features made it onto production models.

Evolving Strategies

From a Model to a Line

In July 1983 the Walnut Strat, Gold Stratocaster, and The Strat all were dropped. As we will see, Fender designers had more important matters to address. But those fancy Strats of the early '80s were significant, signaling a turn in the company's conception of its own instruments.

Fender's previous strategy was similar to that of its rivals in that its line consisted of a few distinct models: Telecaster, Jazzmaster, etc. But with The Strat, Anniversary, Walnut, and Gold editions — all of which were offered concurrently with the Standard — the Stratocaster was no longer a member of a line. It was a line unto itself, a small family of guitars that within a few years would multiply into a sprawling international clan. By the late '90s, its members would range from inexpensive beginner's models built in Indonesia all the way up to U.S.-built, one-of-a-kind custom guitars that retailed for twenty or even thirty times the price of their imported low-end cousins.

The Standard Series Stratocaster, 1983 - '84

At the turn of the decade, players and dealers had sung with one voice in their chorus of complaints: Fender guitars weren't that good, and they cost too much. In 1981 and 1982 the Fender team had dedicated themselves to improving quality. Now, they turned to costs. The result was one of the most distinctive mainstream Strats ever: the low-budget ($650) and short-lived 2-knob Standard Series Stratocaster of mid 1983 to late 1984. It was also controversial; Bill Carson called it "the Stratocaster in its worst-ever configuration." It might have looked like a quickie/cheapie knockoff of a real Strat, but it was a serious redesign, with a new neck profile, a new neck-pitch adjustment mechanism (now working in conjunction with a 4-bolt neck), the brand new Biflex truss rod, the new Freeflyte tremolo (with a snap-in, metal-tipped arm and top loaded strings), redesigned bridge saddles, a single-layer pickguard with 12 screws instead of 11, locking strap buttons, die-cast tuners, white dots (instead of pearloid), and a smaller Fender logo in silver.

Dan Smith: "That concept was mine, and part of it was all about cost. When I got there in 1981, regular Strats were almost a thousand bucks without a case. We had to compete with the stuff coming in from off-shore, so we were looking at ways to cut costs. One was to relocate the jack to the pickguard. That let us remove the ferrule [the standard output jack], which was a chrome-plated part and cost us three or four bucks or whatever it was. I took that guitar all over the country and showed it to retailers, and until I called it to their attention or they went to plug it in, they didn't even notice the ferrule was missing.

"The new wiring harness could be done in one piece and just dropped in, so that cut production time. We also reduced the knobs to one volume and one tone. So you pull out three dollars of your cost here, and another five bucks there, and another couple of bucks somewhere else. We were trying to retail it for about six hundred bucks, a hell of a bargain when you look at all the other guys' guitars at that time."

Another goal was to address modern styles. In the early '80s, a few more players had picked up the Strat, but it was still a relatively faint blip on the radar. It wasn't the guitar of choice in recording studios, for example. Many musicians were still playing the Gibson ES-335, which had been so popular in the late '70s on records by Steely Dan and other influential groups.

Dan Smith: "So to address that market with the new Standard, we went to a flatter fretboard with a 12" radius — same as the Elite [p. 187] — and we put bass frets in there, which is what we use today on the American Series and other things; it's not as big as, say, a Gibson jumbo, but it's bigger than a vintage fret. We think it's excellent fretwire, and that was the first time we used it. We widened the fingerboard at the nut and made the neck a little shallower from front to back. This was all to attract the big-hair bands and other guys who were playing Les Pauls, 335's, and other types of humbucking guitars and were really into string bending.

"The Biflex was a unique design and a great improvement. And we also went with a 4-bolt tilt, which was sturdy but also easier to adjust than loosening the neck and trying to put little shims in there. Leo's design for the tilt-neck that they used with the 3-bolt was slightly different. Our main improvement was closer manufacturing tolerances that gave you a tighter fit and a sturdier joint with the four bolts."

Despite the competitive price tag and impressive features, the Standard suffered from an inferior tremolo. Its spring adjustment was made from the top, so there was no back plate. It had a single knife-edge pivot that went all the way across, so there were no base plate screws. Instead, there was a V-groove block that received the knife edge. Dan Smith: "We felt [the full-width pivot] was the best way to get the tremolo to move back to mechanical center, but it had problems. The balance was actually too good, so you'd get a lot of warble because it was always moving — the V groove was so sharp the tailpiece moved around too much. And then we needed a place for the spring tension adjustment, which was something we added to the bridge shortly before we introduced it.

"We were messing with the geometry, changing the relationship between the pivot point and the intonation point of the string, and we didn't get a chance to test it enough. We ended up giving a lot more power to the string, so when you tuned it up the bridge would pull up off the body further than on a normal Stratocaster, and when you bent strings the bridge would move around more. It was impossible to keep in tune. We didn't realize all that until after we tooled up. The bridge was a cast piece from Schaller. We tried to make it better than [its predecessor], but at the end of the day the tremolo was a nightmare."

Dan Smith believes to this day that if the bridge had been satisfactory, the 2-knob Standard would have succeeded in the marketplace. Fender stopped making it when CBS closed down the factory at the end of '84 in preparation of selling the company. Fender then relied on its well-made imports to tide

them over, until after CBS sold the company and a new U.S. factory was set up.

More Switches? More Knobs? Must Be a Better Guitar — *Right?*

Yet another trend of the '70s and early '80s might be called "super versatility." The Tele, Strat, and Gibson's Les Paul and ES-335 were all famously versatile, their disciples covering the gamut of popular music, but other companies had upped the versatility quotient with models that mixed single-coils and humbuckers or featured coil-tapped pickups, onboard preamps, ever more elaborate switching schemes — even snap-in, interchangeable effects modules.

Suddenly it seemed like a good idea to offer a whole array of available sounds (whether or not they improved upon the electric guitar's few classic tones), or to design guitars supposedly combining the "best of both worlds," the two worlds being Fender and Gibson. Fender hopped on the bandwagon with its Elite Series.

The Elite Stratocaster

Fender touted the Elite Series instruments as its most revolutionary electrics in two decades, which seemed like a good idea at the time. Introduced in May 1983, the Elite Strat featured a long list of innovations, several of which it shared with the Standard Series Strat of the same period: jumbo frets, the new neck adjuster, a flatter 12" fingerboard radius, the Biflex truss rod, locking strap buttons, and the new, ill-fated tremolo.

The Elite's electronics, possibly the most elaborate tone system ever offered on a production Strat, included pickups with Alnico 2 magnets, a hum-canceling dummy coil, a battery powered active preamp, three pushbutton pickup selectors, a TBX control that "adjusts the damping of the pickup's internal resonance for tones you've never heard before" and also boosted the output, and an MDX active midrange boost and top-end rolloff providing a range of tones "from the classic Fender sound to a fat humbucking sound." (Some of the "best of both worlds" ads were even more overt in targeting users of other brands, promising "your favorite Fender — and non-Fender — sounds.") Details included distinctive white plastic pickup covers without polepiece holes, white knobs with black numerals and black rubber jackets, and a side-mounted output jack.

Fender's strategy was revealed in the list prices of the late-1983 Standard Series and Elite Stratocasters. Significantly, the previous Standard of 1981 - mid 1983 had no direct corollary, having been replaced not by one guitar but by two; one cost a lot more, the other a lot less. At $650, the new 2-knob Standard cost $245 less than its more conventional predecessor, while the $995 Elite cost $100 more. Looking at it another way, the Vintage and Elite Strats (all retailing for $995) cost a whopping 53% more than the Standard of the same period.

Still fancier versions included the $1,295 Walnut Elite and $1,155 Gold Elite of 1983 - '84. Both sported gold hardware and fancy pearloid tuner buttons. The Walnut Elite's fingerboard was ebony, an expensive wood rarely used by Fender; its exclusivity befit the guitar's status at the top of the line — what Leo Fender might have called the Cadillac.

Dan Smith: "The Elite went along with the whole 'modern Strat' idea, that '80s vibe. At the time, EMG pickups were really popular. Strats were coming back, but guys didn't want the noise from the pickups. The Floyd Rose thing was also starting to happen in a big way. We were a little misguided, trying to compete with the Floyd Rose. We couldn't do any locking stuff at the time and didn't want to get into legal arguments, so we went with the [Freeflyte] tremolo with the long knife edge. It was fancier looking, polished, sleek. John Page designed how it looked, but it had the same problems as the Standard Strat of the time because it had all the same geometry — same system, just fancier looking."

Like its sister instrument, the Standard, the Elite had some good ideas but also several problems. As with the less expensive guitar, slight changes were made to the size of the Elite's body and pickguard to accommodate the shortcomings of the CNC machinery in use at the time. For example, the body was made a little larger on the right hand side so the pickguard would fit better. Dan Smith: "You have to understand, there was a real question of whether Fender was going to build guitars in the U.S. at all. We made concessions just so we could continue to make guitars. We got through it, and things started to get a lot better in a year or two."

Early-'80s Finishes

For the undercoats on the Standards and Elites of the early '80s, Fender switched from polyester to urethane, which was much thinner, easier to sand, and better sounding. For a time, the color coats were either lacquer or urethane, depending on the color; the clear top coats were urethane. Eventually, all of the lacquer color coats were duplicated in urethane, so the new formula was: urethane for the undercoats, color coats (regardless of color), and clear coats.

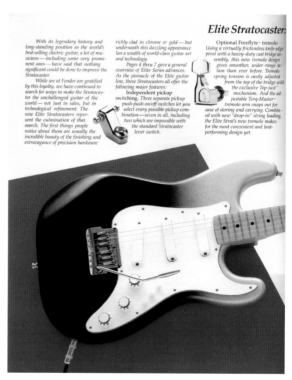

Advertisement for the Elite.

CHAPTER 7

DAWN OF THE THIRD AGE

Buyout '85

Just as compelling a story as Fender's birth in the 1940s is Fender's rebirth in the 1980s. A general economic downturn had hit the music industry in the first part of the decade, and by 1984 CBS had had enough. The word went out in July: Fender was going on the block. Rumors sprouted like weeds as CBS was courted by industry heavyweights, both foreign and domestic.

As Dan Smith suggested, a crucial question was whether Fender guitars would continue to be made in America. An industry insider said that one of the prospective buyers wanted to make all of the guitars overseas, while another wanted to "strip Fender down to a trading company size — very few employees." It may be hard to imagine a time when American-made Fenders faced extinction, but such were the stakes in the summer of '84.

One worker said, "I'm a little patriotic about manufacturing leaving the United States, and if it's at all possible, we should do it here. A lot of employees on the line feel the same way. Some people have been here for 25 years … these workers live and breathe this company. They've been in agony for the past six or eight months, seeing what's been going on." Dan Smith added, "It's not like business is terrible. We probably sold more guitars [in 1984] than anybody, and we're probably making better guitars now than Fender has ever made."

At the U.S. music industry's 1985 trade show in Anaheim, California, the buzz on the expo floor was that Fender employees were trying to buy the company. A press conference was held on February 1st. The atmosphere in the room that day was a mix of cautious optimism and uncertainty. William Schultz took the podium, introduced himself, and announced that Fender employees, backed by investors, would indeed take over the management of their company, having purchased Fender for a reported 12.5 million dollars. Mr. Schultz would remain at the helm but now answer to his colleagues, investors, and employees. The future was uncertain, but one way or another Fender's Middle Ages had come to an end. CBS was out.

Mr. Schultz said they were going to downsize the company, which seemed to address suspicions that recent problems stemmed from Fender's being top-heavy, too corporate, and unresponsive to customers' needs. The other announcement was a shocker: While the reissues would be made in America, all the other guitars, including the regular Strats, Teles, and basses, would be imported from Japan. (As we will see, ultimately it didn't happen that way.) For Fender, the 1980s would turn out to be like the 1960s in one sense, with a mid-decade buyout that in time would radically alter the company's reputation, this time for the better.

Dan Smith: "Things were bad at Fender in the early '80s, but things were bad at *all* the manufacturers. Aside from the economy, it was the beginning of the video game craze. There weren't as many garage bands in the neighborhood. Also, we all loved a lot of the music, but stuff like Steely Dan was more difficult for beginners to get started on. Later on, MTV helped get the guitar business going again, but if you lost those 12-year-olds in the early '80s they're never gonna be your customers."

William Schultz: "CBS decided to get out of the entire music business, and we were the first ones to go. We were the most attractive to sell, they thought. We shut down for a while, and we talked to anybody who thought they had 50 cents in their pocket who would come in and nose around the books trying to find out if they could buy us. It was a demoralizing time. We were simply trying to hold enough of the work force together so we could decide whether to sell it or dissolve it. And there was talk of just dissolving the company."

Dan Smith: "It wasn't until late 1984 that CBS said [to employees], 'Look, we're not getting any offers, so if you can come up with an offer that's better than liquidation, then we'll sell it to you.' If the sale hadn't gone through, Fender could have disappeared."

The wham of that Texas man: Stevie Ray Vaughan drills the big one. Photographer Ken Settle: "I photographed Stevie Ray several times. This was taken during the tour with Jeff Beck, and his playing was especially focused and intense on this particular night. He seemed transported. I remember this moment. He had just hit 'the big note,' and his right arm flew back wildly behind him as he bent the string the way only he could do, and shook the neck. I can still hear that note."

 Rockin' a la SRV!, Track 57

Stevie was known for his heavy strings, starting with anything from a .013 (already beefier than "heavy gauge") all the way to a .016 for the treble E. Fender's Ritchie Fliegler: "We jammed together one time, and at one point we switched instruments. So he hands me this . . . *impossible* Strat, which was literally unplayable — ridiculously high action, incredibly heavy strings. I looked like a guy who'd had his first lesson two days ago. I could hardly get the strings to hit the fingerboard." Ted Nugent: "I played one of his Strats once, and I couldn't bend those strings to save my life."

Pride and joy: Stevie Ray Vaughan and Number One, a battered rosewood-board 1963 Strat (the thick, D-shaped neck is dated DEC. '62). He acquired it in 1973 from Ray's Music Exchange in Austin. Years later he replaced the standard tremolo with a left-hand unit, along with other modifications.

"I didn't even try it out in the store. I looked at it and I knew. I just knew."

Fantasy Blues Jam, Track 59

"To come along at a time when nobody was digging the blues, and to not only make it a credible art form but also to pave the way for so many after him, that's incredible. . . . He was a virtuoso, right up there with greats like John McLaughlin, Wes Montgomery, and Julian Bream. Stevie had the gift."
— *Nile Rodgers,*
producer, "Let's Dance"

"I got to hang with Stevie quite a few times, but I never got to play with him. One time when I was about seven he sat me on his amp and played. I was hooked, man. The last time I saw him we talked about playing, and I think he knew I was for real. The day he died was the worst day of my life."
— Kenny Wayne Shepherd

With his landmark debut album in 1983, Stevie Ray Vaughan almost single-handedly rekindled interest in electric blues. *Texas Flood* made him a modern blues hero, and it inspired a new generation of Texas and Texas-style blues guitarists.

 SRV's Clean Strat Sound, Track 55

William Schultz: "CBS was very cooperative and did everything they could to help me buy the company."

Mike Lewis: "I was a dealer then. That day they made the announcement, I was in the crowd outside the entrance to the NAMM Show waiting to get in. The news that Fender employees had bought the company rippled through the crowd like this incredible wave. There was a huge sigh of relief. Everyone was so happy, and you could feel it sweep through the crowd, because it was on everybody's mind."

John Page: "When Bill and his investors purchased the company we had already gotten real lean. There

Iron Maiden's Dave Murray.

were maybe 100 of us left out of 800. We saw a lot of our friends and co-workers leave."

Dan Smith: "Everyone had invested everything they had to make it happen. We went to Japan and worked on a line of guitars to show at NAMM. On basically a handshake deal, Fuji Gen said they'd continue to make guitars for us, but there was no guarantee there'd be any way for us to pay for them. We had no freakin' clue this whole thing was going to work. It was touch and go."

Shutdown & Reopening

Restoring an old guitar is tricky enough. William Schultz had to restore an old guitar *company*. His first move was to open offices in Brea, only a few miles from Fullerton. The sale had not included manufacturing facilities, so for the first time in 39 years Fender's production line fell silent. Mr. Schultz: "We bought the name but not the factory. We thought we were going to be just a distribution company because we had this fine line of import guitars from Fuji Gen-Gakki. We were also looking for some amplifiers somewhere to buy."

Dan Smith: "The factory was shut down by the end of '84 for all intents and purposes, and officially shut down by February '85. At that point, the company basically started all over from scratch. We offered a whole line of guitars, but except for the leftover U.S. inventory they were all made in Japan. We'd been lucky enough to score some of the most modern equipment, and we had to rent a warehouse for the inventory. After looking around for eight months or so, we set up a little factory in Corona in October '85, but it was real limited — about 14,000 square feet. We made seven to ten guitars a day, all of them vintage reissues."

Mike Lewis: "I toured the factory in January '86, and Dave Maddux was making Strat bodies on the Shoda [router], and then at the end of the production line, here he was again putting the guitars together and setting them up — same guy, running back and forth [*laughs*]. They were just getting started, and it was a skeleton crew."

Fender built no guitars in the U.S. from February to October '85. The imports kept them going in the interim. George Blanda came onboard in October to set up a small Custom Shop, but that project was temporarily back-burnered when the Japan/U.S. currency exchange went from about 250 yen to the dollar to about 125. Fender moved quickly to reconsider its game plan. George Blanda: "When the yen dropped, prices of Japanese products went way up overnight, so importing them wasn't going to save us as much money. Besides, everybody wanted to see some good old-fashioned U.S. technology again."

Fender heard consistent feedback from the field: "You're an American institution. Everyone's pulling for you. We want Fender guitars to be made in America — not just the fancy ones or the reissues, but the basic guitars." Dan Smith and George Blanda went to work. The result would be a new series called the American Standard.

Early-'80s Strats in Review
Aside from reissues and other upscale models (The Strat, Walnut Strat, Elite, etc.), the U.S. production of regular Stratocasters in the first half of the 1980s can be summarized as follows:
- Schultz, Smith and their colleagues inherited the CBS Strat of 1971 - 1981, which they replaced with
- the Standard of 1981 - '82 (sometimes nicknamed the Smith Strat), which was replaced by
- the two-knob, cost-cutter Standard of 1983 - '84, which was dropped when the factory shut down in late '84.

Leftover inventory, imports, and reissues were the only available Strats until the introduction of the American Standard in 1987.

The Contemporary and H.M. Strats
The Contemporary Strat was imported from Japan and introduced in 1985. Aside from helping Fender get through its difficult transition, it also provided an early example of the mix-and-match approach to features that in the coming years would characterize

Duke Robillard is a veteran of two of the most highly regarded bands in recent decades, Roomful of Blues and the Fabulous Thunderbirds. He has offered his blend of jazz, melodic blues, and rock on several acclaimed solo albums as well.

many Fenders, both domestic and imports. The guitar was available with several pickup complements, sported a blackface peghead, and marked Fender's adoption of the increasingly popular locking tremolo.

Another import was 1988's shredworthy H.M. (Heavy Metal) Strat, with a basswood body, a two-octave fretboard, several pickup options, a Kahler locking trem, no pickguard, and appropriately gothic touches (its peghead facing, exposed-coil pickups, and hardware all were black). Later versions featured different cosmetics, circuits, and other variations.

On the H.M. Strat, Fender went for big hardware on the bridge and an edgy look on the peghead.

Eric Johnson: "I like real light wood, and I prefer one-piece bodies if at all possible. I like to play it acoustically to check how well it resonates. I hold my hands on the body to feel if the wood is really transforming the sound, and also at the top of the headstock to make sure there's a lot of vibration of the sound going through the neck."[12]

Jeff Beck: "I've just been listening to Eric Johnson. Bloody great. There are so many great players around now. It's time to take up something else [laughs]."

 Johnson's Thick, Fuzzy Lead & Pristine Clean Tones, Track 61

Lunch With Hank

There's a legend often told about the first Strat in the UK. Cliff Richard was a star, and his backup band was the Shadows, with Hank Marvin. The Shadows also had a career of their own, playing instrumentals, and they were very influential, somewhat like the Ventures in the States. Dan Smith: "The story goes, the Shadows wanted the same guitar like James Burton played with Ricky Nelson. Remember, people often didn't see a lot of photos of the rock stars of the day — they all assumed the Fender they were looking for was the most expensive one. So Cliff Richard's manager was in Manny's in New York City, and he asked for the top of the line. The most expensive Fender in the store that day was a Fiesta Red Stratocaster with a bird's-eye maple neck and gold hardware. That's the guitar that went to Hank Marvin and started a huge trend in the UK."

Flash forward a quarter century or more, to about March of 1986. Hank Marvin was preparing to move to Australia, so John Hill of Fender UK threw a party at a Holiday Inn in a suburb of London, and presented Hank with a recreation of that historic Fiesta Red Strat. George Blanda built it, the first Custom Shop guitar ever.

Front, from left: Stuart Adamson of Big Country, Eric Clapton, Hank Marvin, Steve Howe, Richard Thompson.
Back, from left: Hal Lindes (formerly of Dire Straits), Dan Smith, Bill Schultz, Jeff Beck, David Gilmour.

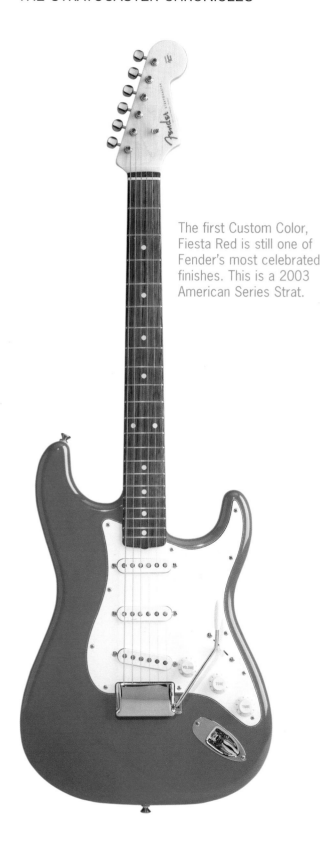

The first Custom Color, Fiesta Red is still one of Fender's most celebrated finishes. This is a 2003 American Series Strat.

Dan Smith: "John invited some of Hank's better known fans and fellow Strat players, but Hank didn't know about all that. The whole thing was a big surprise. Because Hank was getting ready to leave the country, he told John he only had a half-hour, and the only time he could make it was 10 a.m. John panicked, because most of these musicians are never up that early, but they all came, except for Mark Knopfler, who really wanted to come but couldn't make it. They were all hiding behind a curtain. John tells Hank that a few guys had heard about the get-together and wanted his autograph. Hank was in a hurry, but he agreed, and then all these guys came out — Eric Clapton, Jeff Beck, Richard Thompson, David Gilmour, Steve Howe . . . Hank was flabbergasted, and so appreciative. They all ended up spending the whole day together. Some of them hadn't seen each other in years, and they talked about their music and their cars and their families and what was going on in their lives. The last guy to leave was Hank Marvin."

Fullerton Invasion '59: The Strat Arrives in England

"The guitar arrived at a flat shared by Hank, Bruce, and Cliff in Marylebone High Street. When they opened the tweed case, saw the crushed-velvet lining, smelled that smell and saw the pinky-red Strat with bird's-eye maple neck, gold-plated hardware, three pickups and a tremolo arm, no one spoke. No one touched it for a while: they just stared at it. The guitar was the most beautiful thing they'd ever seen. Five years after its creation, this was the first Fender Stratocaster in Britain — an icon."

– from *17 Watts? The Birth of British Rock Guitar*, by Mo Foster

Reinventing a Classic:

The American Standard

You don't mess with an icon. On the other hand, you can't afford to stagnate. (As William Schultz has said, "If you don't grow, you die.") So how would the new Fender company accommodate changing styles and tastes, and adapt its venerable Stratocaster guitar to the needs of the present? During the CBS era, clear answers had often eluded the suits who ran the company. One exec opined in private, "What are we supposed to do — build in the same old mistakes, just to keep the purists happy?"

At the dawn of the Schultz era, things began to come back into focus, and in 1985, with Schultz and his investors now owning the company, Fender faced one of its most daunting design challenges yet: Build a better Stratocaster. Not a reissue, not a cost cutter, not a "Cadillac," not an import — just a basic U.S. Strat. It took courage and confidence for Dan Smith and George Blanda to think they could improve upon Leo Fender's classic design, but then again they knew that Leo himself never rested on his laurels. The idea of leaving technical problems unaddressed would have been as foreign to Leo Fender as goth metal.

A new Strat was developed in 1986, unveiled to key dealers, and introduced to critical raves at the January 1987 NAMM trade show. Details included typical features (three-layer pickguard, one-piece maple neck, etc.), plus a small headstock, 4-bolt neck, a 9½" radius fingerboard with jumbo frets, a TBX tone circuit, a redesigned tremolo with two bearing points instead of six screws, flat-polepiece pickups, a hum-reducing, reverse-polarity pickup in the middle position, a silver transition logo, and a urethane finish. The other key detail: It would be made in the U.S.A. To make sure no one missed the point, the new guitar would be called "American Standard." Conspicuous designation of the U.S. origin of certain models or whole series would be a regular fixture of Fender strategies from now on. (American Standards built in 1994 bear a red, white,

and blue medallion on the headstock, commemorating the instrument's 40th anniversary.)

J.W. Black was a leading guitar repairman in New York City at the time. He recalled: "In the early '80s, Fender was pretty much off the radar as far as my clients and players were concerned, at least in New York. The reissues of '82 were okay, but many players had the real thing and they were still affordable. The buzz was Kramer and Jackson in that mid-'80s era. But when George Blanda and Dan Smith came up with the American Standard, it seemed to be the right thing at

American Standard Stratocaster,
maple-neck version.

the right time. I wonder if Fender would be where it is now, if not for that event from Dan and George."

George Blanda: "Bill Schultz had heard a consistent message from international dealers — the Japanese are targeting the music industry. The fear was,

Cesar Rosas of Los Lobos tries out a lefty 57 Vintage reissue for an impromptu jam.

there goes the guitar market, like cameras or electronics. There had been a defeatist attitude, people thinking American guitars could disappear. So first we looked into countering the imports with low-cost guitars, and then it grew into the more expensive professional guitars as well."

Dan Smith: "Little by little we started to rebuild the company. In October 1985 we opened up manufacturing out in Corona in a 14,000 square foot facility. Within 18 months, we went from building seven guitars a day to 150 a day."

How did you get started on the American Standard?

Dan Smith: "I had experience from the Standards and Elites. I knew what we could get away with and what we couldn't, how far we could push the envelope and still keep everybody happy. Back in the early '80s, we had tried to make an affordable, made in the U.S.A., top quality, modern Stratocaster. By '85 we had learned a lot, and we knew what to do."

Did you ever stop and say, holy cow, I'm about to take Leo Fender's venerated masterpiece and rethink it from top to bottom?

Dan Smith: "No. The respect for him is always there, but I'd had so many years repairing and refretting guitars and flattening out the fretboards, putting different keys on and throwing humbuckers in there and everything else — I'd worked on a *lot* of Stratocasters. I love Fenders, but as I progressed as a player there were things that were more difficult on a Fender. The idea with the American Standard was to make a guitar that would still appeal to the Fender guy but be easier to play. It represented everything I had learned about Fender up to that point."

How did you and George Blanda divide up the labor?

Dan Smith: "George did all the engineering. He took my concept and turned it into something that worked. He is probably the finest and purest engineering talent in the guitar business. There were some things we'd already done that we wanted to keep, like the 2-way adjustable Biflex rod. It had been well received, and we knew that was a solid piece."

The neck radius had gone from 7¼" on the 1950s Strats all the way to 12" on the 2-knob Standard and the Elites. You changed it again on the American Standard.

Dan Smith: "We wanted a neck that was a little easier to play. The flat, 12" radius was fine for Gibson players, but Fender players hated it. So the American Standard's 9½" was a good compromise. We use it for just about everything now, except the reissues. I had James Burton and Steve Cropper try it, and when neither one of those guys said anything I knew it was fine."

The original tremolo was Leo Fender's pride and joy, but the modifications in the '80s turned it into something of a disaster.

Dan Smith: "Yeah, I had learned a lot about tremolo bridges by '85, '86. We thought, okay, we've got to make a bridge that works correctly, we gotta make it simple, something that sounds good, works for production, doesn't cost too much, and still delivers everything Strat players want."

George Blanda: "A fixture of the mid-'80s was the Floyd Rose and similar vibratos, which were well suited to the extreme dive-bomb techniques of the day. Despite those units' popularity, Fender perceived a possible backlash against their complexity, the necessity of tuning it at the bridge, having to use wrenches to adjust it, and its effects on tone. We decided to take a different direction, and go with a unit that was fairly similar to the vintage design but would stay in tune better. It has two pivot points instead of the six screws."

What about the metal used for the bridge components?

Dan Smith: "On the earliest Fenders, they used bent steel pieces. First they'd stamp it with *Fender Pat Pend* or whatever they had to stamp, and then the flat piece went into the forming die that did the bending, like for the little hook in the back for the saddle-adjustment screws; we actually had to make that tool again for the reissues, so the bridges would be authentic.

"Then during CBS there were a lot of die-cast pot-metal parts, and we got rid of them. For the American Standard we used what's called powdered stainless. Instead of a liquid, there's a powdered metal that's forced into a mold and formed under high pressure. It's solid, stronger than the die-cast, and sounds better. In fact, I like the American Standard saddles, because the powdered stainless takes a little bit of the

harshness or brightness out of the Strat. We still use it on the American Series, too."

George Blanda: "The 2-point tremolo design is simple and straight ahead. It's a good sounding, better working system, and it's reasonably cost effective. We wanted a bridge that didn't have to go through the bending process but still sounded good. We eliminated casting, and we didn't want brass. We found out about the powdered-metal process. The tremolo block [which Leo Fender and Freddie Tavares had called the

Funkmaster Nile Rodgers of Chic played "Le Freak" and "Good Times" on a '59 hardtail Strat he nicknamed the Hitmaker. "Whenever I needed a hit, I used that guitar. . . . For my style of playing, the Stratocaster gives me the clarity and brightness I need to play precise rhythm. But it also has enough warmth so I can be bright without being brittle."

inertia bar] is low-carbon steel, like the vintage, but made using the powdered-metal process. The first year or two they were nickel plated, then painted, and from the mid '90s on, powder coated. The base plate is cold-rolled steel that's punched out of a flat sheet."

 Pick out Nile in the Riff Medley, Track 37

Since 1956, most Strats had been made of alder, except for the ash-body transparent finishes.

Dan Smith: "For a while, the environmentalists didn't want us cutting alder. There was an endangered species controversy, with some logging restrictions up in Oregon, so we had to use poplar. Leo had used it on many guitars — Musicmasters and others — and we later used it for the Bullet guitars. It's a good wood. We used it on some American Standards in the early '90s. From the beginning, poplar was spec'd to be used on the American Standard as a substitute."

George Blanda: "All the Strat bodies were alder up until about 1990. When it got so hard to get alder, we were faced with either using poplar or not making guitars. There's a misconception that poplar is not a good tone wood. Actually, it's fine. James Burton actually specified it for his signature Tele in the late '80s, after trying a lot of different bodies. We never regarded poplar as a second-rate wood, but a lot of people preferred alder so when the restrictions eased, we were able to go back to alder in '93 or '94."

Under the pickguard, the American Standard had a big rectangular hole, so you could fit any sort of pickup combination in there.

George Blanda: "Later on, some people said the tone suffered from the big 'hog rout' for the pickups [also known as the 'swimming pool'], but when we devised the Standard, the popular thing wasn't so much the Stevie Ray Vaughan tone or the Texas blues sound. People were looking more for the kind of sound Andy Summers was getting, and lots of Strat players were really into the funky 2 and 4 positions. Our perception was that the big rout actually *enhanced* that sound. We thought there was a little less midrange, and a little more highs and lows."

Some of the guitars had a separate wood veneer on the top and back.

George Blanda: "Remember that in the '80s, those hard, bright, shiny finishes were a big thing. For the solid colors, we went with the veneers because they held those finishes well. Our marketing people perceived this as the way to go. Dealers had been returning some of the previous guitars because mineral deposits sometimes caused the finish to sink into the grain a little bit. The veneering helped solve that problem."

Dan Smith: "Those deposits make hard lines in the wood called aggregate rays, particularly with alder. When the wood dries, it moves around, but the hard mineral deposits don't move, so that can make little raised lines. Dealers complained, because other guitars had thick finishes that hid everything and looked like a piece of plastic. If dealers keep sending them back, we don't have any choice. We change it, using what least affects the sound of the instrument. At first, the American Standard finishes were all urethane — undercoats, color coats and top coats. We went to a polyester undercoat for a while to address the aggregate rays and the complaints about shrinking grain. We continued to use urethane for the top coats, and either urethane or lacquer for the color coat, depending on the color. We then went to the veneer, which we felt was less intrusive and did a better job of covering the grain-shrink problem."

George Blanda: "We had done a veneered maple top on the Strat Ultra, so we knew how to do it. We kept the veneers after we went back to alder, for appearance's sake, so for a while there it was alder on alder."

Dan Smith: "When we eliminated the veneer, we went back to the same type of polyester undercoat we use on the vintage series. We also added a 22nd fret on a fretboard extension — we didn't have to change the neck pocket or move the pickups. I'm not sure what people do up there, but for guys who wanted the extra fret, it's on there."

George Blanda: "That was Marketing's wish; it just seemed what the market wanted at the time. We also put in a reverse-polarity pickup in the middle, which makes it hum-canceling in the 2 and 4 'in between' positions. We still do it on the American Series, and pretty much across the board except for the vintage."

What was the TBX tone control?

Dan Smith: "'TBX' stood for 'Treble Bass Xpander,' one of those marketing names. It was a stacked control — two pots with one knob on top. One was a standard 250k pot; Leo had picked the 250's in the first place because they sound nice. Underneath that was a pot with a circuit on it. At the midpoint — the 5 setting — it was equivalent to a normal control set all the way up, on 10. When you rolled the TBX back toward zero it worked just like a regular tone control except with a short range. When you went back up to 10, it was the equivalent of removing the control altogether from the circuit, and it let a lot more high end through."

The American Standard became Fender's flagship guitar for 13 years, the longest run of any basic, mainstream Stratocaster.

Dan Smith: "It was huge. We're very proud of it. The idea was to go back to the best aspects of the pre-CBS Strats, then get rid of the not-so-good ideas that people had done later, and then improve the consistency of production, update the tremolo so it would stay in tune better, make the neck more comfortable, make the pickups less noisy, get better sounding parts and a more versatile tone control, and make the whole thing simple and affordable. Guitarists are pretty conservative. They may spike their hair and dye it blue, but when it comes to what they play they seem to like things that were designed in the '50s, so what we do is a lot of refinement. We told ourselves, let's build the guitar Leo would be building today if he had evolved the basic Stratocaster himself."

"In an office crammed with solidbodies, fellow workers and curiosity seekers consistently sought out this particular axe for a quick romp. Amazing, how after all these years, a real Fender Strat still exudes such magic."

– *Guitar Player* review of the American Standard, July '92

Highly figured necks await assembly in the Custom Shop.

The Custom Shop's Classic Player Strat: Vintage Noiseless pickups, abalone dots, locking Sperzel tuners, and a gold anodized pickguard, among other premium features.

No Limits: The Custom Shop

Back in June 1977 a CBS Vice President had explained to *Musician's News* that Fender had had "some bad experiences with custom instruments" and went so far as to assert, "Do we create exotic instruments? No! Our products are the basic bread-and-butter heroes of the musical instrument field."

William Schultz' vision was much broader. Following the 1985 buyout, he recognized that even restoring the quality of the mainstream guitars might not be enough to salvage his troubled company. Besides, he never liked the "working man's guitar" idea; it was fine as far as it went, but it was too limiting. Schultz imagined a new kind of Fender guitar, a new kind of Fender company. He told videographer Dennis Baxter: "It's a working man's guitar, yes, but Fender is more than that. People laughed when I said I'm gonna open a custom shop, but a Fender is a top-of-the-line product. It can be used anywhere. It can be a collectible. It can be used with a top artist. There's no limit as to where we can go with quality and playability."

The Custom Shop concept actually stretched back to the late '70s, when John Page built the occasional one-off guitar for Fender artists. Elliot Easton of the Cars was one such player. He explained to Dennis Baxter: "In the Custom Shop, it's one person building that guitar, so you can call and say, 'I have a little idea I would like to try.' You can get into it as deeply as you like — how many winds in the pickup, or what you want the body to weigh, the wood grain you want." George Blanda had been hired to build custom instruments but wound up in R&D, so in January 1987 the establishment of the Custom Shop fell to acclaimed Texas guitar builder Michael Stevens and John Page, by then a nine-year Fender veteran.

Soon after the Shop's inception, its role began to extend far beyond building a few one-offs. Scores of Stratocasters and Strat offshoots were eventually produced in limited quantities: a 27" scale Subsonic with a low B string, signature guitars for Ritchie Blackmore,

Dick Dale, Robert Cray, and others, reissues of Strats from '54, '56, '58, '60, '69 and other years, modern refinements of the basic design (the American Classic, Custom Classic, Classic Player), a Jimi Hendrix Woodstock guitar, Strats commemorating the contributions of Bill Carson and Freddie Tavares, Strats with bodies made out of everything from swamp ash to hand-engraved aluminum, Strats with custom electronics, two pickups, synth pickups, set necks, double necks, bird's-eye maple necks, ebony fretboards, and Floyd Roses, some of them embellished with figured-maple tops, diamond inlays, rhinestones, gold-anodized pickguards, or dazzling custom paint jobs. The quality, artistry and celebrity of these Strats became essential to Fender's claim as the number one guitar company in the world.

John Page: "We knew the biggest thing we lost after the CBS debacle was image. Fender had gone from being the working man's guitar to being the working man's nightmare to some degree. So we had to give it prestige again, give it quality. So the idea was to have these guys out in the 'back 40' woodchuckin' a few exquisite guitars each month, making everything by hand in this little 800-square-foot shop carved out of the Corona factory. At first it was just Michael and me, hand fretting and hand shaping the necks, using some of the machinery from the old Fullerton plant."

The staff was soon augmented by several talented craftspeople and artists, some of whom were well established prior to their arrival at Corona. Those builders and their breathtaking instruments deserve a book of their own, and they have one. The extravagantly illustrated *Fender Custom Shop Guitar Gallery* (photography by Pitkin Studio, text by Richard Smith) is a must-have volume for any Fender enthusiast.

Some of the Master Builders in the first decade were Gene Baker, J.W. Black, John English, Alan Hamel, Mark Kendrick, Fred Stuart, John Suhr, and Stephen Stern, all of whom are profiled in Smith's *Gallery* and some of whom still build guitars in the Custom Shop.

When did it dawn on somebody that the Shop might serve functions beyond producing one-offs and showpieces?

John Page: "In the first few months. We got inundated with orders right out of the chute, especially from Japan. They wanted vintage guitars that were absolutely nailed in every detail, and we could do that. Here's just two guys with 600 orders, so we needed to expand right away. Now the challenge was to do this incredible detail work but in quantity, a limited production run rather than onesies or twosies."

What does the title "Master Builder" signify?

John Page: "When I started that concept, it referred to a person who could do any guitar-building task, make design decisions based on artists' requirements, answer any question, and render exquisite quality in every way. One of the first Master Builders was J. Black." [Note: Black also goes by 'J.W.']

J.W. Black: "Prior to becoming Master Builders, the other craftsmen might take a body from one part of production and a neck from another, or specialize in making only necks or only bodies. Mike Stevens and I were the only Master Builders in the beginning who took an instrument all the way through from planning to completion, sourcing out and building all the components. In the early days, the only shared process, typically, was paint."

The Custom Shop's Dick Dale Stratocaster has a reverse headstock and bridge pickup, a Chartreuse Sparkle finish, a toggle switch to activate the neck and middle pickups together, and bare-bones controls - master volume only. If you've got an .018 gauge string on your guitar, chances are it's a G. On Dick Dale's personal Strat, it's the high E.

Richard McDonald: "As the Shop grew, they staffed it by going through the labor pool and picking the best machine guys, the best sanders — they built a team out of Fender's elite workers."

One of your early models was the Yngwie Malmsteen guitar.

John Page: "Things like that were specialized and would have a limited demand, so it made more sense to go through the Custom Shop. We could also do limited runs like the 35th Anniversary Strat in 1989, the 40th Anniversary in 1994, and the Homer Haynes Strat."

Was every Custom Shop guitar either part of a limited run or built to fill an individual order?

John Page: "We also had 'spec' guitars, where somebody would get a looney idea and go ahead and build it, a one-of-a-kind, even if no one had ordered it. We'd worry about selling it later. This experimentation helps keep the entire company on the cutting edge."

How did the role of the Custom Shop evolve?

John Page: "After a few years we merged the Custom Shop and Fender R&D, and the exchange between the Shop and factory opened up. The Shop dealt directly with artists, so it was a quicker response. As soon as artists would start doing something different, we'd have new designs — boom. We could streamline the R&D process, and pass on to the factory ideas for models or features."

Richard McDonald: "Quick response continues to be a big part of the Custom Shop's value. They can turn on a dime, whereas a big factory trying to make guitars for global consumption is a different story."

J.W. Black: "It was a mutual thing early on. We'd do some things on our own, but Dan Smith would come in from the factory side with his own ideas, like limited runs that could be introduced through the Custom Shop."

John Page: "There was a lot of crossover. The Telecoustic started out as a high-dollar, labor-intensive piece in the Custom Shop but later got sent over to Japan and became an affordable import, so the idea was, we'd experiment with new designs and make one or two pieces that could then be taken in different directions. The Custom Shop is a proving ground for all sorts of things."

Richard McDonald: "That openness and crossover is still the deal, still essential, but now, the Custom Shop activities are being driven more by the people who actually build the guitars. From the creative side, I make a lot of requests, but they're general, and the Custom Shop comes up with great products for a trade show or a retail store's grand opening or whatever the case might be. I ask them if they want to co-brand with someone, or maybe work with particular artists — painters, engravers, carvers. Mike Eldred and I oversee that part of it — some of the artist rela-

At various times available
in Custom Shop and
factory versions, the
long-neck Subsonic has
a hardtail bridge, a 27"
scale, and BEADGB
tuning, low to high.

Built by J.W. Black and pinstriped by Dennis Ricklefs, this unique guitar has stock pickups with lipstick covers. It was auctioned in 2001 at a Petersen Automotive Museum exhibit titled "Cars & Guitars of Rock 'N Roll."

tions and the product development. It's always a team process, and the Custom Shop brings a lot of talent to the table."

Several models started in the Custom Shop and then moved to the factory, like the Stevie Ray Vaughan and Robert Cray Signature guitars. Did you also pass along new production techniques?

John Page: "Yes, a lot of things. We might introduce a new piece of equipment like a neck duplicator, or find a better way of doing the exact contouring of a vintage body, or an improvement in the truss rod geometry. Many new pickups started in the Shop. A lot of the extra fret dressing and extra work on the nut that went to the American Deluxe and later the American Series originated in the Shop as well, thanks to J. Black. He brought in a lot of new ideas."

J.W. Black: "One thing was wood selection. We were discriminating in the Custom Shop, and we passed that along to the factory, that attention to detail. Rolling the fingerboard edges [a technique later applied to the American Deluxe Series and then the American Series] was a critical thing. Mike Lewis really hammered that home. Bringing Bill Turner in from EMG and improving all the pickups was another move. It all fit together. It's such a team thing. Mike would say, can we try this? The Custom Shop would say, we can do it. Dan Smith would say, we can make this happen in the factory, too. Even though the factory and Custom Shop operate independently, there's always a free exchange of ideas, with everybody contributing."

The "art guitars" are a whole separate category.

John Page: "Yes, that's not about the potential for a production guitar. The art guitars are about the guitar being a canvas, if you will, for a particularly gifted artist to use as a starting point. The pieces like Fred Stuart was doing were clearly beyond the normal one-off Custom Shop guitar, and far beyond the idea where a lot of factories just paint graphics on their guitars. It's a much higher level. The other thing was the co-promotion Stratocasters we did with companies like Harley-Davidson or Playboy."

So the functions of the Custom Shop are to build one-off guitars for individuals, build showpiece guitars to demonstrate the highest levels of artistry, build some of the artist guitars and other limited-run models, act as a lab and a proving ground for ideas that might get transferred over to the factory, respond quickly to trends, and help the whole company stay ahead of the curve.

Richard McDonald: "Historically, that's all true. Even today, I might need some designs out of the Custom Shop to be prototypes for new factory guitars or something out of Mexico, but the amount of R&D work coming out of there these days is nowhere near what Dan Smith's own team is doing. About 95% of the Custom Shop is vintage now, which is fine, because the factory's own R&D people — Dan Smith, Bill Turner, Michael Frank-Braun, and George Blanda — are so incredible, so freakin' brilliant. Those guys are a fountain of great ideas."

John Page: "These roles change, but Fender will always put value on having dreamers in the company. If you don't dream, you stagnate. The Custom Shop is always thrilled to build for anybody, whether you're Joe Schmoe or Eric Clapton."

What effect has the Custom Shop had on the worldwide perception of Fender?

Richard McDonald: "It has freed up players' imaginations. The sky is now the limit. The guitar can now be an art form. The Custom Shop inspires dreams, and they can make those dreams come true. It has shown people that almost anything is possible."

John Page: "The Custom Shop introduced a concept that had never been considered at Fender. It helped take the company to a new level, along with a tremendous amount of exposure and marketing benefits, too. Fender was always considered the Chevrolet of electric guitars, which is fine. But the Custom Shop shows that Fender can also be the Ferrari."

John Page, left, and Michael Stevens, posing with a stringless banjo-like object at one of the Dallas guitar shows that sparked a long-running national trend.

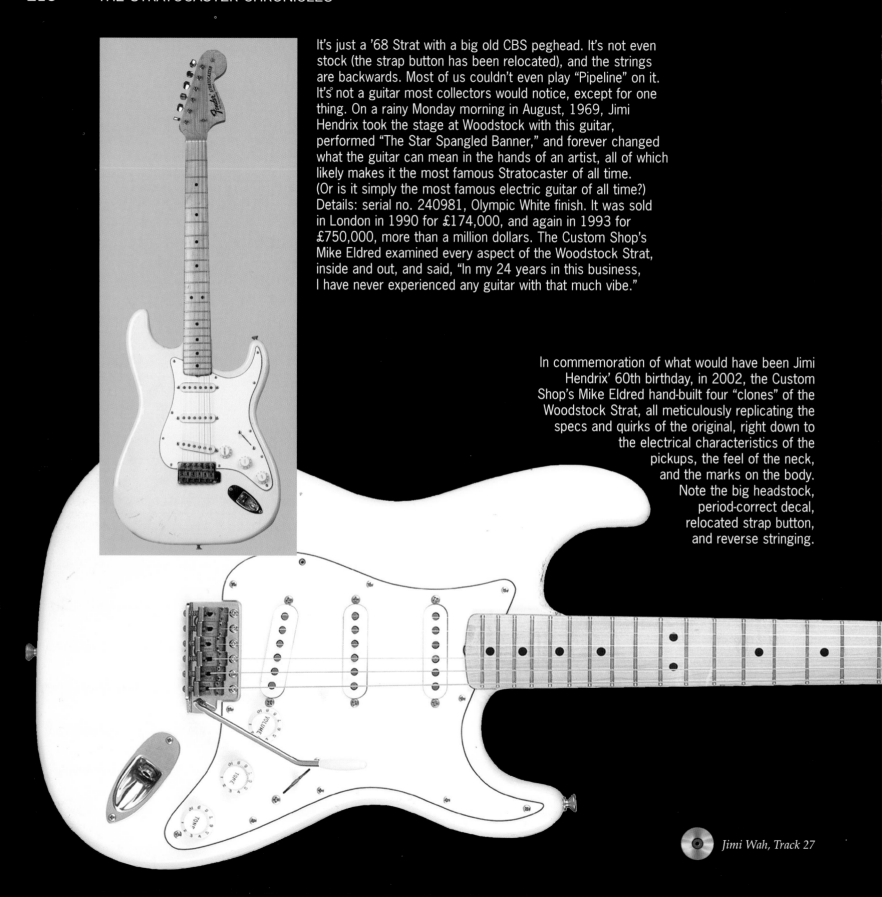

It's just a '68 Strat with a big old CBS peghead. It's not even stock (the strap button has been relocated), and the strings are backwards. Most of us couldn't even play "Pipeline" on it. It's not a guitar most collectors would notice, except for one thing. On a rainy Monday morning in August, 1969, Jimi Hendrix took the stage at Woodstock with this guitar, performed "The Star Spangled Banner," and forever changed what the guitar can mean in the hands of an artist, all of which likely makes it the most famous Stratocaster of all time. (Or is it simply the most famous electric guitar of all time?) Details: serial no. 240981, Olympic White finish. It was sold in London in 1990 for £174,000, and again in 1993 for £750,000, more than a million dollars. The Custom Shop's Mike Eldred examined every aspect of the Woodstock Strat, inside and out, and said, "In my 24 years in this business, I have never experienced any guitar with that much vibe."

In commemoration of what would have been Jimi Hendrix' 60th birthday, in 2002, the Custom Shop's Mike Eldred hand-built four "clones" of the Woodstock Strat, all meticulously replicating the specs and quirks of the original, right down to the electrical characteristics of the pickups, the feel of the neck, and the marks on the body. Note the big headstock, period-correct decal, relocated strap button, and reverse stringing.

Jimi Wah, Track 27

Aside from the Custom Shop clone, there was an earlier Woodstock-inspired guitar, the "Jimi Hendrix Stratocaster" of the late 1990s, shown here. While Jimi played a flipped-over right-handed Strat, the Jimi Hendrix Stratocaster was basically a left-handed guitar – but it was meant to be flipped over, with its heavy strings on top and its strap button on the small horn (now on top), giving right-handers a chance to experience Jimi-style, upside-down ergonomics.

Yet another guitar was the Voodoo Strat of the late '90s, which combined conventional right-hand stringing, trem operation, body shape, and control placement with several reversed, Jimi-esque features: headstock, tuner locations, string lengths behind the nut, polepiece staggers, and treble pickup alignment. Reviewers found advantages in both tone and playability.

The Jimi Hendrix Stratocaster®

Tone king Billy Gibbons with a Custom Shop guitar designed in collaboration with the So-Cal Speed Shop (founded the same year as Fender, 1946). One of the Strat tales spun by the good Reverend came in an interview with Jas Obrecht, who asked, "Do you still have the Strat Jimi gave you?" Billy Gibbons: "Yep, I do. I think I ended up using that on a couple of the cuts on *Deguello*. That's an original pink Strat, a '58 with the tremolo bar. Hendrix gave that to me in '68. It was at Fort Worth, Texas, and I think we had both just finished breaking all the mirrors in the dressing room. . . . After the smoke had cleared we got back to a little blues picking and traded guitars. I had another Strat, a '57, but it was left-handed, so he used it better than I did [*laughs*]! So he got that one, and gave me the pink one."

Roomful of Blues veteran Ronnie Earl, here with the James Harmon Band at the Lone Star Café in New York. "I have all five springs because I can't afford to break a string ... I have to have it set up so that if I break a string, it'll stay completely in tune. All my guitars are like that, so I just have to really bear down when I play whammy."[13]

Guitar Wars: Attack Of The Clones

During the late CBS period, various Strat models had been inspired by the vintage boom, the hot-rod and replacement-parts trends, the top of the line "Cadillac" concept, and the "super versatility" craze. Except for the reissues, all were dropped after two or three years, and production remained severely limited after the factory reopened in the fall of 1985. Ironically, right about the time "Strat Mania" was kicking in, Fender could only stand by and watch as other manufacturers sold *acres* of guitars by exploiting a simple formula: Let's knock off a Stratocaster and load it up with more powerful pickups or a locking trem, or give it a flame maple top, abalone markers, fingerboard binding, or a glued-in neck. The market was saturated with every imaginable sort of Strat clone — souped up, stripped down, glammed out, high-tech, low-rent, you name it.

As Fender ramped up its new facility in Corona, it decided to meet the knockoffs head-on. Dan Smith: "Whenever we made just one kind of Stratocaster, we watched all the other companies making all this stuff with all the options Fender wasn't offering. Every time we left a hole in the line, somebody else filled it up. Some of those products were aimed at just a few players with particular needs or tastes. The classic marketing concept says 80% of your business is done with 20% of your models, so why not drop that other 80% of production and save costs? And the answer is, you lose 20% of your business, that's why. Some of our products aren't about volume sales. They're about showing what kind of quality we can do, or serving players with very specific needs. We decided we had to jump in and specialize."

Fender jumped in, all right, but just how deep the jump into specialization would turn out to be wouldn't be revealed until the 1990s.

The Vintage Plus

In 1986, while Fender may have had a 40-year-old legacy, it was a one-year-old company, having started over after the buyout. To counter the attack of the

Jimmie Vaughan. His brother Stevie Ray recalled, "He really was the reason why I started to play, watching him and seeing what could be done." Jimmie's favorite old Strat is a beat-up '62, and he also gets plenty of mileage out of his Signature models.

Fantasy Blues Jam, Track 59

"I'd always been avoiding the wang bar ... but I was so blown away after seeing Jeff Beck, I got a Fender Strat Plus. There's a lot of good things you can do with it."[14]

— *Nils Lofgren*

The Strat Plus appeared in 1987.

clones, the reborn Fender imported impressive guitars from Japan, soon introduced the promising American Standard, and continued its successful reissues. A parallel tactic was to dust off the Vintage Plus, a concept that went back to CBS. It was intended to invoke Strats from the classic era but also to sport several upgrades, sort of like a Deuce Coupe with fuel injection and a multi-CD changer. Various in-house samples were equipped with alternate pickup designs, a flatter fingerboard, bigger frets, better tuning keys, onboard preamps, different types of hardware, and other features.

The programming shortcomings of the big CNC machines in use at the end of the CBS era had resulted in some Strats with chubbier horns and slightly wider body perimeters. Aside from whatever specialized components the Vintage Plus would ultimately feature, it would also be a way to reintroduce the exact perimeter of the original bodies, and to correct the anomalies of the '80s version of the smaller headstock.

Despite the appearance of an active circuit-equipped prototype at a 1986 trade show, the Vintage Plus was never produced. Still, as a concept guitar, it would inspire designs that manifested the final piece of the emerging strategy: If anyone's going to re-imagine *our* Stratocaster to fit the specialty niches, it ought to be Fender.

Boutique Buddies & The Strat Plus

Don Lace was a successful electronics designer and entrepreneur with decades of experience in several fields, including magnetics. With direction from Dan Smith, he developed devices that resembled guitar pickups but were actually multi-magnet pickup alternatives without separate polepieces. These Fender-Lace Sensors were intended to achieve one of the holy grails of pickup design — single-coil tone without the noise. Several high-end Strats such as the Ultra and the Eric Clapton and Jeff Beck Signature models were eventually outfitted with color-coded Fender-Lace Sensors, each with its own tonal contour. Mr. Lace died in 1992.

On some nonlocking tremolo-equipped guitars, strings scrape back and forth through the nut slots during tremolo operation, sometimes getting stuck and knocking the guitar out of tune (see Leo Fender's comments on the interaction of peghead design and trem function, p. 66). To reduce or eliminate the problem, Englishman Trev Wilkinson designed a string nut that employed needle-bearing rollers for each string at the contact point.

Bob Sperzel's Cleveland-based company specialized in form-tool grinding and worked with clients such as Boeing and Pratt & Whitney before coming to the music industry. He reported: "We're tooling specialists. That's my real game. Our tolerances are plus or minus a half a thousandth, so I could make tuning keys with a precision the business hadn't seen. We were on the 25th Anniversary Stratocaster with non-locking keys, but the thing took off and we couldn't keep up with the orders [*laughs*]. In the early '80s or so we came up with our locking tuner, and I showed it to Dan Smith and George Blanda. We made tuners for Fender for three or four years; after that, we'd still make them from time to time for the Custom Shop."

With his work on The Strat's circuitry back in 1980, Dan Armstrong had broken ground by being the first "name" outsider to join forces with Fender's in-house design team. Now, in 1986, other leading designers were consulted. George Blanda: "Working on the Vintage Plus, we were talking to Don Lace, Trev Wilkinson, Bob Sperzel — all these boutique hardware and pickup people. We were looking for cutting-edge modifications. Some of the new Strat protos even had locking tremolos and humbuckers, but at that time it was decided those things were too far outside the realm of the Strat."

Fender settled on the basic Vintage Plus idea and outfitted the guitar with Fender-Lace Sensors, the Wilkinson roller nut, Sperzel locking tuners, and the two-point tremolo from the American Standard. The name was changed to Strat Plus. Priced between the new American Standard and the two vintage reissues, the Strat Plus of March 1987 was a landmark, the first Strat with Fender-Lace Sensors, and the first boutique-component "super Strat" of the reborn company. In 1989, it received the industry's Music & Sound Award for Most Innovative Guitar.

"Nothing But Strats" — The Guitar Of The '80s

Like any magazine journalists, *Guitar Player*'s editors know that if they're biased toward a particular advertiser, or merely *appear* biased, that advertiser's competitors — and readers as well — will be quick to criticize and rightly so. And yet in 1987 the magazine published an issue that at first glance seemed to throw its 20-year non-favoritism policy out the window. It featured a brand new Stratocaster guitar on the cover, not because it promoted a typical "new gear" article but because the Strat was itself the main event, the cover story. The reasoning: The Stratocaster's unprecedented dominance and influence had altered virtually the entire electric guitar market.

The magazine addressed the welcome reinvigoration of Fender by its new owners and the worldwide popularity of its marquee guitar, as well as a market awash in Strat clones manufactured by many foreign and domestic companies. An offshoot of the trend was a vast array of retrofit parts for real Strats and Strat copies — everything from unfinished necks and bodies to plastic or brass tips for tremolo bars. For the first time, the electric guitar community had what amounted to a virtual standard. Eric Johnson put it this way: "No other guitar really has that modular aspect so completely. You can tailor it to your own tastes."

Then, as now, the extent to which non-Fender SLO's (Strat-Like Objects) borrowed from the genuine article ranged from "remotely Strat-inspired" to "See you in court, pal." This line between somewhat Strat-ish guitars and shameless, legally actionable ripoffs may be in the eye of the guitarist (or the eye of a trademark judge), but in any case *Guitar Player* examined several of these issues and called the whole phenomenon "Strat Mania."

The Edge, describing the "lovely clean tones" on U2's *All That You Can't Leave Behind*: "I have a great '50s Strat, and I plugged it straight into the Bassman. On this record I often found myself simply enjoying the pure tone of the instrument."

"It's overwhelming," reported Bob Capel, from Sam Ash Music in New York City. "Very few manufacturers *don't* make one. Kramer's got 'em, Charvel's got 'em, Jackson's got 'em ... of the people coming into the store, I'd say at least 70 or 80% want a Strat or Strat-styled guitar." Al Julson at Knut-Koupee in Minneapolis agreed: "Every company's got at least one, it seems — Guild, B.C. Rich, Music Man." John Cannon, at Hollywood's Guitar Center, said, "Without a doubt it's the dominant design of the '80s. More specifically,

you need to divide the '80s into two parts. Prior to '85 there was the Explorer, the Flying V, the Randy Rhoads-type Jackson, the wild shapes. Since '85 it's been nothing but Strats."

Mike McGuire built the expensive Valley Arts guitars favored by Larry Carlton, Steve Lukather, and other discriminating artists. He was asked, why make them look like Stratocasters? "Popular demand," he answered. "On a truly custom instrument you'll do whatever the customer wants, and yet the Strat is such a classic we've found that any time you alter it, the customer is less happy. The vast, vast majority request a Strat-type." Such praise acknowledged Leo Fender's foresight, although author Richard Smith reported that the father of the Strat resented "Strat Mania," believing it was rooted in mere nostalgia and also that his later, less celebrated designs had improved upon the Strat in every significant respect.

Despite the advantages to Fender of the Strat's unparalleled popularity, the profusion of clones also burdened the company with legal headaches that persist to this day. After all, while some players may use the term "Strat" as imprecise shorthand for "Strat-type guitar," there is no such thing as a non-Fender Strat. "The ownership of that name is one of this company's most valuable assets," explained Dan Smith, with understandable frustration. "And we spend a great deal of money every year protecting it. Every time somebody misuses the term 'Strat' in reference to another company's guitar, it's not just inaccurate, it's *wrong*. It's a violation of our rights in that name."

The undisputed Guitar Of The '80s seems to be evolving into the Guitar Of The New Millennium. It is still copied by other manufacturers, and still widely heard in funk, rock, metal, neo-surf, blues, fusion, and any number of offshoots and hybrids. It's all over television — blue jeans commercials, beer commercials, MTV, soundtracks. Most session pros wouldn't dream of showing up at a date without one. What Mike McGuire said back in '87 is still true today: "The sound of the Strat — it's everywhere."

Ensenada: No-Excuses Guitars

Fender products have been built by an ethnically diverse crew ever since Lilly Sanchez started wiring up amp chassis and Tadeo Gomez began penciling his now-legendary initials on early-'50s ash bodies and maple necks. This is probably why Fender's factory in Ensenada, Mexico, which opened on May 6, 1987, feels less like a "foreign" operation and more like another world-class Fender factory that just happens to be a few hours south of Corona.

Aside from their employing many Spanish-speaking workers and being located in cities with Hispanic names, the Ensenada and Corona facilities have a lot in common. Mike Lewis: "People are just blown away when they see Ensenada. It's a huge facility with all the modern machines and highly trained workers. They're blasting music in there all the time, the energy is electric, and the pride and love that go into what they're doing is incredible."

Richard McDonald: "There used to be this 'Third World' perception about Mexico, but that's been gone for years. We knew from day one the product had to be not only good but *unbelievably* good because it was from Mexico and would be scrutinized. We got our dealers down there, because when they walk in and see a thousand highly trained people working their butts off in an ultra-modern facility, and you can drop your piece of chicken and pick it up and eat it because the floor is cleaner than your hand, then that 'Third World' thing disappears.

"Here's what it's really about: *Any* Fender instrument, no matter where it's made, has to pass muster with me and people like Ritchie Fliegler, Mike Lewis, Dan Smith, Joey Carducci — this is a tough crowd. And don't forget Bill Carson. If I send a new product to Bill, and there's *one* little thing wrong, the phone's gonna ring and it's Bill Carson and oh my god, you better stand back. So the bottom line is always quality, and the value of the Mexican Fenders is unmatchable. The bang for the buck speaks for itself, so they are no-excuses guitars. We also make our Hot Rod amps down there, our Cyber amps — some of the coolest things we make — so now 'Mexican Fender' has become a positive thing."

The first Mexican-built Stratocaster guitars were produced in 1989. These days, some of the instruments that are finished in Ensenada actually begin life in Corona. Mike Lewis: "This is why the country of origin question is so vague now, and less important. If it says 'American' in the series name, then it's American made, period, but otherwise there can be a lot of crossover. The same guy in Corona who loads up a Shoda [computer-controlled router] or a Zuckerman [multi-spindle copy lathe] for a Clapton Strat might also load it for a 4600 [the in-house part number for the Standard Strat], but with a slightly different body blank. Then he'll just stack the 4600 body on a pallet marked for Ensenada, where they can do sanding, prepping, painting, and assembly."

Richard McDonald: "For us to be responsive, the Corona-Ensenada relationship is fluid, with stuff going back and forth all the time. It changes constantly. We may even do a process in Corona just because a machine's broken or being maintenanced in Mexico. Things come up. We respond and do what we need to do to get great guitars into players' hands, fast, so your 'Mexican-made' guitar may have been painted and buffed in Corona, just because of what was going on that week." According to *The Music Trades* magazine, as of 2000 the Ensenada factory covered almost a quarter-million square feet and employed about 600 workers.

"It belongs in the Metropolitan Museum of Art."

— *Bob Capel, Sam Ash Music, New York*

Artist Series Strats:
Diversity, Quirks & Doing The Whole Job

For many guitars, few attributes are more important to sales than their association with famous players. Duane Eddy with his Gretsches and Guilds, George Harrison with his Gretsches and Rickenbackers, James Burton with his Telecaster, Randy Rhoads with his V-shaped Jacksons — we've seen it time and again. The Strat is an obvious example. It would be hard to name a guitar whose devotees are more numerous, diverse, influential, or successful.

Fender touted its artist endorsements from the beginning, its '50s and '60s catalogs brimming with galleries of neatly dressed musicians with their Jaguars, piggyback amps, steel guitars, and all the rest. Don Randall: "We never paid a dime to any of those artists. We might loan them the gear, and we'd repair it or replace it, but they played it because they chose to do so, because it fit their needs." The roster included red-hot virtuosos (Speedy West, Jimmy Bryant), jazz pioneers (Monk Montgomery), teen idols (Ricky Nelson, improbably posed with a Jazzmaster — but who cares?), and pop stars (the Beach Boys), plus a bevy of other artists (the Kings IV, Roy Wiggins, Nappy Lamare, the Mulcays, etc.) who may have been well known in jazz, pop, or country circles but were best known among rock and rollers simply for their appearance in Fender literature.

Arena rocker Richie Sambora strikes a classic pose with his locking-trem Signature guitar. "You have to have a vision, what you want to sound like, who you want to play like, how you want it to feel. An important part of capturing that is the right tool. That's your lifeblood."

At the urging of Jimmie Vaughan, Fender went ahead with the Stevie Ray Vaughan Signature Stratocaster, in development at the time of Stevie's death in 1990. The SRV Strat is modeled after Stevie's famous Number One. According to former Custom Shop Master Builder Larry Brooks, "Stevie wanted a little more bottom, so we put 600 winds on each pickup." Details: left-hand trem bar, gold hardware, and a thick oval neck with a relatively flat 12" radius fingerboard.

Also shown: a James Burton Signature Telecaster, and a mid-'90s Clapton Strat with Lace Sensors (note the Eric Clapton signature and "Blackie" on the peghead; also see p. 222).

Despite this abundance of candidates and despite the success of rival manufacturers' "signature" guitars, Fender was a latecomer to the concept. Gibson had pioneered the idea with its Nick Lucas flat-top of 1928, and capitalized on it to great success with its Les Paul starting in 1952. By late 1954, Gretsch had signed Chet Atkins, who within a few years would succeed Les Paul as perhaps America's most prominent mainstream pop guitarist. Other companies also offered models ostensibly conceived in collaboration with professional players, including Epiphone (Harry Volpe), Harmony (Roy Smeck), Mosrite (Joe Maphis, the Ventures), Kay (Barney Kessel), and Guild (Johnny Smith, Duane Eddy).

But while Stratocasters were embraced by many influential players throughout the model's first three decades, none of those guitars bore the name of Buddy Holly or Jimi Hendrix or Eric Clapton. (The 1980 reverse-headstock Strat inspired by Jimi Hendrix doesn't count. It appeared a decade after the artist's death, barely resembled the guitars he had played, and was never produced in quantity. And "Mary Kaye," of course, was merely a nickname for blonde Strats with gold hardware; see p. 92.)

It was not until the arrival of Dan Smith and Bill Schultz that Fender adopted the artist guitar concept, but almost as if making up for lost time, it did so in a big way. From the get-go, the mantra was: no compromises. Ritchie Fliegler: "We have the privilege of working for Fender. We're all players. We can talk to these artists. We understand what they do, what they want. Some of our signature guitars are quirky — we use the term 'idiosyncratic' — but we make them that way anyway. Unlike some companies, we don't water them down to make them more sellable. It's more of a tribute to artists in the Fender orbit who have been playing a guitar like this, often well before they're widely recognized. So the object is not to sell a ton of guitars. It's to say thank you, to pay back some of these artists who have done good things for us for no reason other than they love our instruments. They've been good for Fender, and good for the guitar."

One ad for the Tom Delonge Stratocaster says, "You don't have to be a shredding virtuoso to rock."

Ritchie Fliegler: "Players like Eric Clapton, the Vaughan Brothers, or Jeff Beck are the evergreens who remain popular with generations of players. Some of them are the virtuosos, the 'gimme a break' guys. Tom is more like a Keith Richards, a Pete Townshend, or a George Harrison. They might not be the same kind of virtuoso, but personally, those are the guys who got me started on guitar. Getting going is essential. I'd rather start off having to learn 'Dirty Water' or 'Gloria' than 'Eruption,' like some poor guy starting out in the '80s."

Richard McDonald: "We took some heat for the Tom Delonge Strat because he's not an Eric Clapton, but it's all about making a contribution. Guys like Tom or Kurt Cobain make playing approachable, and we try not to forget how important that is."

Ritchie Fliegler: "The truth is, during the period the Tom Delonge Strat has been offered, it far outsells the others. We love Tom for opening up doors for Fender, introducing us — and the guitar — to the next generation. So we work with people who make different sorts of contributions, and the beautiful thing is, they're all part of this mix, the stew, and we get to work with all of them."

Richard McDonald: "We look for a diversity of genres, not just iconic status. The Strat can cross those boundaries effortlessly, and that's important. Look at the Artist Series Strats, and consider the diversity in the last few years — Buddy Guy, Yngwie Malmsteen, Robert Cray, Beck, Clapton, Richie Sambora, Stevie Ray Vaughan, Bonnie Raitt, and on and on."

Ritchie Fliegler: "Our customers have strong feelings about who's 'good' or who 'deserves' a signature model, which is great, but at the same time we try to be open-minded. There's no way I'd ever be confused with a guy who loves country music, but as a player, I appreciate what Buck Owens and Don Rich were doing, and if you're a player, no matter what style, and you're not appreciating what Don Rich has done, then you're missing out, you're not doing the whole job. So this diversity of contribution that we value goes beyond our personal tastes sometimes, and the artist guitar idea, at least at Fender, is about recognizing people who are doing good things — in different ways — for the guitar."

In setting up its Artist Signature Series, the first player Fender spoke to was James Burton, but the development of the Burton Telecaster was delayed by the closure of the factory and James' busy touring schedule. The first Signature guitar to actually see the light of day was the Eric Clapton Strat.

Crash & burn, 2003: Eric Clapton blazes through a solo on a Custom Shop Strat hand painted by Crash.

The Eric Clapton Artist Series Stratocaster

John Page and Freddie Tavares visited Eric Clapton during the ARMS concert tour in 1983, and they brought along one of the first '57 reissue Strats. Dan Smith: "We met with him a few times after that. On April 5, 1985 we got together in Dallas. We agreed to supply his upcoming tour with guitars he could sign. The only Strats left [during the factory closure] were some non-trem Elites, which he asked to test before he would sign them for the promo. They had Alnico 3 pickups, a dummy coil, a TBX tone control, and the MDX midrange boost. The MDX part of the circuit, designed by Jim Demeter and John Carruthers, boosted the midrange and rolled off some of the highs, making the single-coils sound like humbuckers. Eric liked how it sounded. This would evolve into the Clapton circuit, with Eric wanting more and more of what he called 'compression,' so we kept increasing the midrange boost until we maxed out at 25 dB."

Eric Clapton's Signature Strat has a familiar vintage look, and in some respects it's similar to a '57 reissue (the V neck, for example). And yet it's also quirky, with a blocked tremolo; the vintage style trem doesn't work unless the player removes the matchbox-sized wooden block. Although players such as Eldon Shamblin, Robin Trower, Nils Lofgren, and Mick Ralphs had blocked their tremolos to improve tuning stability, there was zero market demand for such a feature. It would be cheaper and more convenient to serve players who don't want a trem by supplying them with readily available hardtail bridges. "But the blocked tremolo is what Eric has on his own guitar, the one he records and performs with," explained Ritchie Fliegler, "so that's how we build it. No matter how quirky, how nutty, if you buy an Eric Clapton Strat, you're getting the guitar Eric plays. It's the same with all our Artist guitars, and these things also get updated. If we send Eric some new pickups that he likes better, and he puts them in his personal guitar, then we put the same ones in the Clapton Strat on the wall in the music store."

Mike Lewis: "The Clapton Strat had Lace Sensor Golds initially. We worked on the Vintage Noise-less pickups for the Deluxe Series for two years, with the idea all along that Eric might like them in his guitar, which is what came to pass. He took some samples out, evaluated them for quite some time, and made suggestions. Eventually we had those new pickups in the Clapton Strat."

Equipment tech Lee Dickson has worked closely with Eric Clapton for more than two decades. He reported in 2003: "These days Eric is playing Custom Shop Eric Clapton models, the two main ones built by Todd Krause. The bodies go to Crash, the graffiti artist in New York City, and he hand-paints them. Then they go back to Todd for assembly and clear-coating, to protect the artwork. Over the years, several Custom Shop craftsmen have all built guitars for Eric — J. Black, Mike Stevens, John Page, Mark Kendrick, and Larry Brooks."

What special requirements does Eric Clapton have for his personal guitars? Todd Krause: "Nothing, that's the thing. He wants his guitar to be the same as the one the guy buys at the music store, so if you get an Eric Clapton Signature Strat, you're getting Eric's guitar. He might want a special finish, like the art guitars that were painted by Crash and other street/graffiti type artists, or he might get a paint job to match his car, but even though he could have anything he wanted, his guitars are pretty much meat and potatoes instruments. There's no fancy inlay or anything like that. Eric likes a body weight between 3.5 and 4.25 pounds, and although some alder bodies can be 4.5 or 5 pounds, that's unusual these days. The trend now is for lighter bodies, but these things go in cycles and if the player wants a heavier body, we accommodate him."

Lee Dickson: "You know, Eric doesn't use a lot of effects. I put together a big rig for him, but he never used most of the things in there. He uses a bit of wah-wah, and maybe a little chorus once in a while if there's no Leslie speaker around. People hear Eric's huge sound, and they look on the floor — where are all the boxes? Where does it come from? But that's just the way Eric plays. It comes from his heart and his brain, through the fingers and the Strat. That's all I can say."

Tom Wheeler, summer, 1987: "Your old Strat is one of the most famous electric guitars in the world. Why get a new one?"

Eric Clapton: "Blackie is simply worn out. It's unplayable. The problem is in the neck. The rest of the guitar is okay, but the neck is worn out. The frets are almost down to the wood, and it's already been refretted once and couldn't take another refret. I've played it so much that even the sides of the neck, running along the length of the fingerboard, are wearing down — the neck is actually getting thinner. It's not even wide enough to support the six strings, so I simply had to go with something else. Dan Smith and I came up with some ideas, and the guitars I'm playing now are the result."

In 2003, Lee Dickson added: "Blackie's still around. Although the neck's a little thin and the high E string seems to have run out of room because of all the playing and a couple of refrets, it's still in great condition."

The Jeff Beck Signature Stratocaster

During the party that Fender threw for Hank Marvin (p. 197), Eric Clapton told Jeff Beck that Fender was building some special Strats for him, and Jeff should look into a similar arrangement. Dan Smith: "But Jeff was so modest — 'Who'd want a Jeff Beck guitar?' Eric tried to talk him into it, and they went back and forth. I did offer to build him a guitar. Jeff liked early-'60s Strats, so I suggested the '62 Vintage reissue. His only special requests were a bright yellow, to match one of his hot rods, and 'the biggest neck you can make.' George Blanda built it, and left the neck unfinished so we could work on the final shape with Jeff. We took it to a rehearsal, and he liked it so much he insisted he take it on tour to Japan — as is, and unpainted."

Beck's landmark *Guitar Shop* album came out during the period when Fender was looking for someone to endorse the new Strat Plus. Dan Smith: "That record had all those amazing harmonic tones and techniques on it. When Jeff tried to get those sounds live, the only guitar that worked was a Strat Plus — a model he hadn't originally cared for. Since the Lace Sensors had little magnetic attraction, very little string pull, plus a wider magnetic field, they're great for harmonics. He also found the Wilkinson roller nut and locking keys made it easier to stay in tune. The Plus became his guitar of choice."

Beck soon agreed to a signature model. The original Jeff Beck Stratocaster was like a Strat Plus, but with the big neck and different pickups: four Gold Lace Sensors, two of them side by side in what looked like a bridge humbucker configuration. Later versions have an LSR roller nut instead of the Wilkinson, Schaller locking tuners instead of Sperzels, special Noiseless pickups (a little hotter than the Vintage Noiseless), and a sculpted heel in back.

Jeff Beck, on playing a melody by manipulating harmonic tones with the tremolo bar:

"There's a purity of tone when you get a natural harmonic at a bent note and it's not interfered with by any mechanical left-hand work .... If you were cynical, you could say it's not really playing the guitar; it's just a mechanical operation. . . . But I disagree. I say, 'Hey! You try doing it [*laughs*].' Try finding that high whistle that's got to be in pitch, [and then] dive and raise and bend in tune to play a melody with the right hand....

I didn't want to cheat. I wanted to be able to perform this thing live. And talk about cutting a big trench for myself. Every night I thought, 'Why did I play this damn thing?'"

Hank Marvin on his Signature Strat, to Guitar Player, *Sept. '87:*

"I wanted a slightly wider neck because with a lot of the Strats you can pull the first string easily off the fingerboard. There's a Teflon nut to make things a bit more slippery, no string trees, and it uses the American Standard bridge. When you use the tremolo on them as much as I do — and sometimes I use it quite radically — they just go out of tune quite easily. But this one stays very much in tune and it sounds wonderful. It's lovely to play, looks great. It has a bird's-eye maple neck and gold plated hardware, in an effort to copy my original Stratocaster." Marvin prefers heavy strings, .011 - .050.

Jeff Beck Signature Strat, 2003 version with custom-tweaked Noiseless pickups.

Pretty Beck-isms, Track 45

Pete Townshend, 1989: "I don't play acoustic on everything now. I can get away with playing what I've found to be a very good guitar which Eric championed for Fender, the Eric Clapton model, a wonderful all-around guitar … the actual rhythm sound on it, the undistorted sound, the pickup, and the string balance are very good. I don't know how they've achieved it, but it's very, very good – it's almost as good as an acoustic."

Townshend's more recent Eric Clapton Strats have an onboard Fishman Power Bridge transducer for acoustic tones, an EMG buffer preamp, stereo output, and an extra volume knob mounted on the body. Alan Rogan had a hand in the guitar's components and layout. He explained: "The EMG preamp is a huge part of the sound. It makes the acoustic side sound far better than a proper acoustic guitar with a pickup on it. The electric and acoustic sides can be used separately, but Pete likes to blend them, which is why I placed the extra volume knob where it is, for easy accessibility and also to leave room for bridge adjustments. Pete loves these guitars, along with his amp of choice, a Fender Vibro-King with a 2x12 extension cabinet. Gordon Wells at Knight Guitars [Weybridge, Surrey] reshapes the necks to the same dimensions of the earlier Clapton Strats, which Pete much prefers."

The New Fender Company Hits Its Stride

1987 had been a crucial, whirlwind year for the new Fender, still only two years old. The first five months alone saw the introductions of the American Standard Strat and the Strat Plus, both seminal guitars, as well as the opening of the Ensenada facility and the establishment of the Custom Shop, soon to be the crown jewel in Fender's expanding production domain. August saw the publication of *Guitar Player*'s "Strat Mania!" cover story. During the rest of the year, Fender laid groundwork for the unveiling of its Signature Series.

Late-'87 price lists included seven Stratocasters: the American Standard, the two reissues, the Strat Plus, a Custom Shop Mary Kaye reissue, and the Clapton and Malmsteen models. Some of the brochures were premature (the artist guitars weren't produced in quantity until the following year), but by mid-'88 the Stratocaster guitar line represented a comprehensive marketing campaign to be conducted on six fronts:

- a basic U.S. model modernized for contemporary playing styles
- authentic reissues
- affordable imports
- a "super Strat" accessorized with boutique components
- limited-edition Custom Shop models
- Artist Signature guitars with the details of their namesakes' actual instruments, quirks and all.

Tom Delonge of Blink 182 specified that his Signature Strat would have a single Duncan Invader pickup, one knob, a big headstock, locking Sperzels, no trem, and no finish on the back of the neck. He told Guitar Center: "I don't need the other pickups and I don't need the extra knobs, and I like the way Fender's '70s headstocks look, and I need different tuning pegs and it just kind of made sense to throw my favorite humbucker in there and change some hardware. I like to keep my rig as simple as possible – plug straight in and play!"

MODELMANIA

The early '90s

One marketing challenge for any company is deciding when an option or bundle of options warrants a separate model name. Fender's tradition had been to maintain a name even when an instrument was extensively reworked. Examples included the 1957 Precision Bass (a top-to-bottom redesign) and the 1959 Stratocaster guitar. However, two late-'80s developments contributed to a different approach. The company was offering more and more options, and players were often combining aftermarket products into similar "packages," so Fender responded by assigning new names to heavily optioned offshoots and upgrades of existing models. For example, the

"Thank God for Leo Fender, who makes these instruments for us to play."

– Keith Richards, upon his induction into the Rock and Roll Hall of Fame

American Standard was joined by the Deluxe American Standard in 1989; the imported H.M. Strat was joined by the H.M. Strat Ultra in 1990.

The trend continued as the line of Stratocasters — reissues, the American Standard, hot rods, "Cadillacs," imports, and Signature models — expanded in the first few years of the new decade. The Strat Plus (renamed the U.S. Strat Plus) spawned the Strat Ultra as well as the Deluxe Strat Plus. During the same period, the Clapton and Malmsteen artist guitars were joined by the Jeff Beck and Robert Cray models.

In 1992 the Collectables appeared. Made in Japan, these were an alternative approach to vintage reissues. Instead of reproducing the features of a model from one year, they combined general features from an era, specifically the '50s or '60s (the exception was the big-headstock, bullet-rod, year-specific 1968 Collectables Series Strat).

A Real Art To It: Relics '95

One of Fender's most remarkable success stories in the past decade has been the Relic instruments, expensive new guitars that look worn, broken in, dinged up, played hard, sometimes even abused. John Page: "That was J.W. Black's inspiration. He nailed it on that one."

J.W. Black: "Repairmen and builders were already doing some of that in their restorations. Before coming to Fender, I worked with Roger Sadowsky in New York. Someone might be unhappy with the finish on their '63 Strat, so we'd hang it in the sun or put it in a freezer and do some sort of distressing. If you were re-topping an old Martin, you'd age the lacquer so it would match the rest of the guitar.

"I was working on Ronnie Wood's old Broadcaster, which didn't have an original pickguard. Vince Cunetto had been making reproduction pickguards for years, with the mark from the five-inch paint can on the underside. He was aging them, and they were just beautiful. He did one for Ron's Broadcaster, and it turned out he had an entire guitar completely aged.

When we saw it we wondered, if we do this at Fender, will people laugh at us — or appreciate it?

"One of my clients was Don Was. He was going to use a brand new bass at the Grammys with Bonnie Raitt, and he said, 'Can you beat it up, make it look old?' He thought new instruments looked geeky, like the kid at the playground with brand new sneakers. I told him aging a new instrument was a little silly, but the more I thought about it, the more I thought it might work."

The 35th Anniversary Strat of 1989 was a Custom Shop guitar with three silver Fender-Lace Sensors and a quilted maple body, built in a limited run of 500.

John Page: "J. comes into my office one day in '94, shuts the door, and says, 'I've got this wacky idea. These distressed guitars — what do you think about releasing them?' I said, 'Great idea! Let's not tell anyone. Let's do a couple for the NAMM show

and put them in a glass case and just shock everybody.' So J. worked with Vince Cunetto and they built a Nocaster and a Mary Kaye Strat. Vince did the paint and aging. We took them to the January 1995 NAMM show. All the dealers said, 'This is so cool for you to honor your legacy by displaying these old classic guitars,' and we said, 'Um, actually, they're spankin' new! How many you want?'

J.J. Cale, whose spare, restrained style had a significant effect on Eric Clapton's work after Cream and Blind Faith. Another artist influenced by Cale was Mark Knopfler, who told Dan Forte: "I listened to a lot of J.J. Cale around the time my style was developing. He's great. He's very, very special to me."

[*Laughs.*] We left that show with hundreds of orders, and the Relics became the number one seller in the Custom Shop."

Did beating up a new guitar strike anyone as bizarre?

Mike Lewis: "Totally. When the Custom Shop brought them to NAMM, nobody knew about them. I think even Dan Smith didn't know. When we found out they were new guitars, it was a shock, but I thought it was genius. Look at all the people who like distressed jeans or old leather jackets. Imagine your favorite guitar didn't make it to the gig, and someone hands you this vintage-type instrument with all this vibe, and it's comfortable and worn and broken in. That would be perfect."

John Page: "For several years we sent them to Vince Cunetto, who did a brilliant job with the painting and aging. Later Fender brought it all in-house."

On a handshake deal with Page, Cunetto hired a couple of helpers and set up Cunetto Creative Resources, Inc. in Bolliver, Missouri. Within a month, he and his crew started aging the bodies and necks and processing the parts they received from Fender. They prepared the wooden components the old fashioned way, hand-sanding everything. They used thin, old-style nitrocellulose lacquers, and they had all the old Fender color charts and original paint formulas. They developed one formula to get the top coat to craze or check a bit, producing the faint surface cracks we sometimes see on old guitars. Another tinted top coat duplicated the look of an aged clear coat. (Cunetto believes the aging process itself doesn't change a guitar's sound, but a very thin finish is indeed important to replicating a vintage Strat's original tone.) After painting, the components were cosmetically distressed. Using various implements and techniques, the crew would apply different wear patterns and strategically placed nicks and scratches.

Vince Cunetto: "A lot of thought was put into it. I took my aging artist to vintage guitar shows to study the old instruments. Why is it scratched over here?

Why does the fingerboard have worn marks up here but not down there? Why are the bridge saddles corroded more on the bass side on this Strat but more on the treble side on that one? It's like archeology. When you study the classics, you can determine how that guitar was played over the years.

"For each guitar we aged, we would actually imagine an individual player with his own style and approach, and everything was done in keeping with that player. Maybe he was a country rhythm guy, so all the finger wear would be in the first positions, with strum wear around the upper frets and pickguard wear consistent with that. There's a real art to it.

"So here you have bodies, necks, and all the visible parts — knobs, pickup covers, pickguards, hardware, everything. When you're aging parts in batches, you get variation. Some knobs are darker; some screws are corroded. The real 'secret' to a convincing aging job is making the aging level of each part consistent with the whole guitar. Before we'd ship a batch back to the Custom Shop, we'd lay out the aged parts on a 24-foot table. We'd start with bodies and necks, then match parts to each guitar to make up sets."

Cunetto shipped the first batch of unassembled Relic components to Fender on June 27, 1995. While a limited number of Relics were built in-house by the Custom Shop during the period Cunetto was involved, he estimates that his company processed about 4,800 Relics of all styles and colors, including catalog items and a few one-offs. In early 1999 the Custom Shop introduced the expanded Time Machine series and began implementing its own version of the

Pearl Jam's Mike McCready has been a Strat man ever since he fell under the spell of Jimi Hendrix and Stevie Ray Vaughan. His two main workhorses are a '59 and a '56, both sunbursts with original pickups.

aging process. Cunetto reported: "Interestingly, none of my proprietary processes or 'trade secrets' were shared with the Custom Shop." After about a six-month transition period of Relics being done in both places, the last batches of "Cunetto Era" Relics were shipped to Fender, in mid June of 1999.

Vince Cunetto: "The success of the Relics is a tribute to the vision and talents of John Page and J. Black and the other great people there at the time. I think the Relics changed the direction of the Custom Shop and changed the way people look at Fenders." [See the Time Machine Series, p. 241.]

Mid '90s Modelmania

The expansion of the line accelerated in the next few years to the point where in 1996, buyers had about 40 Strat models to choose from, depending on how you counted various options. Most were built in the main U.S. factory, just over a dozen in the Custom Shop, and several were imported.

The U.S. factory and import Strats were organized into eight series: Artist Signature (seven artists, nine models), U.S. Vintage Reissue (the continuation of the reissues of 1982), U.S. Plus/Deluxe (with features such as locking trems, locking tuners, humbuckings, or Fender-Lace Sensors), U.S. Standard (including another American Standard offshoot, the Limited Edition, with a painted headstock), the made-in-Japan Collectables, the Special/Deluxe (including, of all things, a Strat 12-string), the made-in-Mexico Standard Series, and the Squier.

Mid-'90s Custom Shop Strats were arranged in four series: Namesakes (the Robert Cray and Dick Dale artist Strats), Set Neck/Contemporary, Relics, and Custom Classics (including recreations of Strats from 1954, 1958, and 1960, among others). Factoring in options such as gold hardware, rosewood board vs.

John Frusciante of the Red Hot Chili Peppers. His favorite Strats include a maple-neck '55 ("the best feeling neck ever") and a rosewood-board '62.

maple neck, various finishes, left-hand models, hard-tail (non-trem) models, etc., it's no exaggeration to say that cataloged mid-'90s Stratocaster variations numbered in the hundreds.

Where in the name of Leo Fender had all these models come from? Well, if the Fender line had multiplied severalfold since the 1950s, so had the needs, tastes, and sophistication of musicians, the styles to which the Strat was suited, the necessity for quick responses to market shifts, and the complexities —

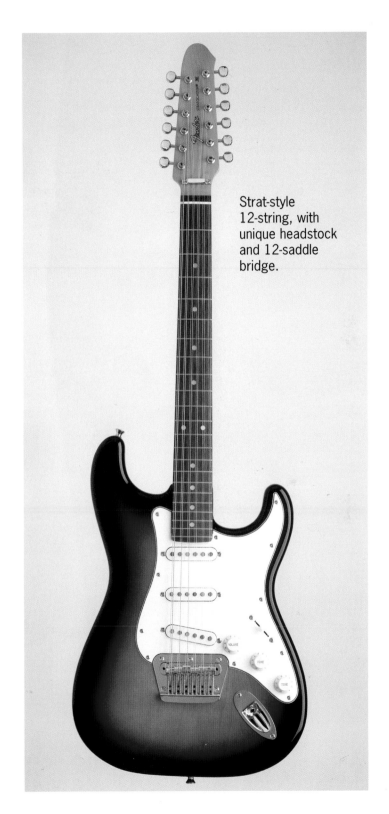

Strat-style 12-string, with unique headstock and 12-saddle bridge.

40th Anniversary Stratocaster, 1994.

Few players are so closely associated with the in-between sound as the hard-touring Robert Cray. He uses few if any effects, and he specified a non-trem bridge for his Signature Strat. "Most effects just clutter up your sound and make it harder to sound like yourself. It's bad enough that we all play Strats!"

and the stakes — of the global guitar industry. *The Music Trades* magazine reported that Fender sold more than 400,000 electric instruments in 2002; sales topped $244,000,000. Dan Smith: "You can't do that on one Strat, one Tele, one Precision Bass, and one Jazz Bass. At the same time, it's incredible to me how many models there are. For one thing, we let products die a natural death. We don't discontinue stuff just to come out with something new. As long as there's a market for it, even a small one, we'll serve that market."

Lone Star, Big Apple, Jimmie Vaughan

Although any number of models could typify Fender's mid-decade strategy of niche marketing, the U.S.-built Lone Star Strat, U.S.-built Big Apple Strat, and the Mexico-built Jimmie Vaughan Tex-Mex Signature Strat are representative examples. The Lone Star and Big Apple have since been renamed, but their inception entailed the quick response to trends that continues to drive Fender marketing and design. The Tex-Mex is a sample of the high-quality models coming out of Ensenada.

Fantasy Blues Jam, Track 59

The Lone Star was introduced in 1996 and grouped in the U.S. Plus/Deluxe Series. Mike Lewis: "This was one of our most significant guitars of the 1990s, the first time we'd ever done a basic Strat with a humbucker. I had a music store for years and did repairs. I can't tell you how many times a player brought in a Strat to fit a humbucker in there, and later at Fender we got requests for it all the time. We had Strats with humbuckers in the line, but those guitars had locking tremolos or other extras. Players wanted something

Jimmie Vaughan Tex-Mex Strat in Olympic White, with vintage-style hardware and a single-ply pickguard.

basic, and the Lone Star had a straight-ahead American Standard body, already routed to accept various pickup configurations. We could drop them right in."

Lewis decided to install a popular after-market pickup, so Fender worked with Seymour Duncan and settled on a slightly modified Pearly Gates for the bridge unit. For the other two, Fender used its own Texas Specials, among the most popular after-market pickups by Fender or anyone else. They gave the Lone Star a pearloid pickguard and several flashy colors, and it was an instant hit.

After the success of the single humbucker Lone Star, a double humbucking Strat was the next obvious model. It was called the Big Apple, appeared the following year, and employed the same modified Pearly Gates in the bridge position that had been used for the Lone Star. For the neck pickup Fender again worked with Seymour Duncan and came up with a slightly modified Duncan '59. Like the Lone Star, the Big Apple was an immediate success.

The Jimmie Vaughan Signature Model came out in 1997, inspired by a guitar Vaughan had found in a music store. Mike Lewis: "He wanted something straight-ahead but with more of a V shaped neck and slightly hotter pickups. He also wanted to see how they do things at the factory in Mexico. He came down for a visit and was blown away by the pride and the passion of those builders. He said he would never look at his guitar the same way. It really moved him, so he said, if you guys will pay for the gas for my bus, we'll play for you. He brought down his whole band. We closed up the factory, had a fiesta for a thousand people, and Jimmie's band played all night. These days he plays the same Jimmie Vaughan model he's always had. He even busted the headstock off and just glued it back on and still plays it."

Revamping the Line

In the mid '90s Fender reconsidered its entire line. Guitars were being built in the U.S., Japan, and Mexico, plus the Squiers in Korea, all with the *Fender* name on them. In some cases Fender had several instruments at the same or similar price points, and perhaps even a few examples where a buyer might actually get more features for less money. It was confusing.

Looking back on it a decade later, the mid-'90s is considered a transitional era. The new company was then about ten years old and still ramping up its production, still integrating its strategies. Their intention all along had been to bring into the U.S. as much production as they could. That took time, but by 1996 Fender was ready to embark on a comprehensive five-year plan to re-do the entire line, from the Squier imports all the way up to the top of the line Corona guitars.

New Factory, New Series

On July 18, 1998, Fender moved into a new facility a couple of miles from its Corona factory. According to *The Music Trades* magazine, as of 2000 the new Corona plant employed more than 300 people. Unlike the previous factory, which was eventually spread among several small buildings in an industrial park, the new one is under one huge roof — about 177,000 square feet.

A herd of Lone Star Strats.

Fender could now complete its five-year restructuring plan by reducing the number of models, having a logical place for each one relative to the others, covering every price point, and simplifying the whole deal. To do all that, the Custom Shop, Artist Signature, and American Standard Series were supplemented with three new or revamped series: American Deluxe, American Vintage, and Classic.

Noiseless Pickups & Ultimate Factory Strats: American Deluxe

The American Deluxe Series of the late '90s took over for the Strat Plus and filled that same niche. It marked a rethinking of the "ultimate Strat" concept, the top of the line among the factory guitars. Fender went back to the original drawings of the 1950s and discovered that the shape of the Strat had gradually "wandered" a bit. So they spec'd out all the CNC machines to re-do the contours of the bodies, to be more like Strats of the 1950s. Mike Lewis: "We also went with a new, comfortable neck shape, and we 'rolled' the edges of the neck, to smooth out the fingerboard/neck joint so it feels nice and worn-in all the way up the neck where your thumb might wrap around. This was when we developed our Noiseless pickups, and we made slight modifications to the machine heads and hardware."

Because the American Deluxe finishes were transparent, Fender selected higher-grade alder and ash, and built bodies with fewer pieces of glued-together wood. They began matching colors to woods — a red that looked good over alder, a teal that complemented the ash. They added locking machines, and fancied up the cosmetics with mother of pearl inlays for the dots and a raised-metal logo for the peghead.

Richard McDonald: "The Deluxe Fat Strat and those sorts of guitars satisfy the player-centric changes that people were making to Strats on their own. You know, we put people in business out there, guys who were putting humbuckings in Stratocasters just because we weren't doing it. So the American Deluxe speaks to the demand for high performance, for upgrades, quieter pickups, and so on. Examples are the Lace Sensors and later the Noiseless pickups. It's for the more technical player."

Mike Lewis: "The American Deluxe Strat is very nice, with a lot of special features but nothing unnecessary. It's beautiful, but it's all about sound and playability and function. The idea was to enhance the Strat's sound and playability, not change it."

Big Apple Strats.

Richard McDonald: "We offer a lifetime guarantee on these guitars, and players don't want to void it, so if they want a certain neck and locking keys and big frets, they can get all that right from Fender and still have their guarantee."

The American Deluxe Series was pivotal, the proving ground for several important features that would later spread to the American Series and other guitars, including detailed nut and fret work, the new neck with rolled edges, and more accurate body perimeters.

The American Vintage Series

The next re-do at the end of the '90s was the American Vintage Series, which were the replacements for the U.S. Vintage Reissue Series and the direct descendants of the Dan Smith '57 and '62 Strats of January '82. Mike Lewis: "You can only do what the facilities allow, and back in '82 those models were the best we could do, and they were great guitars and very successful. But by '98, with our new state-of-the-art factory, we could do anything we wanted. For example, we could use lacquer on more guitars. California has strict environmental regulations, but our containment system is so advanced that the air coming out is actually cleaner than the air going in.

"We had already laid the groundwork by re-doing the body shapes on the American Deluxe series, so the new American Vintage guitars could also be more accurate. As always, you do what you can, and we are always pushing the limits of available technology. Now our neck shapes are more true to the originals. Once again we roll over the necks so they feel already broken in. We got some original '61 pickups, spec'd them out, and duplicated the specs. As replicas, these guitars are more accurate than ever, even down to slightly relocating the fingerboard dots."

The phenomenal Jeff Healey learned to play with the guitar flat on his lap and went on to master a searing blues-rock style.

Left-handed American Deluxe with an ash body, in Aged Cherry Sunburst.

The Classic Series

What if you wanted the vintage Strat vibe but didn't care all that much about picky, year-specific details and didn't have the bucks for an American Vintage reissue? Fender had addressed that segment of the market in the mid 1990s with its Collectables Series, which it evolved into the Classic Series of the late '90s. One goal was to gradually reduce the Japanese Collectables, replacing most of them with Mexico-built Classics. The idea was the same: affordable Strats that captured the vintage mojo and best features of, respectively, the '50s, '60s, and now the '70s era as well, rather than a single model year.

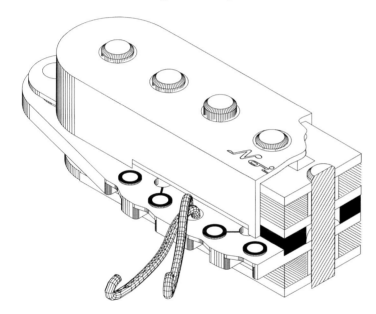

Intended to combine the advantages of single-coil pickups and humbuckers, Noiseless pickups were the result of three years of refinement. Each unit appears to be a typical single-coil but actually entails stacked upper and lower coils. Alnico 5 magnet rods extend through both coils and also through a spacer plate that separates them. Designer Bill Turner reported that the soft ferrous spacer plate "isolates the bottom coil from string vibration, making the top single coil the sound source; the Noiseless sounds like a single-coil because, functionally speaking, it *is* a single-coil." Modeled after a particularly good sounding set of 1963 pickups, these units provide characteristic Strat tones while reducing 60-cycle hum.

American Deluxe in Teal Green Transparent. The tremolo bar differs from the plastic-tipped units on most Strats.

Lenny Kravitz.

Time Machines, Relics Revisited

Fender recognized decades ago that musical instruments can be infused with a magic and meaning far beyond their utility. The continuing success of vintage reissues says something not only about our appreciation of the craft and designs of a bygone era but also about the potency of nostalgia and our reverence for the lore of our instrument.

This realization inspired the Custom Shop's Time Machine Series, introduced in 1999. Not only are these reissues period-correct in their conspicuous features (body and neck shapes, pickups, hardware, etc.), but they are also the result of Fender's use of original materials, original tooling, and even original production techniques whenever possible. This extra detail

reflects a willingness to delve deeper than ever into the vintage sensibility.

Mike Lewis: "Some details can't even be seen, like authentic routing and wiring. One year, Fender drilled the slot for the truss rod a little smaller, and they did it that way for just the one year; well, that's how we do it on the Time Machine version. We also knew it's impossible to recreate a '1956 Strat' per se, because '56 Strats are different from piece to piece. So for each guitar in the Series we took the best features and bent over backwards to recreate them."

Along with introducing the Time Machine guitars, Fender fine-tuned the factory-aged concept and came up with three finish packages. An N.O.S. (New Old Stock) Strat isn't aged at all; rather it appears as it did

Classic Series Strat in
Shell Pink, '60s style.

On albums such as *Texas Sugar/Strat Magic*, Chris Duarte's fiery blues-rock is often compared to that of Stevie Ray Vaughan.

back in the year of the original model's manufacture, "just like it was, right off the line!" The Closet Classic approximates a pampered vintage guitar, with moderate playing wear, a lightly checked finish, oxidized hardware, aged plastic parts, and perhaps a couple of small scrapes or dings; its official description epitomizes Fender's tightly focused, "niche within a niche" marketing strategy: "bought new in its respective year, played perhaps a few times a month, wiped off and put carefully away after each use." The "Relic" designation was now applied to one of the new options and described as "used and abused," with plenty of wear and tear — deeper scratches, more dings, an aged and checked finish, aged plastic parts, even rusty hardware.

Dan Smith: "We use a different finishing material, depending on whether it's N.O.S. or whatever. For the new Relics, we use a finish that's more prone to cracking. On the N.O.S., the finish is softer, more flexible, so it won't check too quickly. The whole process is similar to antiquing furniture. We can cold-check the paint by hitting it with freezing temperatures, and then the guitar is banged around with different implements. If you don't know what you're doing, you would get a guitar that looks brand new but dinged up, instead of truly old and worn — a big difference. It all has to be done in a certain way."

Mike Eldred, Marketing Manager, Custom Shop: "We brought the Relic process in house because we wanted to keep tabs on it and insure the consistency. The majority of what we do in the Custom Shop now is vintage reproductions, for people who want an old Fender but don't want to spend $20,000 or $30,000 for an original. We spend a lot of time examining vintage instruments, and when we're building a reissue we approach each year a certain way. For example, if we're relic-ing a Strat from 1969, we take into consideration that the original finish was done a little differently then, so it would have aged differently. The original necks were starting to be shot with polyester, so it might not have not worn through on the fingerboard. We can be very precise."

For some players, reissue guitars with pre-worn finishes are just plain cool looking or convenient (you don't have to worry about putting nicks in your new guitar if it's already nicked up). For others, the appeal runs deeper. While any authentic reissue allows us to indulge our fantasy of going back in time and picking out the guitar of our dreams, the N.O.S., Closet Classic, and Relic Time Machines take us further into the fantasy, allowing us to imagine the tales our guitar might tell.

Did it spend decades in the company of spiders, entombed in the utter blackness of a sealed closet, just waiting to reflect a laser beam of pure Inca Silver light when its dust-blanketed case creaks open for the first time since Dick Dale was playing the Rinky Dink Ice Cream Parlor for eight bucks a night?

Or did it languish for a year in a sunny music store window, ignored in favor of once trendier guitars and fading from Fiesta Red to salmon pink?

Did it live a life with hard companions, banging across the Texas panhandle in the trunk of an old Mercury, acquiring a burn mark from a Lucky Strike poked in the peghead, belt buckle scratches all the way through to raw wood, and scars around the 12th fret from ripping through "Dust My Broom" pretty much every Saturday night since the Eisenhower Administration?

Billie Joe Armstrong of Green Day.

The 3-bolt neck was recreated (and improved) for the Classic Series '70s reissue.

Time Machine slab-board 1960 Relic.

Gavin Rossdale of Bush.

THE NEW MILLENNIUM

Roadhouse Strats.

Strats 2000: Theme & Variation

By January 2000, many people had given up trying to remember the specs of every Strat model. What was the point? With guitars being added, dropped, and modified faster than the publication of new catalogs, players and dealers were doing well to remember general distinctions among the *series*. Anyone who bothered to do so would have counted several dozen basic Strat models all together in the Custom Shop and factory catalogs of 2000, the exact number depending on whether you adopted Fender's new scheme of listing hardtails as separate models.

Factory guitars were grouped in nine series, five of which, significantly, bore the country of origin as part of the name: American Standard (with the American Standard Strat now in its 13th year), Hot Rodded American Standard (the Roadhouse had joined the Big Apple and Lone Star), American Special (the Jimi Hendrix Voodoo Strat and a couple of Floyd Rose models), American Deluxe (some with locking trems, humbuckers, or both), and American Vintage (the perennial favorites, the '57 and the '62, were now 18 years old — "vintage vintage" reissues).

The other factory Strats of 2000 were grouped in the Artist Series, which had succeeded the Artist Signature Series of the 1990s and now included ten guitars (a few made in Mexico, most in the U.S.), plus three additional series, all made in Mexico: Classic, Standard, and Deluxe (which by now included the Super Strat and the Powerhouse).

In addition to choices in fingerboard wood, trem vs. hardtail bridge, hardware plating, and left-hand models, the catalog now boasted more than 80 different finishes and colors, while the Custom Shop offered each of its three Time Machine Strats in the three finish packages. Anyone attempting to tally every possible combination of Strat models, options, and colors would need plenty of time, several pots of coffee, and extra calculator batteries.

The American Series

A Better Sounding, Better Playing Stratocaster

The American Standard was a good guitar that served Fender long and well, but in the summer of 2000 it was time to raise the bar. After more than 13 successful years, the American Standard would be retired, and replaced by the American Series Stratocaster.

The new guitar didn't look very different from its predecessor. In fact, the guitars pictured in ads seemed indistinguishable from American Standards, unless you happened to notice that the peghead bore a tiny *Original Contour Body* decal and had one string tree instead of two. The apparent similarities posed a challenge: In a market already awash in innumerable Strat variations, the new model might be greeted with yawns. *Just another Strat.*

It was anything but. While it retained the Micro Tilt adjustment, 4-bolt neck, and the shielding from the American Standard, as well as the 5-way switch that dated back to '77, the American Series Stratocaster differed from its predecessor in at least a dozen respects, most of them functional. It was, as Fender promised, a better sounding, better playing guitar.

Note the '50s style spaghetti logo and the shorter heights of the first four tuning posts on the American Series Strat.

American Series: 2-point trem, parchment pickguard, custom-stagger polepieces.

Fender replaced the TBX control with a "no-load" control. Where the TBX had a center detent at the 5 position, the no-load works like a regular 250k tone control all the way up to 10, at which point the knob clicks and the pot is eliminated altogether from the circuit. On vintage Strats, there was no tone control for the bridge pickup, so the no-load on 10 is intended to provide that original wide-open treble sound. To warm it up a bit, the player can back off the knob, bring in the tone pot, and adjust it to his or her liking. The control also works on the middle pickup, and provides more sparkle in the top end when the selector is in the 2 or 4 position.

While the American Series Strat has been described as Mike Lewis' baby, he is quick to set the record straight: "To say it's 'my baby' is misleading. From time to time a particular person is a team leader, but this is a company where everyone has a passion for great guitars, and lots of ideas to contribute. I happened to be in the driver's seat from the marketing side, and George Blanda was the chief designer."

A few members of the Fender team, seated, from left: Dan Smith (V.P. Guitar Products R&D), Jeff Schuch (Director, Manufacturing Engineering), and George Blanda (Manager, Guitar Products Design Group). Standing, from left: Tony Manioci (Manufacturing Engineer), Steve Grom (V.P. Corporate Quality Assurance), Tony Train (Documentation Administrator, Guitar Products R&D), and Bill Turner (Senior Project Engineer, Guitar Products R&D).

The American Standard was successful. Why replace it?

Mike Lewis: "There had been a few changes over the years it was in the line, but it got to the point where all the features we had been asked for were significant enough to warrant a new model rather than just changing an existing one. It wasn't just a feature here and another one there. The whole guitar was reinvented, like a nicely designed car, one end to the other. It was based on years of listening to what people were saying."

Richard McDonald: "That exact same process has been repeated at this company since the day it opened its doors. It's the way Don Randall and Leo Fender did it. Rather than saying it was mandated by marketing, or the factory, it was more a matter of what players were telling us, and then we moved on it. We innovate, but a lot of it is reacting to what people want, just like Leo Fender did."

Dan Smith: "Through the early '90s we were under-capacity to add American-made models because the models we already had were constantly back ordered — we could only do X amount a day. By the time Mike Lewis became marketing manager for guitars [June '95], our capacity had gone up, so we started to expand the line. Mike was responsible for a lot of new models in the mid to late '90s. It looked like the American Standard was dropping off a little bit, so we asked, what can we do to make it better?"

Mike Lewis: "We had gone from the Strat Plus to the American Deluxe, and around the same time we also evolved the U.S. Vintage Reissue Series into the American Vintage Series. We were making changes in the neck shapes and doing a lot more detail work, and many of these things were carried over into a refined regular Stratocaster, which we now called the American Series."

Dan Smith: "Also, as our quality and prices went up, we were competing with high-end companies who were copying our designs but doing all kinds of extra things. We wanted to answer all that."

Mike Lewis: "On the peghead, the first four tuning key posts are lower in height — they're staggered — which provides a sharper angle where the strings go over the nut. We now have only one string tree, because we no longer need the second one. Eliminating a string tree gives us two advantages: Less friction means more tuning stability, and the greater angle over the nut means more tension, which means better tone."

The neck feels a little different than the American Standard's neck.

Mike Lewis: "We borrowed the new shape from the American Deluxe Series. It's a little thicker in back, and rounder on the sides, more natural and comfortable. Where the fingerboard joins the neck surface, along the side, it's been 'rolled over,' which is a process we do by hand: First, we use special scraping tools to shave down the corner; then we smooth it out. There's more handwork on the frets — they're more highly polished — and on the string nut, which gets more hand dressing now. This all takes more time, more equipment, and more training."

George Blanda: "The rolled edges are an ergonomic thing, a noticeable difference and a pleasant feel, especially if you play with your thumb over the neck. It feels like an older neck. Some of those old necks are rounded because they're worn from all the playing, but sometimes they came that way from the factory. When we did the '54 Strat reissue, we carefully measured and detailed one of Richard Smith's original '54 Strats. That guitar had some roundness in the neck, but it wasn't from wear — it was under the original finish. It had hardly been played."

Mike Lewis: "On the back of the neck, we've gone back to original-style volutes up at the peghead and also down at the neck/body joint. We've also gone to the original body radiusing. If you look at the cutaway horns, for example, the contours are more rounded again, and we now use the original body

Doyle Bramhall II grew up among Texas musicians. At age 16 he toured with the Fabulous Thunderbirds, and he's been carrying on the legacy of the Stratocaster in Texas blues ever since.

Alanis Morissette.

perimeter. It's a little more curvy, more comfortable. We have extreme contours on the back as well, like the '50s Strats.

"The bodies are available in alder or ash, all non-veneered. Veneers were separate pieces over the top and back, and we used them on a lot of the American Standards. They made it easier to apply the finish, and this was okay when people liked those harder looking finishes. But the newer, non-veneered body can breathe more. There's no veneer to impede the wood's vibration, so you get a more natural sound."

Might the finish "sink" a bit?

Mike Lewis: "By not having the veneer there's a tendency sometimes, not always, for the finish to sink into the grain a little bit depending on weather conditions, and after a period of time, maybe you can look at it in the light a certain way and see little bits of the grain. Some people think that's a defect, if they prefer that harder, plasticy kind of look, but when I see a guitar with a thinner finish and a bit of grain, I think, oh boy, this guitar is going to sound great."

George Blanda: "When Mike started in marketing, getting rid of the veneer was one of the first things he wanted to do. Some players perceived it as a lesser construction method, even though the veneer held the finishes better. Somewhere in the mid '90s the whole thing kind of turned around and very thin finishes were now preferred for tonal reasons. The sunken grain appearance was more acceptable."

Dan Smith: "We're using a polyester undercoat, a urethane color coat, and a urethane top coat, which looks natural and sounds good."

You got rid of the swimming pool.

Mike Lewis: "Under the pickguard, the previous Strat had one large, 'swimming pool' cavity for the pickups, but on the new one the routing is now hum/single/hum, which lets the player substitute different popular combinations of pickups, and even reposition the middle pickup if the player wants to. We still have the versatility, but with three smaller cavities there's more wood, which allows for more of the original sound of the Strat to come through."

Different pickups?

Mike Lewis: "The pickups are basically the same as before but with custom-stagger polepieces. On the original '50s Strats, with what we call the vintage stagger, the G polepiece is the highest point, or equal to the D, because back then the G, typically the thinnest wound string, needed a high polepiece to pick it up. But now we all use plain G's, so to get proper balance we've lowered that pole a bit. Plus, we're using more overdrive and high gain, and having that G polepiece a little lower gives us a smoother sound in those applications. The stagger was also a little modified from the '50s guitars, because now we are fitting the contour [the pole-pieces' profile across the pickup] to the American Series' 9½" radius. We still have the reverse-polarity pickup in the middle, for hum-canceling."

Any cosmetic changes?

Mike Lewis: "The color of the pickguard and other plastic parts was changed to parchment, which looks great on the parts but also really brings out the color of the guitar. It's a very deep, rich look. One final touch — we thought the peghead should have the *Original Contour Body* decal like the early Strats [the decal had been dropped in 1976]."

On the surface, the guitar looks like the American Standard. With so many Stratocaster variations out there, did you worry that people would think, oh, it's just an excuse to build another Strat?

Mike Lewis: "I thought we might hear that at first, but I knew as soon as any player picked it up, plugged it in, felt it, and heard it, they'd know."

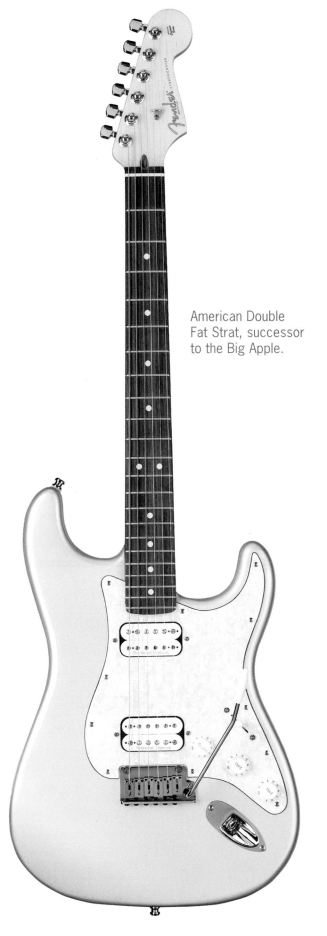

American Double Fat Strat, successor to the Big Apple.

Joe Walsh. In 1988 he offered this insight into the technique of one of his favorite players: "One of the reasons people have such a hard time playing like Jimi Hendrix is that he used an upside-down right handed Strat, so he had his tremolo bar on the top, by the low E string. It's so hard to play like that when you have a regular Strat with a tremolo bar below the high E string. It requires a different technique."[15]

Evolution, 2000-2002

The major development in mid 2000 was the replacement of the American Standard and then the Hot Rodded American Standards with their American Series counterparts. As is typical throughout Fender's history, this shift inevitably resulted in a few transitional models. Examples might include a guitar labeled *American Standard* that actually has a rolled fingerboard, staggered-polepiece pickups, or other features of the newer American Series.

By 2001 the Custom Shop offered eight Strats in several different incarnations. Among U.S. factory guitars, the Jimi Hendrix Voodoo Strat had been replaced with the '68 Reverse Stratocaster Special. The Roadhouse, Lone Star, and Big Apple had been based on the American *Standard*; they were replaced by the similarly equipped American Texas Special, American Fat Strat Texas Special, and American Double Fat Strat, respectively, all based on the newer American *Series*. Mid year, the bare-bones Tom Delonge Strat joined the Artist Series and was an immediate sensation. The Beck and Clapton models were updated with new Noiseless pickups (replacing the Fender-Lace Sensors); and a chrome-pickguard, locking-trem Iron Maiden model jolted the line with a heavy metal attitude adjustment. In 2002, the new Buddy Guy Polka Dot Stratocaster was added.

The organization of the factory's 2002 line continued the nine-group system of 2000: the five U.S.-made series (American Deluxe, American Vintage, etc.), plus the Artist Series and the Mexican-made Standard, Deluxe, and Classic series.

 Find Joe in the Riff Medley, Track 37

Highway Child, the Line of 2003

Everything you need, nothing you don't — that's how Fender pictured the Highway 1 Stratocaster, introduced in 2003. To meet the goal of a more affordable American-made Strat, Fender started with a basic U.S. Stratocaster and removed everything that didn't substantially affect playability and tone. The result is a guitar that fits in the line between a Mexican Standard and an American Series Strat.

Fender saved a few dollars by offering the Highway 1 with only a gig bag rather than the usual package of free hardshell case, strap, and cord, and a few more dollars by duplicating American Series type pickups in Ensenada. The biggest savings was in the finish, a soft, no-gloss matte paint job that has a natural look and feel. Richard McDonald: "It's not a piece of polished Chippendale furniture. It's a thin acrylic lacquer that feels good to the touch and really breathes, and its voice is incredibly powerful and resonant."

The Highway 1's staggered-polepiece pickups and trem are the vintage type found on the Classic Series '60s style Strats. The bodies and American Standard-style necks are made in Corona, and the guitars are also painted and finished there. McDonald estimates that 85% or more of the very successful Highway 1 is American made.

For the most part, the 2003 line continued the general organization of the 2000-2002 line, but with updates within the various series. Aside from the new Highway 1, the prices of the U.S.-made series were arranged as they were in 2000, from least to most expensive: American Series, Hot Rodded American Series, American Special, American Deluxe, American Vintage, and the Artist Series (prices varied within some series by modest amounts, up to a hundred dollars or so).

Despite its complexity, in some ways the 2003 line was actually a bit simplified: The American Special Stratocaster was the only solidbody Strat in that series, and whereas the U.S. Artist Series guitars of 2000 were available at five price points, the 2003 versions all cost the same.

Bonnie Raitt learned slide firsthand from Mississippi Fred McDowell and others. She often plays in open G or open A and uses slides fashioned from the necks of cheap wine bottles. Her soulful artistry, decades of touring, and multi-platinum record sales place her among the best-known and most highly respected slide guitarists in the world. Her "Old Brown" Strat is a '65. "I've played it on every gig since 1969 ... All the people whose playing I love use Strats – John Hall, Lowell George, and Ry Cooder – so I figured it was a good place to start."

Slide Summit, Track 53

Going Global

In the decades since the Stratocaster's appearance in mid 1954, few elements of the musical instrument business have changed as radically as its global aspects. It's no longer a matter of merely countering offshore competition or getting your guitars distributed in other countries. Fender now works with numerous worldwide manufacturers and distributors, and must adjust not only to shifts in musical tastes but also fluctuating currency exchange rates, duties, tariffs, and international trademark issues. The new Fender, although big, must be light on its feet to survive in the complex and frankly cutthroat global music industry of the new millennium.

Richard McDonald: "The windows move by so fast. You either grab them and get in and get out, or you're left behind."

Ritchie Fliegler: "A guitar's features can include chrome plating, gold plating, humbuckers, whatever. Now, in some cases, one 'feature' is the point of origin. In an American Series or a Custom Shop guitar, where it comes from is one of the things people pay for. Other times the primary feature is low cost and high value. In that case, our being able to sell it for $199 and make it a good guitar, a good value, is more important than where it came from. So we've had Squiers made in Mexico, India, Indonesia, China — in a world market, these decisions follow the dollar value around."

Richard McDonald: "Market demands vary in different parts of the world, and we have to be aware of all that. For instance, we've made American Vintage guitars with especially thin nitrocellulose finishes for the Japanese, because that's a very vintage oriented market."

Ritchie Fliegler: "One factory might not be capable of making enough guitars for a particular territory. More than once we've had the same import model — exact same specs — made in two different places for

Shreveport native Kenny Wayne Shepherd's ultra-worn 3-color sunburst Strat is a '61 with graphite bridge saddles and jumbo frets. A devotee of Stevie Ray Vaughan's big tone, he says, "The thicker the string, the better."

two different territories. So the one coming into America is made by one group, but the European one is from a different group."

Mike Lewis: "Once we even had one factory making the rosewood-neck version of an import Strat, and another one in a different country making the maple-neck version of the same model. It's a combination of output capabilities, what materials they're able to source, and demand. In this case, neither factory on its own could make them all."

Ritchie Fliegler: "Let's say one model comes from both China and Korea. We might import the Chinese one into the United States and the Korean one into Europe, based on tariffs or other trade issues. If we can save 5% on tariffs, we'll do it. So this is a multi-national, global phenomenon on every level."

Richard McDonald: "If country of origin isn't always crucial — particularly for younger players — it's only because all of those factories are doing great work for us, and that's because we control it. We're in those factories all the time, rejecting product, re-educating, training — we are *all over* those people with quality control. Some factories are 'captured,' meaning 98% of what they make is Fender, so we are driving not just the design but also the quality and consistency.

"It comes down to this: Our customer wants a *Fender*. Some people will always demand an American product, and we will always serve them. But on the imports, we can't paint ourselves into a corner by saying, this is the *Mexican* Fender, and this is the *Korean* Fender, like it's a fixed guitar. That's the least important thing. What's important is, if it says Fender on it, it better be a freakin' *incredible* guitar, a *great* value, whether it's made in India or Vietnam or Southern California or Ensenada."

Miami Steve Van Zandt.

Dave Navarro, a veteran of the Red Hot Chili Peppers and Jane's Addiction. *All Music Guide*: "With his six-string skills best described as a merger between heavy metal, psychedelia, and modern rock, Dave Navarro became one of alternative's first true guitar heroes."

The Paradigm Shift

In the 1950s and 1960s, the factory crew and marketing staff spent months or years evaluating input from the field. Then they responded with new products that were introduced with fanfare and kept on the market for years in fundamentally unchanged forms: Telecaster, Stratocaster, Jazzmaster, etc.

That approach can't work anymore. It's too sluggish to accommodate the new millennium's diversity of styles, multiplicity of factories, fleeting trends, and the shifting tides of an unpredictable global economy. The new strategy, in a nutshell: flexibility, quick response, and specialized products for niche markets. This makes the line of Stratocaster guitars comprehensive but unavoidably complicated as well, with the methods of grouping the models — import vs. domestic, vintage vs. contemporary, plain vs. fancy, basic vs. high-performance — seemingly cross-mixed every which way:

- top-of-the-line sounding model names do not necessarily denote either a high price tag or U.S. manufacture; the Deluxe Super Strat, for example, is made in Mexico, and even Squier imports come in Special Limited Editions;
- upscale, boutique, or high-performance features sometimes appear on relatively low-cost guitars, such as the Mexican-made Floyd Rose Standard;
- contemporary Strats as well as vintage style Strats all come in Custom Shop, factory, and import versions;
- artist models also come in Custom Shop, factory, and import versions (in fact, the same artist's name might appear on both a U.S. made guitar and an import, or in the case of Tom Delonge, on a Fender import and a Squier import);
- sometimes the same model is carried over from one series to a newer one; the Lone Star Strat, for example, moved from the U.S. Plus/Deluxe to the Hot Rodded American Standard;

- some new models are direct corollaries to previous ones; as noted, the Roadhouse, Lone Star, and Big Apple were updated and renamed the American Strat Texas Special, American Fat Strat Texas Special, and American Double Fat Strat, respectively;
- an otherwise vintage style guitar might be fitted with a flame maple top;
- an otherwise basic Strat might be fitted with a synthesizer-controller pickup;
- some models begin life in the Custom Shop, then move to regular factory production, perhaps in modified form;
- some models were started in the factory, discontinued, then reintroduced as expensive Custom Shop guitars or (at the other end of the spectrum) affordable imports, perhaps years later;
- some Custom Shop Strats are upscale versions of factory guitars, while others have no specific factory corollary;
- in the past decade, the Stratocaster line has included guitars made entirely in Ensenada (e.g., the Standard), guitars made entirely in Corona (anything with "American" in the series name); guitars assembled in Ensenada from parts made in Corona (the Tex-Mex); and guitars whose components are made in Corona, shipped to Ensenada for sanding and painting, then shipped *back* to Corona for final assembly (the late-'90s California Strat);
- as noted, the same import model may be made in different parts of the world, perhaps even at the same time;
- as production techniques evolve, various processes may begin in the Custom Shop, move to a relatively expensive factory line such as the American Deluxe, then to a less expensive factory line such as the American Series.

Clearly, Fender's primary strategy is not to make the line as simple as possible. It's to fill every niche, counter every competitor, serve every taste and every need at every price point — and do it fast.

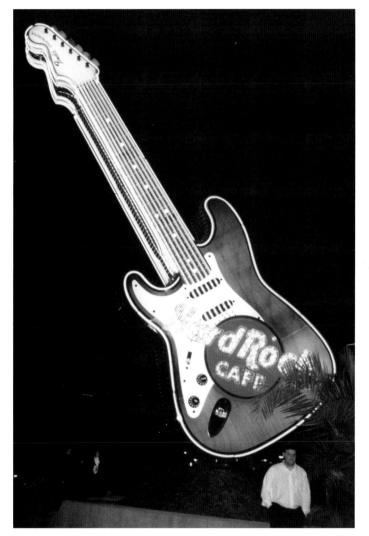

Bigger than life, the Stratocaster has ascended into the rarefied atmosphere of American iconography, easily recognized in detailed images like this one or even in the neon silhouette of a beer sign in a tavern window.

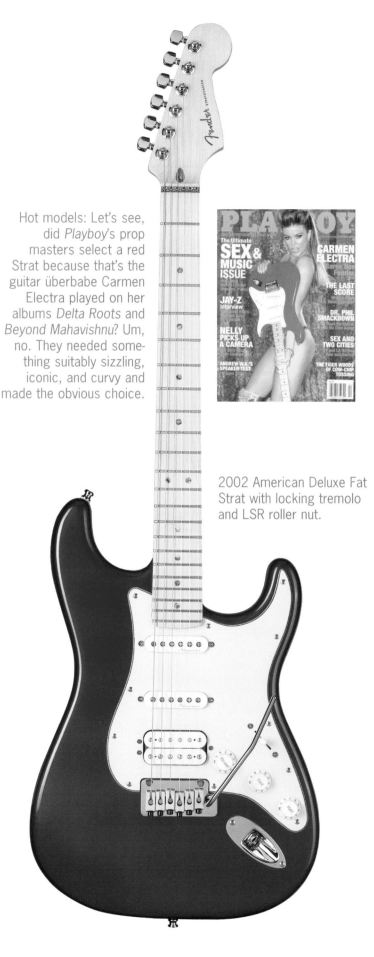

Hot models: Let's see, did *Playboy*'s prop masters select a red Strat because that's the guitar überbabe Carmen Electra played on her albums *Delta Roots* and *Beyond Mahavishnu*? Um, no. They needed something suitably sizzling, iconic, and curvy and made the obvious choice.

2002 American Deluxe Fat Strat with locking tremolo and LSR roller nut.

Approaching the 50th year

In 2003, the Hot Rod Series was discontinued, and some of its features were folded into the existing American Series as options. The reason? Customer demand. Some players wanted one or two Hot Rod features without having to buy, say, a pearloid pickguard or the rest of the package. The American Series became the core line, but it was now broader and more flexible. Even the cosmetic details were more diverse. Richard McDonald: "Not all American Series Strats have to have parchment pickguards, for example. If it's a finish that looks better with a black pickguard, then we'll use that."

In the summer of 2003, the ingenious S-1 system was introduced on most American Series Strats. Essentially invisible, this simple 4-pole/2-position switch recesses into the top of what appears to be a standard volume control. Richard McDonald: "You don't have to pull up the whole knob. You just tap it where it says *VOLUME*. You can't see the switch, so it doesn't disrupt the Stratness of the classic look, but you can wire it different ways — split the coil on your humbucker, get new pickup combinations like neck plus bridge, or switch from series to parallel. There's a lot you could do, and you don't need to drill holes or have pushbuttons or mini-toggles or any of that stuff." In conjunction with the 5-way, the S-1 provides unprecedented flexibility in factory Strats.

The American Vintage guitars continue to be mainstays of the line, their details occasionally fine-tuned to accommodate subtle shifts in market tastes. For example, the early '80s versions were finished in 100% lacquer (undercoats, color coats, and clear coats), and so were the reissues made right after the buyout, in the first Corona shop. American Vintage guitars still use lacquer for the color coats and clear coats but now use polyester (a much thinner application than in the '70s) for the undercoat. Why? Dan Smith: "Because nobody wants a veneer, yet a lot of customers also don't want to see the sinking, aggregate rays, or other natural effects of all-lacquer finishes interacting with wood [see p. 202]. So we adjust to market demands."

The American Special Series will continue to be a home for new ideas, a place to put guitars with appointments that are nontraditional for Fender, such as the Tech-Tonic stop-tail bridge. The American Deluxe Series has been upgraded with several new models including an ash-body Strat, more options such as quilted maple tops, exotic woods for the skunk stripe, and innovations such as the new generation of Noiseless pickups, co-developed with Bill Lawrence.

As we go to press, Custom Shop builders are hard at work on a 50th Anniversary guitar. Billed as the most authentic replication of a 1954 Stratocaster anyone has ever made (right down to the polepiece diameters, original-type plastics, and finish formula), it will be offered only throughout 2004 as a Limited Production Time Machine model in the Closet Classic finish. This commemorative Strat will entail unique serial numbering and include a special certificate.

The Stratocaster has come a long way. A guitar once available as a single basic model with a couple of options now appears with nearly every imaginable combination of features, appearance, attitude, and price. It's almost as if the catalog had turned into a giant brochure of personalized instruments (and if it's not in the catalog, the Custom Shop can build it for you). With every adjustment to the line, Fender attempts to do a better job of matching products to market demands. Richard McDonald: "Responding to players is more important than whether we call some-thing a Special or a Deluxe. Let's say players ask, how about a vintage Strat but with a flame maple top and a flat fingerboard, big frets, and a regular trem but a graphite nut and staggered tuners? If it's valid, then we build it because players demand it. The last thing we think about is whether we stick it in the American Deluxe or the Special or whatever the series is. The old categories were convenient for us and for dealers, but you know what? Consumers don't think like that.

Dweezil Zappa, with his father's semi-cremated Strat, a Feb. '63 model that Jimi Hendrix played and burned at the Miami Pop Festival in 1968. Dweezil on the Strat: "This is excellence in design and it hasn't been surpassed. You can get a lot of sounds out of it — knock on it and vibrate things. It comes alive if you know what to do with it. There have been a lot of imitations and people who have tried to modify it, and those can be good, but it's not as cool as the original concept."

Craig Nicholls of the Vines:

"It's not about the gear. It's what you do with it."

They think about quality, features, value. That's why those old categories and the 'boxes' are coming down all over the place. You're going to see more variety from Fender than ever before."

Carrying A Legacy Into The Future

As the Stratocaster turns 50, players everywhere can celebrate the quirky Southern California guitar that became a global phenomenon. The chronicle of Leo Fender's ultimate 6-string is a story of wood, wire, metal, and plastic but also a story of design, art, music, and unbounded creativity. Ultimately it's a story about people: A stubborn, independent thinker looks at existing products, listens well, steps outside the box, and fashions a guitar so new it's ridiculed at first yet so functional it dominates its market a half century later, and does so in a remarkably similar form when most of the commercial products of its time have either evolved almost beyond recognition or disappeared altogether. Whereas most products are outmoded by shifting tastes, the Stratocaster is adapted and re-imagined time and again, not only proving itself suited to existing musical styles but inspiring new ones as well.

The chronicle of the Strat is also the story of a small shop that served musicians, grew fast, weathered two decades of ownership by a remote corporation, was reborn into an utterly different global marketplace, yet succeeded by rededicating itself to the principles of its founder. It's a story of old-fashioned values and high-tech solutions, of American commerce at its best, of good ideas, uncompromising beliefs, long hours, and vision rewarded by success.

Dan Smith: "If you compare a new Strat to a '54, it's different in every way, and yet there's a lot of Leo Fender in these guitars. It's hard to argue with something that was done pretty damn close to perfect in the first place. We've developed technologies for new styles, but all the lines on the original Strat are just so perfect, and it's balanced so well, it's come to define the instrument. Ask somebody to draw an electric guitar; with all due respect to other brands, chances are you'll get a picture of a Strat.

"People ask, what is your job here? And I say, you know, it's to protect the past, carry on the tradition, and make a future for Fender. That means improvement. If Leo were here today, he wouldn't want it any other way, because he was constantly trying to make a better product, pushing the envelope. He never stopped. Neither do we. If the Stratocaster is going to be viable 50 years from now, it's going to be because somebody's still trying to do what Leo did, which is to innovate."

Bill Schultz: "We would not be here if it weren't for Leo Fender. We never forget that. Leo Fender is legendary worldwide. We accept that, and we will never try to top that. He is the icon of the music business. We try to emulate his philosophy and his principles by building instruments with the same passion that the players bring to them. Fender will never be number two, ever. We are disciples of Leo, and our people here at Fender today live and breathe guitars. If Leo were here, he would be damn proud of them."

The imaginative and evocative improviser Leni Stern plays a gold Custom Shop Strat as well as a 1960 hardtail. She told *Guitar Player*'s Andy Ellis: "I like my Strats to sound sweet on top of mean."

One of the greatest of iconic Stratocasters, this is "Rocky," George Harrison's guitar. In late 1964 or early 1965, John Lennon and George Harrison dispatched roadie Mal Evans to purchase a pair of Strats. He returned with a matched set of rosewood-board models in Sonic Blue. (Although George recalled that they put them to use "straight away" recording late-1965's *Rubber Soul*, John was photographed using his blue Strat during the sessions for *Help!*, released six months earlier.) George played this guitar during the "All You Need Is Love" session, which was broadcast by satellite to an estimated 350 million people on June 25, 1967 and is considered the first live global television event.

George used the guitar on several Beatles hits, but some published reports are speculative. As much as we might like to know every detail, the Beatles' astonishingly prolific output entailed their sometimes using many guitars in a single day. Some songs were recorded dozens of times, and some final versions were composites of different takes recorded days or even weeks apart. Andy Babiuk is the author of the excellent book *Beatles Gear*, and he has researched the band's equipment far more comprehensively than anyone else. His perspective: "I found the Beatles more often than not would forget exactly what went on, and mix things up. Can you blame them? George played the 'psychedelic' Strat on 'Nowhere Man,' but many of the other attributions are guesswork."

The guitar's serial number is 83840; the neck date is Dec. '61. As Harrison explained to *Guitar Player*'s Dan Forte, "When we all took certain substances, I decided to paint mine in Day-Glo colors. And that was on 'I Am The Walrus' and 'All You Need is Love.'" Alan Rogan: "This is a really special guitar, and George used it far more than people realize. The biting sound on 'Sergeant Pepper,' the actual song, is this guitar. I've played it many, many times, and it's easily my favorite Strat ever. There was a period when I had it strung for George as a regular guitar — Ernie Ball Regular Slinkys, .010 - .046 — and it plays so well, but in my years with George it was usually his slide guitar. We had it set up with a high action and Gibson Sonomatic strings, .012 - .056 with the wound G. That light blue was the third most popular color for Strats in England, the first being Fiesta Red, then sunburst. We just called it baby blue. George absolutely loved this guitar. It was a big part of what he did."

In 2004, Fender announced a new American Deluxe series. While these latest Stratocasters offer some original cosmetics packages, their principal features are entirely new pickups co-designed by Fender and Bill Lawrence. Successors to the Fender-Lace Sensors and the Vintage Noiseless units, these new Samarium Cobalt Noiseless pickups mark a significant departure in materials, construction, and testing procedures (Fender even developed new pickup winding machines to accommodate the all-new design).

Dan Smith: "We were literally amazed. No noise canceling pickups we had tested before had come this close to capturing the true essence of Fender's original design." In fact, according to Smith, the new units in some cases actually outperformed the 1956 and 1963 Stratocaster pickups Fender has used as benchmarks for a decade or so.

Slide virtuoso Sonny Landreth:

"Versatility, complex tones, and comfort make the Strat my favorite for slide guitar. Playing one is inspirational because I feel like I'm shaking hands with history and heroes."

RESOURCES & LISTENING GUIDE

RESOURCES

Given the scant in-house documentation of Fender's early years, the assembly of instruments from parts fabricated at different times, the lack of correlation between the sequencing of serial numbers and exact production dates, numerous transition Stratocasters combining old and new features, and the vertigo-inducing number of Strat variants over the years, it's remarkable we know as much as we do. No guitar has been more exhaustively examined than the Stratocaster, and we owe much to the observations of veteran retailers and collectors as well as the authors who have compiled those insights and also interviewed Fender employees. Only a few basic Strat models are historically important, and descriptions of those guitars as well as many less significant models can already be found in helpful books. George Gruhn and Walter Carter's revised *Gruhn's Guide To Vintage Guitars*, for example, lists brief specs for more than a hundred variations.

If you want to know when Fender discontinued the Charcoal Frost metallic finish, or when the Strat control cavity's interior edge acquired a "shoulder," or when the first digit on the peghead's patent numbers switched from "2" to "3," you can find such facts in *Gruhn's Guide* and A.R. Duchossoir's detailed and very useful *The Fender Stratocaster: A Complete Guide to the History and Evolution of the World's Most Famous Guitar*. Ray Minhinnett & Bob Young's *The Story of the Fender Stratocaster: A Celebration of the World's Greatest Guitar* is well illustrated and provides insightful testimonials from more than two dozen prominent Strat players. (My own *American Guitars: An Illustrated History* also contains plenty of Strat lore.)

The history of the Fender company is recounted in several other books, including Richard Smith's *Fender: The Sound Heard 'Round The World*, one of the most compelling and thoroughly researched books ever written about guitars. Other good sources include Tony Bacon and Paul Day's *The Fender Book: A Complete History of Fender Electric Guitars*, Tony Bacon's *50 Years of Fender, Half a Century of the Greatest Electric Guitars*; Richard Smith's *Fender Custom Shop Guitar Gallery*; as well as several books written by former Fender employees (see p. 268-269).

F E N D E R   M E N

"Genius" is a romanticized word invoking images of a visionary who works in solitude and whose mind roams planes of thought beyond the imaginations of ordinary folks. In fact, some of history's best known geniuses were eminently practical, and some had plenty of help (Thomas Edison employed scores of workers at his research facility in New Jersey). Essential to Leo Fender's genius was his ability to filter and to synthesize a blizzard of requests and ideas from sources whose needs and agendas often varied. As a guitar designer who did not play the instrument, he started with suggestions from people who did. He also depended on others who could compensate for his lack of experience in marketing, administration, and organizing a rapidly expanding manufacturing facility.

Fortunately for him, and for us, he found resourceful people to help him do all those things, including Bill Carson, George Fullerton, Don Randall, the late Freddie Tavares, and the late Forrest White. Although their personalities and temperaments varied, they all struck me as polite fellows and no-nonsense problem solvers. Several were Armed Forces veterans, members of what has been called The Greatest Generation. They were tool guys, fix-it guys, men's men.

During the reign of CBS, some of the people who ran the company had little experience in music, and even those who did were stuck with corporate mandates to cut corners. In the post-buyout era, however, the new generation of Fender execs are, by and large, lifelong guitar guys like Vice President Richard McDonald, whose high school yearbook pictured him at the mailbox awaiting the new issue of *Guitar Player*. They had put in countless hours playing gigs, writing songs, recording music, repairing guitars, schlepping gear, and working in music stores before

they came to Fender. The corporate offices are full of guitars and amps, and the atmosphere is informal (Ritchie Fliegler: "Around here, a business suit is a Halloween costume").

Mr. Fender is profiled in Chapter 1 and interviewed in Chapters 1 and 2. Several recent and current employees or associates are identified in the text, including Joe Carducci, Vince Cunetto, Mike Eldred, Bob Hipp, Mark Kendrick, Todd Krause, Larry Moudy, and Bill Turner. Here are background sketches on other interviewees.

– TW

J. Black (also "J.W.") started work as a Master Builder in 1989 and was instrumental in some of the Custom Shop's most innovative and important projects, including the Relic series and the Artist Signature guitars. He transferred to Quality Assurance in 1998 and left Fender in 2002.

George F. Blanda, Jr. came to Fender in October 1985 to start the Custom Shop, was reassigned to R&D, and designed or co-designed the two-point tremolo and the most significant Stratocasters of recent decades, including the Beck and Clapton Signature models, the Strat Plus, the Strat Ultra, the American Standard, and the American Series. Dan Smith called him "probably the finest and purest engineering talent in the guitar business."

Bill Carson epitomizes the modern version of the plain-spoken Texas gentleman/hombre. He scorned the now-prized Burgundy Mist custom color because he suggested, in different words, that real men don't play purple guitars. In the old days, employees who got on his bad side could find themselves the target of outrageous pranks. People who have enjoyed his friendly, calm demeanor might be surprised to learn he once bit off a guy's ear in a bar room fight (hey, the fool had put the moves on Bill's wife). His contributions are discussed in Chapters 1 and 2 and also in his own book, *Bill Carson: My Life and Times with Fender Musical Instruments*.

Ritchie Fliegler played guitar and toured with such diverse artists as Tom Verlaine, John Waite, John Cale, and Lou Reed. He was already well known in industry circles for his work at Marshall when he joined Fender in May '95 as Marketing Manager for Fender amplifiers; players knew him for his book *Amps! The Other Half of Rock 'n' Roll* (he later wrote *The Complete Guide to Guitar and Amp Maintenance*). Ritchie served as Senior VP of Marketing for all Fender products and is currently Senior VP of Market Development. An example of how products are developed at Fender: "When Mike Lewis was the Marketing Manager for guitars and I was his boss, we came up with this idea for the American Series. The market said what it needed to say, Mike put together the business plan, I sold it to the powers that be, and Dan Smith and the people in the factory made it a reality. It's very collaborative. The whole company signs off on it, top to bottom, because it involves a lot of people."

George Fullerton was Leo Fender's oldest associate on the factory floor, co-builder of the Telecaster prototypes, and later the "G" to Leo's "L" at G&L. His contributions are discussed in Chapters 1 and 2 and in his book *Guitar Legends: The Evolution of the Guitar from Fender to G&L*. He recalled, "Leo had a radio repair shop. I used to go in there and buy records and visit with him, and he started asking, 'Why don't you come over here and work with me?' Later he moved into some new buildings, and there were only about two gals working with him. I told him I wasn't interested in steel guitars and amplifiers. And then one

day he said, 'Well, I'm thinking of trying to come up with a solidbody electric guitar.' Now, *that* sounded interesting."

Mike Lewis was a professional guitarist and music retailer who came to Fender in 1991 and later served as Marketing Manager for amplifiers, Marketing Manager for guitars and basses, and VP of Marketing for electric guitars. He is currently the Marketing Manager for Gretsch guitars, now part of the Fender Specialty Brands division.

Richard McDonald joined Fender in 1993 at an entry-level position and has served in many capacities. As head of the amp division he spearheaded projects such as the Cyber-Twin, the Pro Tube series, and others. As Marketing Manager for guitars he helped develop several of the most interesting Stratocaster guitars and Strat-inspired models of recent years, including the Tom Delonge Strat, Highway 1, Acoustasonic, and Strat-o-Sonic. He is now a Vice President in charge of marketing Fender, Guild, Gretsch, Jackson, Charvel, Squier, and others.

John Page (Chapter 7) came to work for Fender as a neck buffer in 1978 and worked with Freddie Tavares. He directed the Custom Shop from its inception and later took over R&D. He left the factory after 20 years to head up the Fender Museum, and now works as a consultant.

Don Randall (Chapters 1 and 2) was responsible to a great degree for Fender's success, although he downplays his role, calling it "inconsequential." After World War II, he came out of the service and began to distribute the products of K&F and its successor, the Fender Electric Instruments Company. In 1953 he established Fender Sales, Inc., which marketed and distributed Fender products worldwide and also designed its groundbreaking literature. Mr. Randall was credited by Forrest White as having built the "finest organization ever created to sell guitars." He left Fender over disagreements with CBS management and later founded Randall Instruments.

William Schultz is the Chairman of the Board and CEO of Fender Musical Instruments Corporation. His reinvigoration of product innovation, dealer pride, and employee morale are discussed in Chapters 6 and 7. He supervised the expansion of Fender's production and distribution capabilities as well as the inauguration of the Ensenada factory (Chapter 7) and the Custom Shop (Chapter 7); he also established a licensing agreement under which Fender manufactures, markets, and sells Gretsch guitars, and he directed Fender's acquisition of Guild, Jackson, Charvel, and SWR.

Dan Smith is quoted throughout several chapters. He came to Fender in August 1981 as Director of Marketing for electric guitars, and became Vice President of Guitar Products Research and Development in 1995. From late 1999 to mid 2002 he also directed the Custom Shop. He's had a hand in every new Fender guitar for the past two decades in one capacity or another — marketing, R&D, or design.

Freddie Tavares came from his native Hawaii to live in the U.S. in the late '40s. A very accomplished player of both standard and steel guitars, he was also self-taught in the fields of audio amplification and electronics. One of his seemingly typical freelance studio gigs brought him pop-culture immortality, when he slid his bar up the strings to kick off the familiar Looney Tunes cartoon theme. He came to Fender in March 1953, worked on the embryonic Stratocaster, and later became head of guitar research as well as a key consultant in both product design and engineering. Mr. Tavares died in 1990. His memory was honored with one of the most beautiful of all Custom Shop instruments, the Freddie Tavares Aloha Stratocaster. See Chapters 1 and 2.

Forrest White came to work at Fender on May 20, 1954. Eventually ascending to the position of Vice President and General Manager, he reorganized the factory operation and took over the handling of day to day problems. A stickler for quality control, he put through the Stratocaster's first production run in the fall of '54, stayed on at CBS after Leo's departure, and resigned after refusing to sign off on products he felt were not worthy of the Fender name. Leo named the Fender-built White lap steels and amps after Forrest. Mr. White's recollections appear in Chapters 1 and 2 and also in his book *Fender: The Inside Story*.

"We are disciples of Leo, and our people here at Fender today live and breathe guitars. If Leo were here, he would be damn proud of them."

– *William Schultz*

C D   L I S T E N I N G   G U I D E

Introduction to the Leo Fender excerpts

I interviewed Mr. Fender several times in the late 1970s and 1980s, never intending to use the transcripts beyond their appearances in my book *American Guitars*, my Rare Bird column, and a *Guitar Player* feature story. Had I foreseen a project such as this one (or imagined a future technology that would allow readers to actually hear Mr. Fender's words), I would have brought along studio-quality recording gear instead of my little hand-held Sony with the dent on the side, and I would have conducted the interview far away from the clatter of dishes at a sandwich and coffee joint. (Despite the funky gear, the less than pristine conditions, and the effects of time, the tapes sound pretty good.)

I held onto those old cassettes simply because there are some things you never throw away. Prior to writing *The Stratocaster Chronicles* I seldom if ever went back and listened to them, but they were precious to me all the same, just knowing I had a piece of guitar history stashed in a box somewhere. Now, listening to the tapes again, I am reminded how fortunate I was to spend time with this quirky, brilliant man and his close associates from the early days of Fender. A few bits of those conversations are included here on the CD, cross-referenced in the text and indicated on the page with the little gold CD icon. I'm happy to share them with you, and I hope you enjoy hearing Mr. Fender talk about the Stratocaster as much as I did a couple of decades ago when he sat across the table and spelled it out for me.

– Tom Wheeler

Greg Koch
He Came, He Saw, He Pummeled

The CD that accompanies this book is much more than a bonus or a mere perk. Inspiring, enlightening, and occasionally hilarious, it continues the 50th anniversary celebration of the Fender Stratocaster guitar with brilliant demonstrations of many of its best loved sounds and styles – 50 of them, to be exact.

I can't think of a better player to pull this off than Greg Koch. In fact, I'm not sure *any* other player could pull it off. Aside from establishing his own musical identity on jawdropper CDs such as *Radio Free Gristle, The Grip!,* and *13x12* (and on this CD's intro and outro), Greg can reproduce the sounds and styles of dozens of famous players.

Here, many of what Greg calls the "potentates of Stratdom" are captured with uncanny authenticity in all their twangy glory — from Eldon to Yngwie, from Bonnie to Stevie Ray, from Buddy Holly to Buddy Guy, from Jimi Hendrix to Jimmie Vaughan. Wielding a Custom Shop Relic '56 Strat, another Custom Shop Strat also similar to a '56, and a Voodoo Strat (for the Hendrix and Malmsteen cuts), Greg doesn't just mimic these players; he inhabits them, conjuring up moods and emotions along with licks and sounds.

So crank up this CD and let Greg Koch be your spirit guide into the soul of the Strat. You'll be nodding in appreciation, slapping your forehead in amazement, and once in a while laughing out loud. In the words of our own Jam Master G: Let the good times roll.

CD TRACK LISTING

On Tracks 1-8, you'll hear Leo Fender, in his own words, discuss the following topics:

TRACK #

1. Development of the Stratocaster body
2. Need for a vibrato
3. Benefits of a multiple-springed vibrato
4. Offset design and the utility of the Strat
5. Pickup selector
6. Electrical layout
7. Origin of the Fender headstock design
8. Additional benefits of the having the tuners all on one side
9. Production manager George Fullerton explains how he developed the first Custom Color, Fiesta Red

10. Introduction to *Fifty Sounds of the Strat,* developed and played by Greg Koch
11. Introduction to Track 12 – **Eldon Shamblin**
12. Example of Playing Style
13. Introduction to Track 14 – **Buddy Holly**
14. Example of Playing Style
15. Introduction to Track 16 – **Dick Dale**
16. Example of Playing Style
17. Introduction to Track 18 – **The Beach Boys**
18. Example of Playing Style
19. Introduction to Track 20 – **Hank Marvin**
20. Example of Playing Style
21. Introduction to Track 22 – **Curtis Mayfield**
22. Example of Playing Style
23. Introduction to Track 24 – **Jimi Hendrix** Rhythm/Octavia

24. Example of Playing Style
25. Introduction to Track 26 – **Jimi Hendrix** Middle Pickup/Blues
26. Example of Playing Style
27. Introduction to Track 28 – **Jimi Hendrix** Wah Pedal
28. Example of Playing Style
29. Introduction to Track 30 – **Jimi Hendrix** Univibe
30. Example of Playing Style
31. Introduction to Track 32 – **Eric Clapton** False Harmonics
32. Example of Playing Style
33. Introduction to Track 34 – **Eric Clapton** Laid Back
34. Example of Playing Style
35. Introduction to Track 36 – **Eric Clapton** Modern Clean & Dirty
36. Example of Playing Style
37. Introduction to Track 38 – "Riff Medley" **Joe Walsh, John Fogerty, Ed King, Rick Derringer, Steve Miller, Ron Wood, Nile Rodgers**
38. Example of Playing Style
39. Introduction to Track 40 – **David Gilmour**
40. Example of Playing Style
41. Introduction to Track 42 – **Robin Trower**
42. Example of Playing Style
43. Introduction to Track 44 – **Ritchie Blackmore**
44. Example of Playing Style
45. Introduction to Track 46 – **Jeff Beck** Volume Slurs/Harmonics
46. Example of Playing Style
47. Introduction of Track 48 – **Jeff Beck** Warbles

48. Example of Playing Style
49. Introduction to Track 50 – **Mark Knopfler**
50. Example of Playing Style
51. Introduction to Track 52 – **George Harrison**
52. Example of Playing Style
53. Introduction to Track 54 – **"Slide Summit"**
    Bonnie Raitt, Lowell George,
    Rory Gallagher, Ry Cooder
54. Example of Playing Style
55. Introduction to Track 56
    Stevie Ray Vaughan – Clean
56. Example of Playing Style
57. Introduction to Track 58
    Stevie Ray Vaughan – Dirty
58. Example of Playing Style
59. Introduction to Track 60 – **"Blues Jam"**
    Stevie Ray Vaughan, Buddy Guy,
    Robert Cray, Jimmie Vaughan
60. Example of Playing Style
61. Introduction to Track 62 – **Eric Johnson**
62. Example of Playing Style
63. Introduction to Track 64 – **Yngwie Malmsteen**
64. Example of Playing Style
65. Introduction to Track 66 – Koto Sound
66. Example of Playing Style
67. Introduction to Track 68
    Volume Slur w/Delay
68. Example of Playing Style
69. Introduction to Track 70
    Behind The Nut Pings
70. Example of Playing Style
71. Introduction to Track 72
    Whammy Warble Madness
72. Example of Playing Style
73. Outro

THE STRATOCASTER CHRONICLES

FEATURING RARE
INTERVIEWS AND PERFORMANCES
OF FAMOUS PLAYERS' STYLES

See page 272 for complete listing of each track

HAL•LEONARD®

A B O U T   T H E   A U T H O R

Tom Wheeler

After freelancing for *Rolling Stone*, Tom joined the staff of *Guitar Player* and became its Editor in Chief four years later. He served in that capacity for ten years, was also the founding Editorial Director of *Bass Player*, and continues to provide a monthly column for *Guitar Player*. He has interviewed Muddy Waters, B.B. King, Chuck Berry, Keith Richards, Eric Clapton, and many others. His first encyclopedia, *The Guitar Book: A Handbook for Electric and Acoustic Guitarists*, was published by Harper & Row in various languages over a period of 14 years; a new Japanese translation was published in 2000. His next book, *American Guitars: An Illustrated History*, has been in print for more than 20 years and was called by one retail catalog "the best book ever written about guitars."

Tom co-edited Richard Smith's *Fender: The Sound Heard 'Round The World*, and also wrote the foreword. He wrote the foreword for *The PRS Guitar Book*, and contributed chapters to *Gibson Guitars, 100 Years of an American Icon*; *The Electric Guitar*; *Electric Guitars of the Fifties*; and *Electric Guitars of the Sixties*; among others. He has been interviewed by *The New York Times*, *The Wall Street Journal*, *U.S. News & World Report*, MTV, NPR, and CNN. He is a consultant to The Smithsonian Institution, host of the *American Guitar* video series, and the writer and host of informational videos for Fender and Guild. He holds a Juris Doctor degree from the Loyola School of Law, is currently a member of the faculty of the University of Oregon's School of Journalism, and gigs regularly with soul singer Deb Cleveland.

CREDITS

Footnotes:
All footnoted quotes are excerpted from interviews in *Guitar Player* magazine and are reprinted here with gratitude to both the publication and the two footnoted authors, Jas Obrecht (notes 1, 2, 4, 5, 7, 12, 14, 15) and Dan Forte (3, 6, 8, 9, 10, 11, 13).

Photo credits:
FOREWORD & INTRODUCTION: p.7 Courtesy Fender Musical Instruments Corporation (FMIC), p.9 Bob Leafe/STAR FILE, p.12 Holly photo MICHAEL OCHS ARCHIVES.COM, illustration Hal Leonard Corp., p.13 FMIC, p.14 Experience Music Project, p.16 Holly photo S&G/Redferns/Retna Ltd., statue photo courtesy of Eddy Grigsby, p.17 Frank Driggs Collection, p.18 MICHAEL OCHS ARCHIVES.COM, p.19 Frank Driggs Collection, p.20 courtesy of Art Greenhaw, www.lightcrustdoughboys.com, p.21-22 FMIC, p.23 Peter Amft, p.24 Experience Music Project

CHAPTER 1: p.26 Jon Sievert, p.27 FMIC, p.28 Richard Smith Collection, p.29 Leo Fender, p.30 Robb Lawrence, p.31 Robert Perine, p.32 John Sprung, p.34 Bill Carson, p.35 FMIC, p.36 John Peden, p.38-39 Ray Flerlage/MICHAEL OCHS ARCHIVES.COM, p.41 Ray Flerlage/MICHAEL OCHS ARCHIVES.COM, p.42 Val Wilmer/MICHAEL OCHS ARCHIVES.COM, p.45 courtesy Bill Carson, p.46 Richard Smith Collection, p.47 Bill Carson, p.49 John Peden, p.51 Bob Hipp Collection, p.53 John Peden

CHAPTER 2: p.56 Courtesy of Jon Sievert, Bill Carson, George Fullerton, Robert Perine, p.58-59 Guitar magazine, Japan, p.61 Robert Perine, p.65 Richard Smith Collection, p.66 Experience Music Project, p.67 Bob Hipp Collection, p.68 Robert Perine

CHAPTER 3: p.71 John Peden, p.73 Richard Smith Collection, p.74 Experience Music Project, p.75 Tom Wheeler, p.76 Robert Perine, p.78 Frank Driggs Collection, p.79 John Peden, p.80 Robert Perine, p.81 Frank Driggs Collection, p.83 courtesy of Robert Perine, p.84 MICHAEL OCHS ARCHIVES.COM, p.85 FMIC, p. 86,87 John Peden, p.88 Robb Lawrence, p.89 Robert Perine, p.90 album cover courtesy of Joel Whitburn, guitar photo John Peden, p.91 Robert

Perine, p.92 Richard Smith Collection, p.93 guitar photo Iain Hersey, Kaye portrait Robert Kley, p.94 FMIC, p.95, Richard Cummins/CORBIS, p.96,97 Robert Perine, p.98 Richard Smith Collection, p.99 John Peden, p.100 John Sprung, 102,104,105 John Peden, p.106 Robert Perine

CHAPTER 4: p.108,109 Robert Perine, p.110 MICHAEL OCHS ARCHIVES.COM, p.111 John Peden, p.112 Terry Cryer/CORBIS, p.113,115 John Peden, p.116 Robert Perine p.117, Richard Smith Collection, p.118 John Peden, p.119 Robert Perine, p.120 Richard Smith, p.121 Raeburn Flerlage/ASMP/Frank Driggs Collection, p.122-123 Robert Perine, p.124 John Peden, p.125 Bob Gruen/STAR FILE, p.127 John Peden, p.128 Bruce Fleming/MICHAEL OCHS ARCHIVES.COM, p.129 guitar FMIC, Hendrix guitar piece Experience Music Project, p.130 Paul Haggard, p.131 Dave Peabody/Redferns/Retna Ltd., p.132-133 John Peden, p.134 Hulton-Deutsch Collection/CORBIS, p.135 John Van Hasselt/CORBIS SYGMA, p.136 Experience Music Project, p.138 John Peden/courtesy of R. Friedman, p.139 John Van Hasselt/CORBIS SYGMA, p.140 Chuck Pulin/STAR FILE

CHAPTER 5: p.142 John Peden, p.143 David M. Tannen, p.144,145 Neil Zlozower, p.146 FMIC, p.147 Neil Zlozower, p.148 Ron Pownall/STAR FILE, p.149 Bob Alford/STAR FILE, p.150 poster from Bob Hipp Collection, guitar photo FMIC, p.151 courtesy of Joel Whitburn, p.152 Neil Zlozower, p.153 Neal Preston/CORBIS, right photo Jon Sievert/MICHAEL OCHS ARCHIVES.COM, p.154 Ken Settle, album cover courtesy of Joel Whitburn, p.155 Larry Hulst/MICHAEL OCHS ARCHIVES.COM, cover courtesy of Joel Whitburn, p.156 cover courtesy Joel Whitburn, photo John Peden, p.157 Neal Preston/CORBIS, p.158 Jon Sievert, p.159 Neil Zlozower, p.160 MICHAEL OCHS ARCHIVES.COM, guitar photo FMIC, p.161 Aldo Mauro, p.162 Gems/Redferns/Retna Ltd., p.163 Neil Zlozower, p.164 Chuck Pulin/STAR FILE, p.166 Bob Gruen/STAR FILE

CHAPTER 6: p.169 Barry Schultz/Sunshine/Retna UK, p.170,172 FMIC, p.174 Joseph Sia/STAR FILE, album cover courtesy of Joel Whitburn, p.175 Jeffrey Mayer/STAR FILE, p.176 cover courtesy of Joel Whitburn, p.177 Neal Preston/CORBIS, p.178 Ken Settle, p.179 ad courtesy of Bob Hipp Collection, photo Todd Kaplan/STAR FILE, p.180 Bob Hipp

Collection, guitar photo FMIC, p.181 Tim Mosenfelder/ CORBIS, p.182 Bob Hipp Collection, p.183 Ken Settle, p.184-185 FMIC, p.188 Bob Hipp Collection

CHAPTER 7: p.191 Ken Settle, p.192 Jay Blakesberg/ Retna Ltd., p.193 Aldo Mauro, album cover courtesy of Joel Whitburn, p.194 Ken Settle, p.195 Jon Sievert/MICHAEL OCHS ARCHIVES.COM, p.196 Neil Zlozower, guitar photo FMIC, p.197-199 FMIC, p.200 John Peden, p. 201 Claudio Bresciani/Scanpix/Retna Ltd., p. 203-208 FMIC, p.209 John Peden/courtesy FMIC, p. 210 Hendrix guitar courtesy of Experience Music Project, replica and poster FMIC, p.212 photo on left John Peden, Gibbons photo FMIC, p. 213 Ken Settle, p.214 FMIC, p.216 Neal Preston/CORBIS, p.218 Neil Zlozower, p.219 John Peden, p.221 David Atlas/Retna Ltd., p.222,224 FMIC, p.225 Al Pereira/MICHAEL OCHS ARCHIVES.COM, p.226 Neil Zlozower

CHAPTER 8: p.228 CORBIS, p.229 FMIC, p.230 W.B.L. Photo Lomitola/Frank Driggs Collection, p.231 Neal Preston/CORBIS, p.232 Neil Zlozower, p.233 Bob Hipp Col-

lection, 12-string photo FMIC, p.234 David Seelig/STAR FILE, p.235-237 FMIC, p.238 Healey photo Ken Settle, guitar FMIC, p.239 FMIC, p.240 Ken Settle, p.241 FMIC, p.242,243 Ken Settle, p.244 guitar FMIC, Rossdale photo Ken Settle

CHAPTER 9: p. 246-248 FMIC, p.249 Tim Mosenfelder/CORBIS, p.250 Jeffrey Mayer/STAR FILE, p.251 FMIC, p.252 Ken Settle, p.253 CORBIS, p.254 Neil Zlozower, p.255,256 Ken Settle, p.257 Bob Hipp Collection, p.258 guitar photo FMIC, magazine cover reproduced by Special Permission of *Playboy* magazine. Copyright © 2003 by Playboy, p.259 Reuters NewMedia Inc./CORBIS, p.260 Rune Hellestad/ CORBIS, p.261 John Peden, p.262 courtesy Balafon Image Bank as seen in Backbeat Books' *Beatles Gear* by Andy Babiuk, p.263 FMIC, p.264 Travis Gauthier

CHAPTER 10: p.271 Jim Wieland/Ricco Photography, p.274 Luis M. Salazar

The guitar on page 24 was used by the Kingsmen's Mike Mitchell for the solo on 1963's "Louie Louie," recorded for fifty bucks at a local studio in Portland, Oregon. Courtesy Experience Music Project.

INDEX

Bolded page number indicates photo on this page.